PRAISE FOR ANTON PA...

"The most brilliant theoretician of libertarian communism."
—Mike Davis, author of *City of Quartz*

"Good, solid, working-class literature."
—Noam Chomsky

THE WORKERS' WAY
TO FREEDOM
AND OTHER COUNCIL COMMUNIST WRITINGS

Anton Pannekoek

Edited by Robyn K. Winters

The Workers' Way to Freedom and Other Council Communist Writings
Anton Pannekoek
Edited by Robyn K. Winters © 2024
This edition © PM Press

ISBN: 979-8-88744-008-8 (paperback)
ISBN: 979-8-88744-009-5 (ebook)

Library of Congress Control Number: 2023930614

Cover design by John Yates/www.stealworks.com

10 9 8 7 6 5 4 3 2 1

PM Press
PO Box 23912
Oakland, CA 94623
www.pmpress.org

Printed in the USA

To all my fellow workers around the world who seek
a life of freedom and cooperation for all.

"Just as we obtained our doctrines through many difficult struggles,
they [the younger generation] too will have to do the same, and the most
we can do is to help them see the variegated possibilities in everything,
in order that they can form their own judgments. To teach them to
use their own brains is the best doctrine that can be handed down."
—Anton Pannekoek, letter to Ben Sijes (January 21, 1953)

CONTENTS

ACKNOWLEDGMENTS

This book, as with all things in life, is not the result of the efforts of a few but rather of many, regardless if some were directly involved or not. Of course, this book would not exist without Anton Pannekoek, but there are others worth mentioning who contributed to spreading these emancipatory ideas further into the world.

Since the night I first met her during an all-night labour protest, Em has inspired me to be more thorough in contemplating, discussing, and digging into the history of revolutionary ideas. She has been a constant source of support during this project. From helping me decipher the odd word in Pannekoek's handwriting, to reading and discussing which of Pannekoek's writings are his best to include in this book, to urging me to take ibuprofen when a migraine set in. I cannot imagine a dearer friend.

John L. has been someone I have worked with on Working Class History (WCH) for half a decade now. He has always been easy to talk to about both revolutionary projects and everyday life. Though my contribution to WCH has become more sporadic over the years, he knows he can rely on me for help and I on him, as was the case when I proofread his introduction to *Working Class History: Everyday Acts of Resistance and Rebellion* (2020, PM Press) and he proofread my introduction to this book.

About a year after I got the idea for this book I contacted the Association Archives Antonie Pannekoek (AAAP). Without the AAAP this book would be half the size and half as accurate. I began corresponding with Kees I. What started with me asking for a letter of Pannekoek's evolved into an insightful discussion of broader revolutionary politics. Over the years that followed, I reached out a handful of times to ask more questions and even to contribute to the AAAP. Kees has always been patient and diligent in helping.

Nina v.d.B., Joppe S., and Julie H., though from two different institutions on either side of the Atlantic Ocean, added enormously to this book by providing minute details I was missing from original sources—an extract of a letter, a single sentence, a short article. The Internationaal Instituut voor Sociale Geschiedenis and the University of Michigan Library are fortunate to have such kindhearted people involved in not merely preserving but, more importantly, distributing knowledge to those who are curious.

PM Press was my first choice for a publisher, so it was a thrill to get positive feedback so shortly after submitting the manuscript. Ramsey K., Joey P., and Claude M. have all provided superb encouragement, suggestions, and insights as this book reached the final stages of publishing. Quite literally, this book would not exist as it does without these three.

Unexpected but much appreciated generosity came suddenly one morning from Chaokang T.—not with the written content of the book but with the cover. Chaokang scanned many of the exquisite drawings of the Milky Way by Pannekoek for *Anton Pannekoek: Ways of Viewing Science and Society* (2019, Amsterdam University Press), and they graciously shared them with me and PM Press. The swiftness of Chaokang's kindness perfectly matches the beauty of Pannekoek's drawings.

Finally, I must express my gratitude to everyone who has ever contributed to and everyone who continues to maintain the invaluable libcom.org and Marxists Internet Archive. Combined they served as the cornerstone for this book as I formed the first rough list of Pannekoek's council communist writings from what they had freely available online. As a communist society would never be without mistakes—since its very existence would depend on being continuously created by all for all, with the diverse and conflicting input that implies—so too these archives are not without mistakes, yet they are inspiring resources of extensive knowledge. The ideas and history that has come out of our class in our gradual steps towards a better world can be found in these two archives. Agreeing with all their content is impossible, but, like this book, they can spark important discussion among us workers, and for that they are worthy of everyone's support.

EDITOR'S NOTE

Anton Pannekoek was quite particular about his writings being published accurately, noting in a letter to Jim Arthur Dawson dated October 12, 1947, that "the omission or displacement of one comma can entirely change or revert the meaning of a sentence." With that in mind, every effort has been made to preserve his original intent and unique voice while minimal edits for readability were made.

When writing in English, Pannekoek tended to use both British and American spellings, even in the same piece of writing. For the sake of consistency and readability, the content of this book has been edited so that the American spelling (which seemed the most prevalent) is the standard throughout.

Finally, I have transcribed every piece of writing in this book from original manuscripts or publications except for the following: chapter 20, "On Workers' Councils" (1952); the first letter of chapter 21, "The Need for the Workers to Lead Themselves" (1953–54); and appendix A, "Anton Pannekoek by Paul Mattick" (1962).

—Robyn K. Winters

EDITOR'S INTRODUCTION

After the Russian Revolution of 1917, Marxism was increasingly seen as a synonym for Leninism. This was due, in part, to a myth—consciously and unconsciously crafted by many of those in favour and many of those against the revolution—that the revolution was the product of the Bolsheviks led by Vladimir Lenin.

Mistaken as such, Marxism is eager to ride on the coattails of the rising working class in order for the party of professional revolutionaries to conquer state power (of course quickly rebranding the state as a workers' state, the dictatorship of the proletariat, etc.), to command the means of production and the workers to get the highest output for industrial growth, and, of course, to crush anyone who might challenge the current whims of the party leaders—capitalists, peasants, workers, revolutionaries, or even fellow members of the party. Through the propaganda of both those in favour of and against such means, this distorted conception of Marxism has lasted in the minds of millions for over a century. Whether one considers themselves a Marxist or not, this ought to be recognised as a shame, for it only makes the task of creating a better world more difficult.

To restrict the scope of Marxism to Leninism is to restrict many from taking the valuable ideas and lessons from Marxism. There are countless workers who yearn for change, a few even identify as revolutionaries, yet they refuse to even skim a few pages of Marx's *Capital* or will only give a most cynical reading of his *Civil War in France*. Even ideas and analytical methods Marx merely utilized along with many of his contemporaries, such as materialism and dialectics, which were part of the repertoire of Marx's anarchist rival Mikhail Bakunin no less, get outright dismissed due to the sanctification many Marxists built around their ideological leader. This rejection of all things associated with Marx results in skewed understandings of Marxism, which interpreted and expanded upon his ideas in various directions. Thus, these skewed understandings lead to critiques of Marxism limited in their depth, quality, and usefulness.

For those who have not fallen for propaganda and instead have searched beyond the swamp of Leninism, they have learned that a wide variety of Marxist perspectives have existed and continue to exist, even after 1917. Anton Pannekoek (1873–1960), the Dutch astronomer and Marxist revolutionary, was a key theoretician of one such variety: council communism. Though immersed in revolutionary socialism from the turn of the twentieth century, it was during the last three decades of his life that his most refined and stirring ideas arose. These council communist theories—developed after witnessing the rise and fall of social democracy, the rise and fall of the Russian and German Revolutions—encompass lessons all revolutionaries can learn from.

The anarchist and Marxist alike can find insights on why the working class must liberate itself rather than rely on parties or trade unions leading the way, and, most importantly, how council organisation is arguably the fullest expression of that self-emancipation to date. As Pannekoek points out in a personal letter from 1949, workers' councils can be seen as a synthesis of the best elements of these two great revolutionary traditions—freedom and organisation. Both anarchists and Marxists therefore will find in his writings ideas they agree with and ideas that challenge their views. By engaging, analysing, and critiquing these writings, like those of Marx, we can take important lessons and develop a broader understanding for our future struggles.

* * *

As for this book, it is divided into two parts: Part I: The Workers' Way to Freedom and Part II: Other Council Communist Writings.

The former is a transcription of a handwritten manuscript that had never been published in its entirety until now. Though undated, six of the chapters were edited into shorter, stand-alone articles and published in *International Council Correspondence* during 1935–36, therefore it must have been written in 1935 or sometime shortly before. Read as a whole piece, as was intended, *The Workers' Way to Freedom* is an early walk-through of council communist ideas and how they came about for a working-class readership in 1930s America. One feels a sense of Pannekoek trying to ease new ideas that challenge the old dogmas of the socialist movement—both those obvious in the social democracy of the Second International as well as those thinly painted over in the Bolshevism of the Third International. In this way, the manuscript could be seen as a precursor to Pannekoek's magnum opus *Workers' Councils*, which he secretly wrote years later during the Nazi occupation of Holland.

The latter part of this book is an assortment of writings—essays, articles, and letters—which have been chosen for their subject matter, their coherency, their placement in Pannekoek's council communist phase, and their potential to spark discussion among workers today. Many are available online, however most have been incorrectly transcribed, e.g., changes in wording or restructuring of sentences. The versions found here have been transcribed from their original publications or archival sources. Through these writings we can see the development of council communism in the decades when the shrinking movement was becoming more and more forgotten. Similar to *The Workers' Way to Freedom*, these assorted writings often mirror points made in Pannekoek's *Workers' Councils* and his 1938 book *Lenin as Philosopher*. It is suitable, then, that this latter part of the book is similar in size to the former; the two complement each other just as they complement Pannekoek's books.

* * *

I was inspired to compile Pannekoek's shorter works into a book in October 2018 after reading a collection of Daniel Guérin's shorter works titled *For a Libertarian Communism* published by PM Press. Oftentimes people focus on the large published works of thinkers; we can see this with, for example, Marx and *Capital* or Kropotkin and *The Conquest of Bread*. This is no surprise; these thinkers obviously put great effort in writing these works, and they tend to be the authors' greatest works. Readers do miss out though on brilliant snippets of theory condensed into a few pages, especially when the writings have gone unpublished. Not only do shorter works provide an easier access point for those apprehensive or unable to read theoretical tomes, but by being originally limited in space these works can get to the heart of the matter in such a way that may very well be lost in a larger, more general work.

Some six or seven years ago, I read Pannekoek's *Workers' Councils* on the forty-five-minute bus rides to and from work over the course of a handful of weeks. The ideas were impactful but gradual—I agreed with much of the content, though found some statements a bit harsh. It was a few years later, after gaining more experiences within the socialist and trade union movements, as well as delving deeper into working-class history, when I began reading his shorter writings online. With reading these, more and more of Pannekoek's ideas clicked.

It was around this time when I also noticed an increase in people, especially younger folk, referencing Pannekoek and council communism on social media. A combination of things surely has caused this: from the ever-increasing number of people using the internet to the various Leninist sects crumbling as fresh radicals learn the shortcomings of such restrictive organisational methods. Unfortunately, many of those referencing Pannekoek and his ideas online seem to only have a surface level or even skewed understanding. A book like this will hopefully aid in widening the reach of Pannekoek's ideas while also deepening people's understanding of them.

After reading as many shorter works of Pannekoek's online as I could find, often while on my bus ride to and from work, I put together a list of what I considered his best or most important. The list was fine, though the content could be more substantial. So, following off-and-on research during the precious little free time I had after work, over weekends, on vacations, and sometimes during slow days at work, I eventually stumbled upon Pannekoek's handwritten manuscript for *The Workers' Way to Freedom* on the Association Archives Antonie Pannekoek (https://aaap. be). Many of the chapters were already on my list as articles, but these chapter versions were longer and had differences—some slight, some substantial. There were also chapters that never got published as standalone articles. Furthermore, these chapters melded into each other to create a cohesive, flowing work.

Not long after I began transcribing the handwritten manuscript— learning how Pannekoek rarely crossed his *t*'s and was little better with dotting his *i*'s—the COVID-19 pandemic caused me to work from home. Work was sadly no less exhausting from my couch next to my cat, though when opportunities came I could at least transcribe without fear of my boss sneaking up behind me. It took longer than I expected, but I finished three years after I first conceived of this book.

* * *

Pannekoek did not have all the answers—the same can be said about Marx, Bakunin, you, me, everyone past, present, and future. This book is not meant to be swallowed whole without criticism, the words inside are not meant to be parroted; neither a panacea nor a dogma it is merely a tool to spark discussion among us workers. The core notion, however, of all of Pannekoek's writings is something I hold firm: the working class can attain freedom only through self-emancipation. If any of my fellow workers reach this same conclusion from reading any number of the pages of this book, then my efforts researching, compiling, and transcribing whenever I had time to spare across the past few years have been worth it.

PART I

THE WORKERS' WAY TO FREEDOM (C. 1935)

CHAPTER 1

CAPITALISM

This chapter is from Pannekoek's handwritten manuscript, and was never published in *International Council Correspondence*. —Ed.

Work is the basis of human existence. Nature produces everything needful to the life of beast and man. But it must be searched for and won at the cost of pains, of labor.

This labor has assumed many forms, from the hunting and root digging of the primitive savages to modern industry and agriculture by means of perfect machines and highly developed science. It shows an uninterrupted progress, in that labor is growing more efficient. Its productivity increases, i.e., the same product costs ever less labor. This increase was extremely rapid, and is growing more so, in modern times.

What is the outcome of this tremendous progress? A steady increase of productivity means that finally an abundant amount of all necessities for all mankind can be produced at the cost of a moderate labor task for each. That the imperious demands of our bodily needs no longer enslave us. It means the possibility of abundance, leisure, and freedom for mankind.

This point has already been reached in modern times. It has been computed that in order to ascertain an easy middle-class living for every citizen in the United States by the best modern technical means, two or three working hours a day, during ten years of our life, would be sufficient.

Why then instead of abundance all this misery and poverty for the great masses? Why instead of leisure the long exhausting hours of work? Why an often tyrannical sway instead of freedom? The answer is given by an examination of the capitalistic production system.

Capitalism means private ownership in big industry. Mainly industry and transport works with large machines. These big instruments of production cannot be owned by everybody separately; every man could have his own wheelbarrow but he cannot have his own railway. Big industry could be owned whether by all collectively, or by some few very rich people privately. Big industry arose out of a world of small industry and small producers: settlers, small farmers, craftsmen, to whom private ownership of their tools, their lots of land, was a necessity in their work. Private business was the foundation of society. Then out of small private business, by means of mechanical progress, big private business developed.

How does capitalism work? The possessor of capital buys a factory, buys the machines, buys the raw material to be worked in the machines. He hires poor people, who own nothing but the labor power of their body. He buys their labor power and consumes this his property by having them work with his machines; the product being also his. He pays them the value of their labor power, i.e., what is necessary to produce this labor power anew, i.e., the value of the necessities a man needs for his living. He sells the goods produced. Now the value a man can produce during a week's work exceeds the value of what he needs for one week's living. The difference, the surplus value, is the capitalist's profit. This profit is the aim, the object, the goal, the reason of his taking the trouble of producing goods.

Thus the capitalist class is exploiting the labor of the workers, its richest mine of wealth. Such an exploitation is not new. Always during the history of civilization the working masses have been able to produce more than the necessities of their own life. The surplus was taken from them by the ruling classes—kings, feudal lords, priests—and it was this surplus that formed the basis of their masters' "civilization," whilst dire necessity reigned in the homes of the workers. This surplus, small at first, increased by the increasing productivity of labor. Now it has become so large, that through it capital itself grows at an enormous rate. The whole capitalist class and all its attendants live on this surplus, big finance taking the greatest share.

What share falls to the workers themselves? They only get—if they do get it—the bare means of existence for them and their family. Hence they are doomed to remain have-nots, to remain proletarians forever.

Such is the economic structure of capitalism. This is bad enough: this gigantic power of mankind to produce abundance for everybody, whilst the majority of the people are poor, dependent, slaves of their work, without hope of a better future. But in reality it is even worse.

Capitalism is competition of private enterprises. The weapon in competition is cheap production. Big machines with few workers produce the same goods at a smaller cost than small machines with many workers. The increase in productivity of the work means substitution of machines for men. The whole history of capitalism is a turning out of workmen, made jobless, through the perfection, the rationalization of machinery. They form the army of the unemployed that have to wait [to find out] whether by an increase in production they may perhaps find work again.

Capitalism can only exist by continually extending its domain. For its increasing production it must seek foreign markets. When the home markets restrict their buying power, foreign markets are sought all the more eagerly. Foreign continents are opened to the products of capital-ism; countries of barbaric tribes as well as empires of old civilization are revolutionized. Here a fierce strife arises between capitalist groups and capitalist stakes over the domination of markets, of colonies, of foreign countries. Their opposing interests break out into wars, where the mass of the people, the working class, has to fight, to die, to be crippled for the interests of the capitalist's profit. The last world war has ruined the economics of Europe; America entered only at the last moment. The next world war will ruin the economics of America and of the whole world.

Capitalism is production for profit. Of course it must produce goods that can be sold, else there is no profit; thus it is at the same time production of the necessities for the life of mankind. But with regard to purpose and directing force it is production for profit. When the profit ceases or is doubtful the capitalist stops the production. He is the master. Thus the providing for the needs of society, the first condition of life for every community, is left to the profit hunger of private capitalists. That this cannot be relied upon is shown by the crises. Periodically, through the inner laws of capitalism, a time of prosperity when production expands year by year, is followed by a breaking down, a depression, a crisis, when the armies of the unemployed increase and the production is restricted. What a crisis means, the workers can experience today, now that a world crisis is reigning to an extent never witnessed before, a crisis so long and deep that it looks as if capitalism will never recover from it.

Crisis and world war show that capitalism cannot master the mighty productive forces it has developed. Society is like a powerful motorcar with a baby behind the wheel. Production is like a brainless monster, composed of mighty disjunctive parts directed by no common consciousness. Governments may try to make some regulations, to institute a leading superior power; but so long as profit is the basis and the moving force of the economic system, a real conscious order cannot exist.

For the working class the situation is this. They see before them the big apparatus of production, the factories, the machines—the products all of their own hands—idle and inactive. They themselves have hands to work, and a will eager to work, yet they also are enforced to be idle and inactive. They are hungry and badly in need of all the necessities of life. When they set in action the production apparatus and work with it, they can produce all they need. But they are not allowed to do so; the capitalist class is the master and prevents the workers from produceing what society requires.[1]

---

1   [This paragraph was followed by this passage, though Pannekoek crossed it out: "There has been an analogous situation in history, on a smaller scale. In France, before the Great Revolution, a large part of the soil belonged to the Church and the

Can anybody believe that forever the machine and the workers, which for the existence of mankind must be united, can be kept separated? And how are they kept separated? Only by a spell. A spell, called the right of property.

Hence it is clear that capitalism is a passing, temporary form of society. It has a beginning and it will have an end. In its beginning it was a new and necessary form of production: only by the eager competition of capital and the steady accumulation of capital out of the surplus value, the slow progress of the petty world of small producers could be accelerated to the world-conquering rapid technical progress of today, to the extent that an abundant living for all should be possible. But now capitalism stands in the way of progress, it cannot master the economic powers it has generated, and it becomes a power of destruction and regress. It is bound to disappear.

Capitalism is a transitory form of production, which itself points to a further, a higher form.

We call it private capitalism, private enterprise. But private is only the juridical form of ownership, not the technical form of the labor process. Labor is a collective process. In a big factory, or in a railway, a collectivity of men is working and handling the complicated apparatus of production. It is highly organized collective work; only by a strict adaptation of each member of the whole an accurate running and a high performance is secured.

But while the work is collective, the ownership is private. The outcome of the collective labor is seized by the capitalist as his private property. The juridical form is in straight contradiction to the technical form. In the old modes of small production and craft, work and ownership were in harmony: the worker owned his tools. Whoever had to work with the technical implements, must also command them. In developed capitalism this harmony has been broken.

---

nobles and was not or badly worked. The farmers wanted it, and they lived in poverty, because also in the use of their own land they were restricted. The Revolution gave it to them, and they produced an abundance of food, which made it possible to France to sustain a twenty years' war against the whole of Europe." —Ed.]

Can we restore the harmony by changing the technical form back to the old small craft? That is impossible. The result of a progress of centuries, the high technique and knowledge of modern society, warranting coming riches for all mankind, cannot be abolished. The only possible means of removing the contradiction is to adapt the juridical form to the technical reality. The collectivity of workers, who use and handle the modern machinery should also command and possess them. Collective work implies collective ownership. And since the factories and means of production of the whole country—of the whole world even—form a unity and must work together as one large apparatus of production, this should be the property of the working people as a body. This is the next necessary change needed in the world, indicated and foretold by the contradictions of present-day capitalism.

Socialism or communism is the name of the new form of production. Whether there is a real difference in meaning between these names will be seen afterward.

Defenders of capitalism will say that we have too easily dismissed the capitalist in the process of production. For he also has a necessary function, just as much as the workers. He is the leader of production; by his command the unity and the organization and consequently the efficiency of the collective process is secured. In petty capitalism this is certainly true; because the capitalist is the owner of the means of production he is at the same time the leader of the work. But in highly developed capitalism these two sides have been separated. As the leader we find a director, and the owners are the shareholders. This leadership consists only in leading the difficult process of profit making; he has to buy cheap to sell dear, to beat competitors out of the field, he has to direct matters in such a way that the greatest profits for the owners are made. The technical process of production of necessities is the simple duty of the workers, the engineers, and the technical staff.

In the shareholders the juridical character of the capitalist appears pure and simple. They have no function at all in the process of production. They are sitting at home, or at some country place or in Key West or in a mountain hotel; all they have to do is to receive the dividends, the divided-up surplus value, and to spend them. They are parasites of society; they have the same function in society as pests in agriculture. They show us the real part played by private property in modern capitalism.

Collective ownership of the apparatus of production instead of private ownership means in the first place the throwing off of these parasites. But it means more. Collective ownership means that the workers, instead of being paid a salary as the price of their labor power, are direct masters and owners of the products. Collective ownership means the production directed and managed by the workers themselves. Not for the sake of profit, but simply to provide the necessities of life. It is production for use, guided only by the needs of society, hence led and directed by clear consciousness of the result. By making use of the best technical means abundant wealth will be produced for all. Instead of a society based on exploitation of the numerous poor by the ruling few we get a real commonwealth. The productive forces are dominated by man and used for his welfare. Then mankind will have secured forever its life subsistence. It is, as Engels said, the transition from the reign of necessity into the reign of freedom.

It is the task of the working class to bring about the new society. For the workers the capitalist system is a lifelong curse; hard work and a poor living in times of prosperity, unemployment and pauperization in times of depression. Communism means the prospect of wealth, of freedom, of happiness to them. They must desire communism with all their heart.

But the capitalist class hates communism. It will take away their profit, the basis of their existence as capitalists. The scientists of capitalism have brought forward some dozen reasons why communism will be a disaster, a calamity, the destruction of all civilization, the fall of mankind into deep barbarism. So in defending their profits the capitalists have the conviction that they defend human culture against greedy barbarian hordes.

Thus the contest between capitalism and communism is a contest between the two opposing classes. It is a class struggle between the capitalist class and the working class. The workers will have to fight, if they want to have communism. And when they fight they will be right; for the progress of mankind is with them. It is their honorable task, imposed upon them by history, as their share in the rising of the human race, to fight, to vanquish and to beat down the capitalist class, and in this social revolution, to establish communism.

At the present day we are living in the beginning of this struggle. Hence it is a matter of first importance to inquire, what are its conditions, and how it has to be fought.

CHAPTER 2

THE POWER OF THE CLASSES

This chapter is from Pannekoek's handwritten manuscript. A shorter version was published in *International Council Correspondence* vol. 2, no. 6 (May 1936) under the same title. —Ed.

Let us first consider the adversary.

The power of the capitalist class is enormous. Never in history was there a ruling class with such power.

Their power is firstly money power. All the treasures of the world are theirs, and modern capital, produced by the ceaseless toil of millions of workers, exceeds all the treasures of the old world. The surplus value is partly accumulated into ever more and new capital; partly it must be spent by the capitalists. They buy servants for their personal attendance; cannot they also buy people to defend them, to safeguard their power and their dominating position? In capitalism everything can be bought for money; muscles and brain as well as love and honor have become market goods. Said Rockefeller, old John D: Everybody can be bought, if you only know his price. The statement is not exactly true; but it shows the capitalist's view of the world.

The capitalists buy young proletarians to form a fighting force. In the same way as against strikes they buy Pinkertons, they may, in times of greater danger, organize big fighting armies of volunteers, provided with the best modern arms, well-fed and well-paid, to defend their sacred capitalist order.

But capitalism cannot be defended by brutal force alone. Being itself the outcome of a high development of intellectual forces, it must consequently be defended by these same intellectual forces. Behind the physical fight in the class struggle stands the spiritual contest of ideas. Capitalists know that, often better than the workers do. Hence they buy all the good brains they can get, by paying them accordingly, of course. Often in a coarse, open way; but most often indirectly, for instance, by spending money for cultural aims. Numerous students of science all the world over have profited in their researches from the "Rockefeller Foundation"; so the name Rockefeller sounds well in the world of natural sciences, where Ludlow is never heard of, and it serves capitalism well. Capitalists have founded universities all over America, where among other sciences also sociology is taught, to demonstrate the impossibility and the wickedness of communism. The young people leave the universities imbued with these ideas and they know that high salaries and public honor await them if they do not deviate from the straight capitalist path.

The capitalists buy the press, buy editors, buy all means of publicity, and in this way they dominate public opinion. It is an invisible spiritual despotism, by which the entire nation is thinking just as the capitalist class will have them think. Money reigns over the world, in the first place because it can buy all the brain power of the world.

Capitalist power, in the second place, is political power. The state is the organization of the capitalist class. Its task is to render possible private production, and to enable the separate capitalists to carry on their separate business, by protecting them and regulating their intercourse. Government is the executive board of the capitalist class.

The government makes laws to protect honest businessmen against thieves and murderers. Shall it not make laws too against strikers, who are more dangerous, and against red revolutionists who threaten the future of all business?

Behind the authority of law, police and jail stand to enforce it. In every strike, in every political demonstration, the workers find the police power against them, clubbing their heads, throwing them into jail, for the benefit of the capitalist class and to protect the capitalist's profit. Gangs of hired thugs are sworn as deputy sheriffs and given police authority. And when the workers cannot be beaten down in this way, militia and citizen guards are mobilized against them.

In each capitalist state the army is the strongest force in the service of the capitalist class, because for its contest with other capitalist states it needs the entire fighting power of the whole country, all classes included. The army is a highly organized body, bound together by the strictest military discipline, provided with the most cruel, refined, and effective means of killing and destroying. If it is used in political wars, where in the worst case the capitalist class suffers only heavy losses, is it not then to be used in case of revolution, where the capitalist class is menaced with complete loss of all it possesses?

Thus the state is the stronghold of capitalism. As a strongly organized power, over the whole country directed by one will of the central government, provided with a heavily armed powerful force, it protects the capitalist class.

Physical force, however, is not sufficient to subdue a people or a class. How many strong governments in history, though well-armed, have been overthrown by rebellions! Spiritual forces in most cases are decisive above mere physical power. Also in capitalism the rule holds good that in the long run it is more effectual to fool people than to beat them.

Capitalist power then, thirdly, consists in its intellectual power. The ideas of a ruling class, as a rule, pervade the whole of society. Certainly, the capitalist class could not buy guards and intellectuals, if these fellows did not, in the main, share its ideas and feelings. Capitalist government could not govern, even with its strong physical power, if not the mass of the people were filled with the same spirit as the government itself. How is it possible that in the mass of the people, even in the working class, this capitalist spirit is current?

Firstly by tradition and inheritance. The capitalist frame of thought and the capitalist spirit are nothing but the spirit and the frame of thought of the former middle classes, the petty producers. The idea of private property as a natural right, the belief that everyone should build his own fortune and that free competition guarantees the best result for each, the maxim that everyone has only to care for himself and to let God care for all, the conviction that thrift and industry are the virtues which secure prosperity, and that America (or whatever may be your nationality) is the best country and should be defended against other nations—all this is inherited from the time and the class of small business. And this is the very creed big business wants the masses to believe in as eternal truths.

The fathers or grandfathers of the proletarians of today were such small businessmen themselves: small farmers, settlers, craftsmen, even small capitalists, ridden down by competition; either in America, or somewhere in Europe. They too have inherited these ideas, and in their youth they found them to be true. Then society changed rapidly, big industry developed, and forever they became proletarians. Their ideas, however, could not change so rapidly and their mind clings to the old things.

Still, the school of life is powerful and impresses the mind with new ideas in line with the new real world. Now, however, the capitalist school comes into action. With all possible means the capitalist ideas are propagated and artificially enforced upon the minds. At first in the actual schools, in the years when the children's minds are flexible and impressible; afterward, for the adults, from the pulpit, in the daily press, by the radio and the movies. Their task is not only to keep the capitalistic way of thinking alive in the working masses, but still more to prevent them from thinking. By filling their time and their minds with exciting futilities and killing every wish for serious reading and thinking they work as morphium for the mind.[2]

May this be called fooling the workers? The capitalistic class is sincere in this propaganda, it believes what it tries to urge upon the workers; it is their own middle-class feeling and its highest wisdom. But

---

2   [Morphium was the original name German pharmacist Friedrich Sertürner gave
     morphine. —Ed.]

capitalistic wisdom is foolishness to the workers. The workers have to foster the new ideas that are growing up out of the changing world, they have to acquire the knowledge of the evolution of labor and of the class struggle as the way to communism.

Thus the power of the capitalist class is more than their money power and their political power alone. The small businessmen, the small farmers who believe that they will succeed by personal effort—as sometimes they do—are a part of the capitalist power. Every workman, who only cares for himself and not for the future of his class, every workman who only reads his capitalist paper and finds his chief interest in boxing matches, by so doing contributes to the power of the capitalist class.

In the rapid development of technical and economic forms of production the mind of man is left behind. This mental backwardness of the working masses is the chief power of the capitalist class.

* * *

What power can the working class set forth against it?

Firstly, the working class is the most numerous class in society. By the growth of industry it continually increased and still increases, whereas the number of independent businessmen has relatively decreased.

If, by means of statistical data, we go more into details, we have to consider that these data always relate to the past; they can show, however, the trend of the change in conditions. In all capitalist countries the general aspect is the same, but the degree of development is different. We will take Germany and the United States as specimen cases.

In Germany in 1907 among 25 million somehow occupied, 5 million were independent (in 1882 they were 5 million also), and 16 million working for wage or salary (1882, 10.5 million). Among the latter we find 1.5 million servants (1882, also 1.5 million), 3 million technical employees or staff (1882, only 1 million) and 11.5 million wage workers (1882, 8 million) Among the independent businessmen 2 million were farmers, 1.5 million small craftsmen and shopkeepers, and only some hundred thousands were real capitalists. Of the whole population 22 percent lived on the land, 78 percent in the towns (in 1882 these figures were 32 and 68 percent).

In the United States agriculture takes a more important place. The town population, in 1880 only 29 percent, had increased to 46 percent in 1910, and is certainly still higher now. Of course the rural population is not all agricultural; a number of industries are located in the country. The number of persons occupied in agriculture was nearly 11 million in 1900, as well as in 1926; since the number of farms was 6 million there is a strong minority of employees among them. The number of wage workers in manufacturing industries increased from 5 million in 1900 to 9 or 10 million in 1925, the number of salaried employees from 6 to 16 hundred thousand. If we add the people employed in mining, transport, and construction trades we come to 19 million employed in the entire industry. Compare to this the number of nonagricultural enterprises: 300,000 factories, 1½ million trade enterprises, nearly 2 million other small enterprises—and we see how far the number of dependent exploited persons exceeds the number of independent persons. Another statistic gives for 1927 the total number of 27 million of wage workers, 8 million of salaried employees, whereas the total number of "gainfully occupied" persons (all businessmen therefore included) was 44 million in a population of 118 million.

That here also big industry grows more rapidly than small industry may be seen from the following figures. In 1914 the number of small, middle and big factories was 185,000, 82,000, 8,000; in 1925 these numbers were 55,000, 111,000, 20,000 (with an average of 3, of 21, of 330 workers). The workmen occupied in these three groups were in 1914: 560,000, 4 million, 2½ million; in 1925 160,000, 2 1/3 million, 7 million. The change is manifest: the bulk of the industrial workers, instead of in the middle sized factories is now occupied in the large factories, where several hundreds of men, and even thousands are collected.

The figures show that in the United States the working class is the most numerous class. Only the farmers and the salaried employees follow at some distance as important classes. The capitalist class proper is insignificant in number; and the small and middle-class businessmen and the petty dealers, are much less numerous than the wage workers.

But number is not the only thing that counts. A number of millions, dispersed in widely separated homes all over the land, cannot exert the same power as the same number of millions pressed together in the towns. The big towns, the metropoles, are the centers of economic, cultural, and political life. The millions of workers, forming the majorities in the population of these centers, assembled into big class agglomerations, must with this state of affairs be able to exert a strong social power.

In ancient Rome the proletarians were numerous also and strongly concentrated. Their social power, however, was nothing, because they did not work. They were parasites, they lived from public spending. With the modern proletarians the matter is the reverse.

The second element of power for the working class is its importance in human society. It is on their work that society is founded. The capitalists might be dismissed, the petty producers and dealers might be dispensed with without impairing the production of life necessities, which mostly takes place in the big factories. But the working class cannot be dispensed with. With its essential fundamental role only the work of the farmers can be compared.

The workers have their hand on the production apparatus. They manage it, they work it, they command it, they have direct power over it. Not legally; legally they have to obey the capitalists; and police or soldiers may come to enforce this legal right. But actually it is theirs; without them the living producing machinery is a dead carcass. If they refuse to work, if the whole working class refuses to work, society cannot exist. It has happened already that a general strike paralyzed the entire economic and social life and thereby wrung some important concessions from the unwilling ruling class. Then for a moment, like a flash of lightning, that mighty power of the proletarian class, its intimate connection with the production apparatus, was disclosed.

To be sure, if this possible power is to become a living actual power, a weighty condition must be fulfilled. Such united action of the whole class is not possible, if it is not sustained by a strong moral force. So as the third element of proletarian power we find the solidarity, the spirit of unity, organization. Solidarity is the bond that unites the will of all the separate individuals into one common will, thus achieving one mighty organized action.

Is it right to speak here of a specifically proletarian virtue? Does not capitalism itself practice organization and united action in its factories, in its trusts, in its armies? Here the unity is based upon command, upon fines, upon penalties. Certainly, for common interests combined action must take place in each class; but then always again the true economic position manifests itself, that capitalists are competitors, and workers are comrades.

Capitalism is based on private business, private interests. The more eagerly the capitalist pursues his personal interests only, the better for his business. Hence a hard egotism is developed, that ever again overthrows natural human sympathies. The workers, on the other hand, cannot win anything by egotism. So long as they faced capital individually, they were powerless and miserable; only by collective action could they win better conditions. The more they pursue personal interests, the more they are beaten down; the more they develop a feeling of fellowship, mutual aid, self-sacrifice for their class community, the better it is for their interests.

When at the dawn of civilization private property arose, men separated, to work each on his own lot, in order to develop the productivity of labor in mutual competition. In this century-long development from small crafts to modern industry, civilized man rose to a sturdy self-determination, to independence, to confidence in his own powers, and to a strong feeling of individualism. All his energies and faculties were wakened in service of his fighting powers. But at the cost of moral losses: egotism grew, and cruelty, distrust, and enmity against his fellowmen.

Now the modern proletariat is coming up, for the first time a class without property, hence without real interests one against the other. Still endowed with the personal energies and faculties inherited from their ancestors—though at the first moment often helplessly beaten down by the overwhelming new power of capitalism—they are trained by the machine into the discipline of common action. And their common interest against the employer first, then against the capitalist class, awakens in them the feelings of brotherhood—which slept in their hearts as in all human hearts, as an inheritance of the prehistoric times of tribal communism—the necessary condition and the guarantee for a successful fight against capitalism, the dawn of the complete brotherhood of future communism.

So the working class finds strength in its moral superiority over the capitalist class. But not less in its intellectual superiority. To the feeling is added the knowledge. First comes the deed, certainly, the action of solidarity, that springs spontaneously from the depth of emotion and passion. After that comes the insight, that here is an unavoidable conflict of opposing class interests. It is the first form of class consciousness. With the deepening of knowledge the ways of action, the fighting conditions are seen more clearly, and, just as is the case with all science, this insight may lead future actions along the most efficient ways.

After their number, their social importance, their moral force of solidarity, this knowledge is certainly the fourth element in proletarian power. It is the science developed chiefly by Marx and Engels, which explains, firstly, the course of history as the growth of society from its primitive beginnings, through feudalism and capitalism to communism, based upon the development of labor and its productivity. And secondly it explains the structure of capitalist production, and shows how capitalism must break down through its own forces, by producing the proletarian class, by exploiting the workers, by driving them into revolt through its own collapses, the crises, and by increasing their fighting powers.

This science, Marxism, is a truly proletarian science. The capitalist class rejects it; its scientists deny its truth. Indeed, it is impossible for the capitalist class to accept it. No class can accept a theory that proclaims its certain collapse and death; for by accepting, it could not fight with full confidence and with its full force. And to fight against annihilation is a primary instinct, in a class as well as in an organism.

The capitalist class cannot see beyond the horizon of capitalism. So it sees the growing concentration of capital, the growing power of big finance, the heavy crises and the impending world wars, the rising tide of the proletarian fight and its threat of revolution—it sees all these phenomena, and not one rational outcome. It sees no sense in history, though its ablest scientists investigate every detail; it sees no light in the future; uncertainty and mysticism fill its mind. But it is determined to fight for its supremacy.

For the workers this science enlightens their arduous course to the future. It makes clear to them their own life, their work, their poverty, their relation to their employers, to the other classes. It explains to them the reality of the world, as they experience it themselves, different from the capitalist teachings. Whereas the school of life impresses their minds with new ideas in line with the new world, it is this science of society that molds these ideas into a firm consistent knowledge. And so the workers acquire the wisdom they need in their fight for freedom.

* * *

If now we compare the classes, this is what we see.

The capitalist power is enormous, oppressing. It is an aggregate of heavy, hard realities. The working class also has strong elements of power; but these are still imperfect, hence the history of labor is a series of defeats. They are expectations rather for the future than realities for today. But they are growing. By the innate forces of society themselves, they are increasing. And this is a stronger reality than any other. Just as the young sprouting plant is a stronger reality than the hard dead branch.

The working class is the class of the future. All the forces of the real material world drive and help her. They assure her victory. That is her strongest power. She is a vigorous plant, growing out of the soil of the world's development itself. Capitalist power is a big tree, molding in its core. It will be hard work yet to fell this tree.

The power of the workers consists in elements, which lie partly outside, partly inside their own conscious strivings. Their number and their importance in society are results of an economic development entirely outside their will. They have to accept and use them, but they cannot change them. If by special causes in some country the economic development should take another course, should stagnate or decay, they would also have to accept it and to make the best of it according to the possibilities.

Their moral and their intellectual power, however, consist of faculties within themselves. These faculties arise out of the praxis of their life, of their fight; every victory, every defeat after an honest fight is a new experience, tending to raise their solidarity and their insight. On the other hand the pursuit of illusions and false side ways may temporarily darken their view and narrow their feelings. As in every community of men these faculties are strengthened by mutual intercourse, by praise and blame, by teaching and propaganda; they are objects of zeal and devotion to enthusiastic propagandists. Thus the moral forces are exalted and directed toward unity of action; thus the intellectual forces are raised and directed to wisdom of action.

Unity and wisdom, these are the great qualities the workers need for victory. They are the essentials of the working-class power. They are the outcome of all the struggles and pains and sacrifices of the labor movement. To acquire unity and wisdom for the victory, this is the purpose and goal of every fight. The test of every tactics and every mode of action in the labor movement is this, whether the unity and the wisdom, i.e., whether the power of the working class is increased by it.

CHAPTER 3

TRADE UNIONISM

This chapter is from Pannekoek's handwritten manuscript. A shorter version was published in *International Council Correspondence* vol. 2, no. 2 (January 1936) under the same title. —Ed.

How must the working class fight in order to win? This is the all-important question facing them every day. What efficient means of action, what tactics can it use to conquer power and defeat the enemy?

No science, no theory could tell them exactly what to do. But they knew it themselves, instinctively, and they stood up to fight against misery and oppression. Spontaneously, by feeling out, by sensing possibilities, they found their ways of action. And as capitalism grew and conquered the earth and increased its power, the power of the workers also increased, new modes of action, wider and more efficient, came up beside the old ones or instead of them. It is evident that with changing conditions the forms of action, the tactics of the class struggle have to change also.

Trade unionism is the primary form of labor movement in fixed capitalism. The isolated worker is powerless against the capitalistic employer. The union binds the workers together into a common action; with the strike as their weapon. Then the equality of powers is restored, or even reversed to the other side, so that the isolated small employer is weak over against the mighty union. Hence in developed capitalism trade unions and employers' unions stand as fighting powers one against the other.

Trade unionism first came up in England, where industrial capitalism first developed. Afterward it spread to other countries, as a natural
companion of capitalist industry, where this made its appearance. Among
these America was in very special conditions. In the beginning there
was an immensity of free unoccupied land all around open to settlers.
So there was a shortness of workers in the towns, and high wages and
good conditions could easily by obtained. The American Federation of
Labor became a power in the country and, generally, was able to uphold
a relatively high standard of living for the workers.

It is clear that in such conditions the idea of overthrowing capitalism
could not for a moment arise in the minds of the workers. Capitalism
offered them a sufficient and fairly secure living. They did not feel themselves a separate class, whose interests were hostile to the existing order;
they were part of it, they were conscious of partaking in all the possibilities of an ascending capitalism in a new continent. There was room for
millions and millions of people, coming partly from Europe; for these
increasing millions of farmers a rapidly increasing industry was necessary,
where, with energy and good luck, workmen could rise to free artisans,
to small businessmen, even to rich capitalists. It is natural that here a
true capitalist spirit prevailed in the working class.

The same was the case in England. Here it was due to England's
monopoly of world commerce and big industry, to the lack of competitors
in foreign markets, and to the possession of rich colonies, which brought
enormous wealth to England. The capitalist class had no need to fight for
its very profits and could allow the workers a reasonable living. Of course
fighting was at the first necessary to urge this truth upon them; but then
they could allow unions and grant wages in exchange for industrial peace.
So here also the working class was imbued with the capitalist spirit.

Now this is entirely in harmony with the innermost character of
trade unionism. Trade unionism is an action of the workers, which does
not go beyond the limit of capitalism. Its aim is not to replace capitalism by another form of production, but to secure good living conditions
within capitalism. Its character is not revolutionary but conservative.

Certainly, trade union action is class struggle. There is a class antagonism in capitalism; capitalists and workers have opposing interests. Not
only on the question of conservation or subversion of capitalism, but also
within capitalism itself, with regard to the division of the total product.
The capitalists try to increase their profits, the surplus value, as much as
possible by cutting down wages and increasing the hours or the intensity
of labor. The workers try to increase their wages and to shorten their
hours of work—their own private life begins where the work for the boss
is finished. What a worker needs in order to live, the price of his labor
power, is not a fixed quantity, though it must exceed a certain hunger
minimum, and it is not paid by the capitalist of his own free will. So it is
the object of a contest, a real class struggle. It is the task, the function
of the trade unions to carry on this fight.

It is thus that trade unions serve the interest of the workers. But
they also serve the interest of capitalism itself and of the capitalist class.
By securing the payment of the labor power at its right value they are
a regular and indispensable member of capitalist society. Suppose for
a moment that there were no trade unions; what would be the consequences? The employers, now the strongest, and each one only thinking
of his personal profit, could lower the wages, increase the hours of work,
at the cost of heavy damages to the health, the strength, the working capacity of the laboring class, i.e., at a serious risk to the future
productivity of labor. Irregular strikes would then break out, continually
and unexpectedly disturbing the course of production. Now the trade
unions regulate this class struggle; by tariff contracts with the employers'
unions they guarantee peace in industry and they guard the employers
against one of them attempting unfair competition by underpaying his
men. When the workers' class has developed to the point that they let
themselves be subdued, when they have a certain fighting force, then
it is in the interest of the capitalist class, that this fighting should be
led into the regular bed of trade unionism. This is its function in capitalism. Capitalism is not complete, it is not true capitalism, without
trade unionism.

This character of trade unionism must be borne in mind if we consider its effect upon the workers. It tries to make capitalism endurable to the workers; and for this it must propagate the theory that by its action capitalism can be made endurable. Sometimes, up to a certain point, it meets with success. Under such circumstances as mentioned above, in England and the United States in the nineteenth century, existing conditions seemed to confirm this theory. So the workers did believe in capitalism there.

These were, however, very special circumstances. When capitalism arose in many other countries, when England's monopoly on foreign markets was broken by German, French, American, Japanese competition, when in America all the land was occupied, and new millions of immigrants of a low standard of living followed in, not as settlers but as industrial workers, matters changed. Sharp competition compelled the capitalists to strive for the highest possible profits. They tried with all their might to press down the life standard of the workers and to increase their exploitation. Now the teachings of capitalism were in direct opposition to the teachings of trade unionism; they pointed toward revolution.

Of course the practice of trade unions was still necessary. Even more so than ever. Against these very attacks of the capitalist class, the unions had to wage a continuous and fierce fight, sometimes, in years of prosperity, with some positive effect, but usually on the defensive, with the only success that they prevented a downfall.

Yet these apparently fruitless struggles were of the utmost importance for the working class. Trade unionism was always the first training school in proletarian virtue, in solidarity as the spirit of organized fighting. It embodied the first form of proletarian organized power. In the early English and American trade unionism this virtue often petrified and degenerated into a narrow craft-corporationship, a true capitalistic state of mind. It was different, however, where the workers had to fight for their very existence, where the utmost efforts of their unions could hardly uphold their standard of living, where the full force of an energetic fighting and expanding capitalism attacked them. There they learned that trade unionism is only one side of their fight; that their aims must be widened; that capitalism itself must be destroyed. There they learned the wisdom that only the revolution can definitely save them.

So there comes a disparity between the working class and trade unionism. The working class has to look beyond capitalism; trade unionism lives entirely within capitalism and cannot look beyond. Trade unionism can only represent a part, a necessary but narrow part in the class struggle. And now it develops sides which bring it into conflict with the greater aims of the working class.

With the growth of capitalism and big industry the unions too must grow. They become big corporations of hundreds of thousands of members, extending over the whole country, having sections in every town and every factory. Officials must be appointed presidents, secretaries, treasurers, to conduct the affairs, to manage the finances, locally and centrally. They are the leaders who negotiate with the capitalists and who by this practice have acquired a special skill. The president of a union is a big man, as big as the capitalist employer himself, and he discusses with him on equal terms the interests of his members. The officials are specialists in trade union work, which the members, entirely occupied by their factory work, cannot judge or direct themselves.

So large a corporation as a union is not simply an assembly of single workers; it becomes an organized body, like a living organism, with its own character, its own policy, its own mentality, its own traditions, its own functions. It is a body with its own interests, apart from the interests of the working class. It has a will to live and to fight for its existence. If it should come to pass that it were no longer necessary for the workers, then it would not simply disappear; its funds, its members, its officials, its papers, its spirit, all these are realities that cannot disappear at once, but continue their existence as elements of the organization.

The union officials, the labor leaders, are the bearers of the special union interests. Originally workmen from the shop, they acquire, by long practice at the head of the organization, a new social character. In each social group, once it is big enough to form a special group, the economic function in society, the nature of its work, molds and determines its social character, its mode of thinking and acting. Their function is entirely different from the workers', they do not work in factories, they are not exploited by capitalists, their existence is not threatened continually by unemployment. They sit in offices, in fairly secure positions, they have to manage corporation affairs and to speak and discuss with employers and on workers meetings. Of course they have to stand for the workers, and to defend their interests and wishes against the capitalist. This is, however, not very different from the position of the lawyer who, appointed secretary of an organization, will stand for its members and defend their interests to the full of his capacity.

There is a difference, surely. Because the labor leaders came from the ranks of the workers, they have experienced for themselves what wage work and exploitation means. They feel themselves members of the working class and the proletarian spirit often acts as a strong tradition in them. But the new reality of their life continually tends to weaken this tradition. Economically they are not proletarians any more. They sit in conferences with capitalists, bargaining over tariffs and hours, pitting interests against interests, just as the opposing interests of capitalist concerns are waged one against the other. They learn to understand the capitalists' position just as well as the workers', they have an eye for the needs of industry; they try to mediate. Personal exceptions occur, of course. But, as a rule, they cannot have that elementary class feeling of the workers, that does not understand and weigh capitalist interests over against their own, but will fight for their proper interests. So they get into conflict with the workers.

The labor leaders in advanced capitalism are numerous enough to form a special group or class with a special class character and special class interests. As representatives and leaders of the unions they embody the character and the interests of the unions in them. The unions are necessary elements of capitalism; so the leaders feel as necessary items, as most useful citizens in capitalist society. The capitalist function of unions is to regulate class conflicts and to secure industrial peace; so labor leaders may see it as their duty as citizens to work for industrial peace and mediate in conflicts. The task of the union lies entirely within capitalism; so labor leaders do not look beyond capitalism. The instinct of self-preservation, the will of the unions to live and to fight for existence is embodied in the will of the labor leaders to fight for the existence of the union. Their own existence is indissolubly connected with the existence of the unions. This is not meant in a petty sense, that they only think of their personal jobs when fighting for the union; it means that primary necessities of life and social functions determine opinions. Their whole life is concentrated in the unions, only here they have a task. So the most important part of the world, the most necessary organ of society, the only source of security and power for the working class is for them the unions; hence it must be preserved and defended with all means.

Even when the realities of capitalist society undermine this position. And so the real capitalism does, as with its expansion the class conflicts become sharper.

* * *

The concentration of capital in mighty concerns and their connection with big finance render the position of the capitalist employers much stronger against the workers. Powerful industrial magnates are reigning as monarchs over large masses of workers, they keep them in absolute subjection and do not allow "their" men to go into unions. Now and then the heavily exploited slaves break out in revolt, in a big strike. They hope to enforce better terms, shorter hours, more human conditions, the right of organization; union organizers come to aid them. But then the capitalist masters use their social and political power. The strikers are driven from their homes, they are shot by militia or by hired thugs, their spokesmen are put into jail and court-martialed, their relief actions are inhibited by court injunctions, the capitalist press denounces their cause as disorder, murder and revolution, public opinion is aroused against them. Then, after months of standing firm and of heroic suffering, exhausted by misery and disappointment, unable to impress the capitalist steel structure, they have to submit and to postpone their claims to a more favorable opportunity.

In the trades where unions exist as mighty organizations, their position is weakened by this same concentration of capital. The big funds they had collected for strike support are insignificant in comparison to the money power of their adversaries; a couple of lockouts may totally drain them. No matter how hard the capitalist employer presses upon the workers, by cutting down their wages or intensifying their labor, the union cannot wage a fight. When tariffs have to be renewed, it feels itself the weaker party, because in a fight it cannot hope to win. It has to accept the bad terms the capitalists offer; no skill in bargaining avails. But now the trouble with their members begins. The men want to fight; they will not submit before they have fought, and they have not much to lose by it. The leaders, however, have much to lose: the financial power of the union, perhaps its very existence. They try to avoid the fight, which they consider as hopeless. They have to convince the men that it is better to come to terms and not to fight. So they must act as spokesmen of the employers to force the capitalists terms upon the workers. It is even worse when the workers insist on fighting in opposition to the decision of the union. Then the union power must be used as a weapon to subdue the workers.

So the labor leader has become the slave of his capitalistic task of securing industrial peace—now at the cost of the workers, though he meant to serve them as best he could. But he cannot look beyond capitalism; and within the horizon of capitalism he is right that fighting is of no use. The criticism can only mean that trade unionism here stands at the limit of its power.

Is there another way out then? Could the workers win anything by fighting? Probably they will lose the immediate issue of the fight. But they will gain something else. By not submitting without having fought, they rouse the spirit of revolt against capitalism itself. They proclaim a new issue. But here the whole working class must join in. To the whole class, to all their fellow workers they show that in capitalism there is no future for them, and that only by fighting, not as a trade union, but as a class unity, they can win. This means the beginning of a revolutionary fight. And when their fellow workers understand this lesson, when solidarity strikes break out in other trades, when a wave of rebellion goes over the country, then in the arrogant hearts of the capitalists there may appear some doubt as to their omnipotence and some willingness to make concessions.

The trade union leader does not understand this point of view, because trade unionism cannot reach beyond capitalism. He opposes this kind of fight. Fighting capitalism in this way means at the same time rebellion against the trade unions. The labor leader stands beside the capitalist in their common fear for the workers' rebellion.

When the trade unions fought against the capitalist class for better working conditions, the capitalist class hated them; but it had not the power to destroy them, it had to arrange matters with them—only clever capitalists appreciated them. If the trade unions should try to raise all the forces of the working class in their fight, the capitalist class will persecute them with all its means. They may see their action repressed as rebellion, their offices destroyed by militia, their leaders fined and thrown in jail, their funds confiscated. On the other hand, if they keep their members from fighting, the capitalist class may consider them as valuable institutions to be preserved and protected, and their leaders as deserving citizens. So the trade unions find themselves between the devil and the deep blue sea: on the one side persecution, which is a hard thing to bear for people who meant to be peaceful citizens, on the other side rebellion of the members, which may undermine the union. The capitalist class, if it is wise, will recognize that a bit of sham fighting must be allowed to uphold the influence of the leaders upon the members.

The conflicts arising here are not anybody's fault; they are an inevitable consequence of capitalist development. Capitalism exists, but it is at the same time on the way to perdition. It must be fought as a living thing but at the same time as a transitory thing. The workers must wage a steady fight for wages and working conditions, while at the same time communist ideas, more or less clear and conscious, awaken in their minds. Great thoughts arise in them of a better future for mankind, deep feelings of a golden world of freedom, to be won at the cost of immense self-sacrifice and devoted fighting. At the same time they cling to the unions, feeling that they are still necessary, trying now and then to transform them into better fighting institutions.

But the spirit of trade unionism, which is in its pure form a capitalist spirit, is not in them. The divergence between these two tendencies in capitalism and in the class struggle appears now as a rift between the trade union spirit, mainly embodied in their leaders, and the growing revolutionary feelings of the members. This rift becomes apparent in the opposite positions they take in various important social and political questions.

Trade unionism is bound to capitalism; it has its best chances to obtain good wages when capitalism flourishes. So in times of depression it must hope that prosperity will be restored, and it must try to further it. To the workers, as a class, the prosperity of capitalism is not at all important. When it is weakened by crisis or depression, they have the best chance to attack it, to strengthen the forces of the revolution, and to take the first steps toward freedom.

Capitalism extends its dominion over foreign continents, seizing their natural treasures in order to make big profits. It conquers colonies, subjugates the primitive population and exploits them, often with horrible cruelties. The working class, driven by sympathy for these fellow victims of a mutual oppressor, denounces colonial exploitation and opposes it. Trade unionism often supports colonial politics as a way to capitalist prosperity.

With the enormous increases of capital in modern times, colonies and foreign countries are being used to invest large masses of capital. They become valuable possessions as markets for big industry and as producers of raw materials. A race for getting colonies, a fierce conflict of interests over the dividing of the world arises between the great capitalist states. In these politics of imperialism the middle classes are whirled along in a common exaltation of national greatness. Then the trade unions side with the master class, because they consider the prosperity of their own national capitalism to be dependent on its success in the national struggle. For the working class, imperialism means increasing power and brutality of their exploiters, increasing taxes, increasing oppression, increasing danger of war.

These conflicts of interests between the national capitalisms explode into wars. World war is the crowning of the policy of imperialism. For the workers war is not only the destroying of all their feelings of international brotherhood; it is also the most violent exploitation of their class for capitalist profit. The working class, as the most numerous and most oppressed class of society, has to bear all the horrors of war; they have to give not only their labor power, but also their health, their life, their little bit of safety and happiness; their bodies molder in the trenches, their limbs are torn by explosives, not only they themselves but also their wives and children at home are poisoned by gas. And when they die, it is not as heroes of a new happier world to die for which is happiness, but as worthless victims of the gold hunger of worthless masters.

Trade unionism, however, in war must stand upon the side of the capitalist class. Its interests are bound up with national capitalism, on the victory of which it must wish with all its heart. Hence it assists in arousing strong national feelings and national hatred, it helps the capitalist class to drive the workers into war and to beat down all opposition.

Trade unionism abhors communism. Communism takes away the very basis of its existence; in communism, in the absence of capitalist employers, there is no room for the trade unions and labor leaders. It is true that in countries with a strong socialist movement, where the bulk of the workers are Socialists, the labor leaders must be Socialists too, by origin as well as by environment. But then they are right-wing Socialists; and their socialism is restricted to the idea of a commonwealth where instead of greedy capitalists honest labor leaders will manage industrial production.

Trade unionism hates revolution. Revolution upsets all the ordinary relations between capitalists and workers. In its violent clashes all those careful tariff regulations are swept away; in the strife of its gigantic forces the modest skill of the bargaining labor leader loses its value. With all its power, trade unionism opposes the ideas of revolution and communism.

This opposition is not without significance. Trade unionism is a power in itself. It has considerable funds at its disposal, as material elements of power; it has its spiritual influence, upheld and propagated by its periodical papers, as mental elements of power. It is a power in the hands of leaders, who make use of it wherever the special interests of trade unionism come into conflict with the revolutionary interests of the working class. Trade unionism, though built up by the workers and consisting of workers, has turned into a power above the workers, a power over the workers. Just as government is a power over and above the people. This is the natural outcome of every firmly built organization.

* * *

The forms of trade unionism are different for different countries, owing to the different forms of development in capitalism. Nor do they always remain the same in every country. When they seem to be petrifying, the fighting spirit of the workers sometimes is able to transform them or to build up new types of unionism. Thus in England in the years 1880–90 the "new unionism" sprang up from the masses of poor dockers and other badly paid unskilled workers, bringing a new spirit also into the old craft unions. It is a consequence of new developments of capitalism which, in replacing skilled labor by machine power or in founding new industries, accumulates large bodies of unskilled workers, heavily exploited, unorganized, living in the worst of conditions. Till at last in a wave of rebellion, in big strikes, they find the way to unity and class consciousness. They mold unionism into a new form, adapted to a more highly developed capitalism. Of course, when afterward capitalism grows to still mightier forms, the new unionism cannot escape the fate of all unionism, and then it produces the same inner contradictions.

The most notable form sprang up in America, in the Industrial Workers of the World (IWW). They originated from two forms of capitalist expansion. In the immense woods and plains of the West, capitalism reaped the natural riches by Wild West methods of fierce and brutal exploitation; and the worker-adventurers responded with as wild and gallant a defense. And in the eastern states new industries were founded upon the exploitation of millions of poor immigrants, coming from countries with a low standard of living and sweating labor or other most miserable working conditions.

Against the narrow craft spirit of the old unionism of the American Federation of Labor (AFL), which divided the workers of one industrial plant in a number of separate unions, the IWW put the principle: all the workers of one factory, as comrades against one master, must form one union, to act as a strong unity against the employer. This is the principle of "industrial unionism."

Against the multitude of often jealous and bickering trade unions the IWW set up the slogan: one big union for all the workers. The fight of one group is the cause of all. Solidarity extends over the entire class.

Contrary to the haughty disdain of the well-paid old American skilled labor toward the unorganized immigrants, it was these worst-paid proletarians that the IWW led into the fight. They were too poor regularly to pay high fees and build up ordinary trade unions. But when they broke out and revolted in big strikes, it was the IWW who taught them how to fight, who raised relief funds all over the country and who defended their cause in its papers and before the courts. By a glorious series of big battles it infused the spirit of organization and self-reliance into the hearts of these masses.

Contrary to the trust in the big funds of the old unions, the Industrial Workers put their confidence in the living solidarity and the force of endurance, upheld by a burning enthusiasm. Instead of the heavy stonemasonry buildings of the old unions, they represented the flexible construction, with a fluctuating membership, contracting in time of peace, swelling and growing in the fight itself.

Contrary to the conservative capitalist spirit of trade unionism, the Industrial Workers were anticapitalist and stood for revolution. Therefore they were persecuted with intense hatred by the whole capitalist world. They were thrown into jail and often tortured on false accusations; a special new crime was even invented on their behalf: that of criminal syndicalism. This is contrary to all law and justice because syndicalism (the French name for fighting unionism), in making use as it does of legal means, cannot be a crime against existing laws, any more than the growth of the revolution itself can be a crime against law.

But this attitude is in accordance with the feelings of the capitalist class for whom revolution is the worst of all crimes.

Industrial unionism alone as a method of fighting the capitalist class is not sufficient to overthrow capitalist society and to conquer the world for the working class. It fights the capitalists as employers, on the economic field of production, but it has not the means to overthrow their political power, their political stronghold, the state power. Nevertheless the IWW so far has been the most revolutionary organization in America. More than any other it has contributed to rouse class consciousness and insight, solidarity, and unity in the working class, to turn its eyes toward communism, and to prepare its fighting power.

* * *

The lesson of all these fights is that against big capitalism trade unionism cannot win. And that if at times it does win, such victories give only temporary relief. And that yet these fights are necessary and must be fought, always anew. To the bitter end?—no, to the better end.

The reason is obvious. An isolated group of workers against an isolated capitalist boss, this might make equal parties. But an isolated group of workers against a boss, backed by the whole capitalist class, that is hopeless. And such is the case here: the state power, the money power of capitalism, public opinion of the middle class, excited by the capitalist press, all attack the group of fighting workers.

But does not the working class back the strikers? The millions of other workers do not consider this fight as their own cause. Certainly, they sympathize, and often collect money for the strikers, and this may give some relief—if its distribution is not forbidden by a judge's injunction. But this easygoing sympathy leaves the real fight to the striking group alone. The millions stand aloof, passive. So the fight cannot be won, except in some special cases, when the capitalists, for business reasons, prefer to grant concessions. Because the working class does not fight as one indivisible unity. Because there is too little unity and still less wisdom in the workers.

The matter will be different, of course, if the mass of the workers really consider such a contest as directly concerning them; if they find that their own future is at stake, and they stand with all their power behind the strikers. If they go into the fight themselves and extend the strike to other factories, to ever more branches of industry. Then the state power, the capitalist power has to be divided and cannot be used entirely against a separate group of workers. It has to face the collective power of the working class.

Extension of the strike, ever more widely, up to a general strike in the end, has often been advised as a means to avert defeat. But, to be sure, this is not to be taken as a truly expedient recipe, luckily hit upon, and ensuring victory. If such were the case trade unions certainly would have made use of it repeatedly as regular tactics. It cannot be proclaimed at will by union leaders, as a simple tactical measure. It must come forth from the deepest feelings of the masses, as the expression of their spontaneous initiative; and this is aroused only when the issue of the fight is or grows larger than a simple wage contest of one group. Only then the workers will put all their force, their enthusiasm, their solidarity, their power of endurance into it.

And they will need them. For capitalism also will bring into the field stronger forces than before. It may have been defeated, taken by surprise, by the unexpected exhibition of proletarian force, and so have made concessions; but then, afterward, it will gather new forces out of the deepest roots of its power and proceed to win back its position. So the victory is not lasting and not even certain. There is no clear and open road to victory; the road itself must be hewn and built through the capitalist jungle at the cost of immense efforts.

But even so it will mean great progress. A wave of solidarity has gone through the masses, they have felt the immense power of class unity, their self-confidence is raised, they have shaken off the narrow group egotism. Through their own deeds they have learned new wisdom: what capitalism means; how they stand as a class over against the capitalist class; they have seen a glimpse of their way to freedom.

Thus the narrow field of trade union struggle widens into the broad field of class struggle. But now the workers themselves must change. They have to take a wider view of the world. From their trade, from their work within the factory walls, their mind must widen to encompass society at large. Their spirit must rise above the petty things around them. They have to face the state; they enter the realms of politics; the problems of revolution must be dealt with.

CHAPTER 4

THE POLITICAL FIGHT AND SOCIAL DEMOCRACY

This chapter is from Pannekoek's handwritten manuscript and was never published in *International Council Correspondence.* —Ed.

Political power is the most important stronghold of the capitalist class. If the workers want to win freedom, if they strive to overthrow the capitalist system, they will have to vanquish this power. They have to wage a political fight to conquer the state.

In America politics have always been the battlefield of capitalist parties, organizations or gangs of politicians, to whom government and state power meant business. Business for themselves and their adherents, who took possession of the government offices, business for their capitalist friends, who got land, concessions, profitable contracts, mines, all the treasures of the soil. Politics was a dirty business here.

In Europe politics had a different meaning. Politics were a fight of fundamental principles. Formerly government had been in the hands of kings and nobility. The people—collective name for middle and small capitalists, artisans, farmers—had to conquer it in a series of revolutions: in England 1648, in France 1789. These revolutions were class fights, necessary for the progress of society. The greatness of their aims incited the young capitalist class and its representatives to great deeds of heroism and self-sacrifice. Without enthusiasm and idealism they could not win power.

Henceforth the political fights partly in parliament, partly in revolutionary street actions, retained this character of class struggle, the source of idealistic exaltation. The party platforms were expressions of opposed class interests; the party struggles were contests between classes, first between capitalists and landed aristocracy, then between small and big capitalists, between agrarian and industrial capital, between capitalists and workers. Though in later times the full and uncontested capitalist power brought decay of political morals and abuse of power for personal graft, this was not the distinctive character of politics. To serve their class honestly was, as a rule, the aim of capitalist politicians.

In America the young capitalist class won its liberty and dominance by a war of independence against a foreign power. It never knew what a class fight against a feudal dominating class means. Therefore politics, which always are a contest of interests, could never take on the idealistic character of a general fight for the common necessary life interests of the whole class. It could only be a contest of mean egotistic personal or group interests.

The workers have to conquer political supremacy from another ruling class. As the capitalist class did in Europe. Hence European, not American standards of politics have to guide them here.

As in former revolutions the rising capitalist class conquered the political power from the feudal classes, the rising working class in the coming proletarian revolution will conquer the political power from the capitalist class. The workers will use this political power, as the new dominant class, to destroy the capitalist system and to replace it by communism.

This was the principle first set up by Marx and Engels in the *Communist Manifesto*. Afterward it was taken up as its basis by social democracy.

Is it possible for a government, when in the hands of the working class, to change the economic system from capitalism into communism or socialism? This change is a change from private property to collective property. The right of property is fixed and regulated by law; the laws are made by the government. The class that is master of the political power can make the laws according to its needs and interests. This the capitalist class does now, this the working class will do after the victory.

The state of today is the repressive power of the ruling class; but after the victory of the working class it will be the collective representative of this class. As the instrument of the workers the state—or its smaller parts, provinces, communes, towns—takes production in hand. Its function, instead of a governing of persons becomes a management of affairs.

Is collective management of production, by a state or a town, possible? The answer is given by such public services as are now managed by the capitalist state on behalf of the capitalist class. As for instance the postal service. Everybody recognizes that this is more efficient than if it were left to the competition of a number of capitalist enterprises trying to make profit out of it. Why not do the same thing with food provisions, with electric power distribution, with railways? In many countries the railways are a state service. Competition, it is said, lowers the prices and makes the services more efficient for the public. However, "public be damned" was the device of Jay Gould the railway king. Competition means an immense waste of labor, especially in times of rising capitalism with its many petty affairs. Once they are monopolized public management means that the large profits do not come into a few private pockets. Private management, it is said, is more efficient and cheap. This is partly true, in so far as red tape bureaucracy reigning in public services; partly it means that in private enterprises the workers can be and must be more heavily exploited.

Social democracy tries to bring about socialism by means of democracy.

Democracy means reign of the people. With universal suffrage, the majority of the people determines the majority of parliament. If there are no other independent aristocratic powers, as a senate or a monarch, the majority in parliament determines government.

The workers have been growing into the majority of the people. If they want to replace capitalism by socialism, they have only to vote for social democracy, which as the "Socialist Party" fights the capitalist parties in parliament. When by their majority they bring government into the hands of this party, it will be the instrument of the workers to effectuate socialism. Hence by parliamentary means, by voting and by fights in parliament, they may attain their goal in an easy way.

Stated thus, the matter seems quite easy indeed. In reality it is beset with enormous difficulties. Who believes that the ruling class will suffer itself to be turned out of power so easily?

We see that this easy scheme of things presupposed democracy. But the working class did not find democracy spread for it as a soft bed. In many countries the suffrage was restricted to the wealthy classes. Almost everywhere senates, chambers of privileged groups, had and have to test the laws voted by parliament. In many countries kings or emperors, military or aristocratic classes control and command the government. Hence before being able to use democracy the workers had to establish democracy. The fight for democracy was one of the forms of proletarian class struggle.

The most famous case was the fight for universal suffrage in Belgium 1891–93. Led by the Belgian Workers Party and the trade unions, a series of street demonstrations, general strikes and vehement parliamentary discussions brought about the conquest of this primary right. The resistance in parliament was beaten down, because part of the capitalist class, considering universal suffrage less dangerous than the continual unrest of the masses, soon consented to the demands. Their point is that universal suffrage gives a regular outlet to deep discontent and prevents it from breaking out in serious rebellions. This campaign contributed more than anything to arouse class consciousness and fighting spirit in the Belgian workers. Other countries followed, in most cases with less trouble.

The success of the workers in this fight shows that up to a certain point, democracy is necessary in capitalism. To such a point, namely, that the working class may take part in the general interest fights in capitalism on the same terms as the other classes. But not to the point that simply by voting it could gain supremacy. This latter truth is evident; the capitalist class, so long as it rules society, cannot tolerate that the exploited class should control government.

The former truth, becoming apparent by the very result of these suffrage fights, rests on the economic structure of capitalism. The working class must consist of free owners of their labor power, and, by their personal liberty, as free contractants they must be able to sell it to the capitalist. If not, they would be coolies or slaves. And capitalist production, with its intricate and complex system of cooperation and its highly developed technics, requiring workers with strong responsibilities, cannot be run by slaves or coolies. These rights of legal freedom and equality are safe against encroachments from the separate capitalists or functionaries only if the working class is able to defend them in regular parliamentary fight. If not, destructive outbursts of class rebellion must ensue.

These are the deeper causes why a resolute fight of the working class for universal suffrage must meet with success. It means at the same time that hardly more can be obtained while the capitalist class has the superior power. Princes, senates, courts of justice, armed forces and other independent undemocratic powers, dependent only on capital, are maintained to prevent real democracy. And should it be necessary, should the existing bit of democracy appear dangerous, then it will be done away with also.

The Socialist Party grew up as an organization of workers inspired by the radical socialist goal, stirring up their fellow workers to the class struggle and fighting the capitalist parties outside and inside parliament. Young intellectuals, even some members of the capitalist class, joined them, moved by the great idea of socialism, of freedom for all mankind, and sometimes became prominent spokesmen and capable political leaders. In public meetings and in parliamentary speeches, in their weekly or daily papers and in a number of books, pamphlets, and leaflets the Socialists expounded to the workers how capitalism is the sources of their wrongs, and its development to socialism is the necessary result of the working-class struggle. They denounced on all occasions the abuses and the tyranny of the capitalist class, they showed the conflict of interests between the classes, and defended the interests of the working class, wherever it was oppressed. They proposed laws or amendments to laws for reform and relief. They stood up for all the poor oppressed classes, for all the victims of oppressing and exploiting capital.

In this way social democracy in Germany first, and then in many other countries in Europe, did what trade unionism had done in England. It wakened the workers to class consciousness, led them in their first fights against the capitalist class, and taught them class solidarity and idealism. It was closely allied to trade unionism; many labor leaders were Socialist parliamentarians at the same time. It embodied the proletarian class struggle in a wider, more general and more abstract form: it fought not only industrial capital but also agrarian capital, colonial capital, big finance. It aroused in the workers a feeling of unity of the whole class, above the trade divisions. It fought a theoretical fight against capitalist scientists. In an increasing number of valuable studies they developed and defended, as followers of Marx, the science of the world's development through class struggle to freedom. For many dozens of years it embodied the noblest hopes, the deepest idealism, the best revolutionary ideas of the working class.

In its propaganda the future socialist aim and reforms for the present formed a natural unity. This was the basis of its growing power. For the poor oppressed masses, when they listened, socialism was the sweet hope of future happiness, but more important was the immediate relieving of their wrongs: abolition of long working hours, of child labor, of night labor, insurance against accidents, lower taxes, health measures, school reforms. Only Socialists could stand up for them to the utmost: to all objections of the capitalist parties that such reforms were impossible as they could not be financed, their answer was: so much the worse for capitalism, and all the more proof that the latter should disappear. Socialism was the strong arsenal at the back of the fighters for the betterment for the workers.

Thus social democracy grew to be an important political factor. From a herald of the future, in its first beginnings, it became a reality of the present. Though discussion and propaganda spoke of the future, the real parliamentary and electoral fights dealt with the actual position of the workers in capitalism. They were class struggles over the opposing class interests within capitalism.

The economic conditions intensified this character. During the first development of the socialist parties, capitalism lived in a continuous depression; only a short flair-up of prosperity now and then alternated with long periods of crisis. Hence capitalism appeared untenable, no reforms could avail, nothing but socialism could save the workers. But by about 1895 a new period of prosperity began, which, with short interruption of crisis, lasted till the world war. Capitalism again was full of vigor, and now reforms appeared to be possible. But more difficult also, because of the increasing power and self-confidence of the capitalist class. So fighting was necessary, fighting with all powers, for immediate aims, in attack, but still more in defense. All attention was concentrated upon the struggle of the moment.

Like trade unionism, social democracy had to defend the present-day interests within capitalism. Parliamentarism, the struggle of political parties within parliament and their contest at the polls, is the way in which all the different and varying class interests and group interests in capitalism are struggling and adjusting themselves, each according to its importance in society. Among these are also working class interests. The Socialist Party has to stand for these against other parties. Thus the Socialist Party is a natural and necessary member in capitalist society. Capitalism is not really complete without a political workers' party.

In England the workers had no special party; they voted Whig or Tory. But then a bill was proposed in parliament to prohibit picketing during strikes. Immediately the trade unions, up to that time nonpolitical, resolved to found a separate party, the Labour Party, without a socialist program, having only some moderate socialist tendencies, exclusively to defend the actual interests of workers. In their further development, the English Labour Party and the continental socialist parties gradually took the same course.

Social democracy became a power in politics. The party members increased to tens and hundreds of thousands, its number of votes at the polls to millions; its delegates in parliament, in provincial boards, in town councils formed big bodies. These votes were not all workers' votes; the Socialist Party defended the interests of all small people, even of small capitalists against big capital. To get more votes it inserted into its platforms wishes and interest of such groups. The guiding spirit of many of its parliamentarians was not the working class against the capitalist class, but the workers and the petty capitalists against big capitalists and landlords. The line of proletarian class struggle was dropped. They argued that in this way a working majority could sooner be won to crush the power of the big capital. They forgot that even in this case the small capitalists, clearly conscious of their capitalist interests, would prevail over the fooled workers.

Party power, not class power, became the great goal. Party power not in the sense of clear socialist thinking and feeling in the masses, but in the sense of parliamentary power, big parliamentary fractions and a high number of votes. Party consciousness was confounded with class consciousness. Not the party, a means to socialism as the great aim, but socialism, the attractive slogan, the means to the party as the immediate aim.

With this the masses of socialist workers were content. They wanted reforms, they wished to be protected against "reaction"; and they felt that a big and powerful Socialist Party in parliament could better protect them than a small group. So it seemed. They forgot that for the working class the only protector lies in itself, in its real class power, not in the sham power based upon votes of other classes.

Also in this way a majority did not come soon enough. So to attain some of its aims the Socialist Party had to make alliances, alliances with other parties. Sometimes in parliament, sometimes already at the polls, sometimes after the polls. This was called then "constructive policy," which means: reduction of the workers' demands to that minimum that even the capitalist class cannot seriously object to.

Now Socialists get government posts; they become town mayors, aldermen, even ministers. Not as independent delegates of the working class, but by the consent of their allies, delegates of the capitalist class. This is called "conquest of power step by step," or "not being afraid of taking responsibilities."

What are these responsibilities? As aldermen or ministers, they have to manage the general affairs of state or town under capitalism. Of course they cannot take socialist measures. They have to conduct affairs for capitalism. They certainly try to get some reforms for the workers. As far as capitalism allows it. But most things they have to see to are interests of capitalist society.

So Social Democrats grow into the role of capitalist politicians. Surely they are different from the hardboiled brutal type of capitalist politicians, who uphold the authority of the ruling class by brute force. They have more humanity, they introduce reforms, they try to smooth down the class antagonism and to render capitalism more endurable. They think themselves Socialist politicians, taking the first steps in transforming capitalism into socialism. But when fierce struggles arise, strikes or hunger revolts, they have, as public officials, the duty to send police or militia against the revolting workers. A Socialist mayor who assists the strikers from public funds, and sends the police against the Pinkertons, is a white raven and would be removed by a higher authority very soon.

Viewed from this ideal of a peaceful capitalism, consisting of satisfied workers and capitalists held in check, Socialist politicians consider their method as the clear-sighted progressive democratic policy against the brutal reactionary politics of the other parties. The dividing line is drawn not between the capitalist class and the workers' class, but between progressive and reactionary parties. Politics to them are a world in itself, not determined by the world of class interests, but a play- and battlefield of party interests, where greedy money magnates buy the other parties. They attack the ruling politicians, not because they stand for capitalist interests against workers interests, but because they are stupid politicians. They recommend themselves as sensible politicians, who would be able to run the affairs of state much better. Of course the capitalist class, full of class consciousness as it is, did not believe these politicians to be better. It prefers a strong power holding the exploited class in subjection with a firm hand. But it draws its conclusions and bears them in mind, in case of a future necessity.

What was the effect of these politics upon the working class? The party members were haunted by the fear of "reaction," i.e., capitalist parties trying to repress the workers by force, taking the place of their party officials in public office. They spent all their energy in the fight for keeping up the influential position of their party. But the great attraction which the socialist ideals exerted upon other workers was gone. All parties now put "social reforms" into their platform. The workers largely remained followers of these parties, sticking to their old traditional, often religious divisions. The growth of unity of the working class came to an end in a permanent division. A narrow-minded faith in foul party slogans came instead of class consciousness. The enthusiastic devotion to the liberation of the class was drowned in this muddle of dirty politics.

The relation between the workers and their political leaders had changed too. When in the beginning the few Socialists in parliament raised their voices, accusing capitalist society, the eager energy of the workers behind them, protesting in public meetings, gave weight to their words. But in "constructive politics" afterward it was the skill and the knowledge of the parliamentarians that determined the results. Every day they were active in parliament, discussing, speaking, accusing, defending, fighting or persuading; they did the real work of the class fight while the workers themselves did nothing but vote once in four or five years. Only small groups of party members were aiding in distributing leaflets, organizing meetings, and making speeches there. The politicians in parliament were the important men. Through their knowledge of politics they had the greatest influence. It enabled them to determine, though in the form of decision by party majority, the politics and the tactics of the party.

And when they became big men, mayors and ministers, they rose still higher above the masses. Their goodwill, or their maneuverings between the contending interests, determines what the working class shall get. The party becomes a tool in their hands for the carrying out of their politics. The political power of the party is concentrated and embodied in its great political leaders.

When a Socialist Party grows up to [become] a big organization, it becomes a body with separate interests and a life of its own. It feels like an organism with a will to live and to fight for its existence. According to its own theory it is the vanguard of the working class, it embodies the working class, its victory will be the victory of the working class. It has a large membership animated by a common spirit, a lot of daily and scientific papers to propagate its doctrines, a great literature of books and reviews, an influential system of ideas, a number of able politicians and leaders. For the great political leaders, for the lesser politicians and all its officials, the party is the basis of their existence. In them the will of the party to fight for existence and power is concentrated.

They talk, in accordance with the socialist ideas, of revolution in the far future as eventually necessary to the victory of socialism. But when revolutionary movements break out, or threaten to break out, it becomes evident that they fear the revolution. Revolution indeed, by its heavy clashes of the classes, is not an atmosphere conducive to quiet parliamentary work. When the workers break loose in street actions, in general strikes, what will become of the party, built up at one time with so much labor? And imagine the party itself summoning to revolution! Capitalist government by its military force would be able to crush the whole party without any difficulty.

The Socialist Party is closely bound up with capitalism. It can live and flourish only in capitalism as its natural world, as a fish can live only in water. It has its functions entirely in capitalism—the function of assembling all the discontent and all the rebellious spirit of the working class and leading it into the quiet bed of parliamentary contest. Not only its roots, the workers' exploitation, but all its organs and members live in and by capitalism; parliament, funds, offices and officials, papers, leaders, they are all capitalistic relations. Social democracy, in its youth a clarion waking the workers to unity and class consciousness, now by its growth, by natural causes, has been tied hand and foot to capitalism.

One test, only, still remained to be made. When capitalism is strong, it is said, there is no other way to fight than by means of trade unionism and parliament. And revolution cannot be made at free will. But when a revolution comes and the power of capitalism is shaken, then everything changes. Then social democracy will step into its original function and realize socialism for the workers.

The test was made.

The Great War broke out. In all countries social democracy voted for war credits and with its great influence aided their masters, the capitalist class, to divide the workers into the war and to rouse their national spirit. During four years the Socialist leaders were the obedient servants of the Kaiser in Germany, of their government in other countries, to crush every rising resistance of the workers.

November 1918, the war was over. The military power of Germany broke down; the whole imperial and aristocratic ruling apparatus crumbled to pieces. In most countries more or less serious revolutionary movements of the workers ensued; in Russia the Communist Party had been holding government for a year already. In Germany the power fell into the hands of the working class. They had not conquered it in a revolutionary fight; the mighty armor of the capitalist class had simply disappeared. As in an empty space they chose their soldiers' and workers' councils. The leaders of the Socialist Party took the government in their hands. It had been the great opposition party before the war and represented the majority of the working class; so there was nobody to oppose them.

The capitalist class also hailed the new regents. It knew them. It had still its money power, its spiritual power, its hold on the production; the revolution was only a breakdown of military power, not a breakdown of capitalist power. The working class was not victorious through real superiority; only it constituted an extreme danger owing to the lack of a strong capitalistic government. Hence the Socialist Party was necessary. The capitalist class knew by instinct—and thereby it showed itself the strongest class still—how to act in the right way: by treating the workers with circumspection, by giving them an appearance of power in putting their leaders at the head of the state. Until capitalism should be sufficiently restored, until it should have built up its political power again. The Socialist Party was the instrument wherewith to fool the workers.

The working class expected measures to carry through socialism. For now that their party, the workers' party, social democracy was master of the state, it could make socialist laws to abolish capitalism. Nothing of this kind, however, happened. The new government—to put an end to the workers' councils—ordered a new parliament to be chosen by universal suffrage; and they installed a commission of Socialist theorists and professors to study the question of how production could be socialized. After some years this commission came to the conclusion that this was an enormously difficult matter; society was not yet ripe for socialism; only they recommended that, as a first step, banking, big finance and the great concerns should be brought under state control. Big finance heartily laughed at that, because it had already the state under its control.

Socialist theorists said the working class was still too weak for a socialist society. To be sure; but their chief weakness was their very socialism, their confidence in the Socialist leaders.

Was there any other way possible? There certainly was. For the working class the November upheaval could only be the beginning of a revolutionary development. Only a minority was clearly conscious of ways and means; a larger part felt vaguely what ought to be done; a big but for the moment unorganized capitalist power stood against it. The only way was to bring the whole working class into the field to fight for their interests, and thereby to prevent the capitalist class from organizing its forces into a new political power.

A truly revolutionary party, if the government power had fallen into its hands, would have armed the workers, disarmed the military forces, prevented any efforts of the capitalist class to form armed groups; it would have organized production and traffic by means of factory and shop delegates, so that the workers kept them firmly in hand; at the same time by a wide propaganda explaining the great aims and rousing energy and enthusiasm in the masses. Thus the course would be freed for the whole working class to take active part in the fight, to find their way of efficient class struggle, and to take their future into their own hands.

This was the way of the small groups of communists, the so-called Spartacus groups, which sprang up everywhere in Germany. Against them the Socialist leaders in power associated with the generals of the kaiser's former army. The Communist workers were crushed by a rapidly organized military force, under the command of the Socialist leaders. So the path was clear now for a restoration of capitalist power. The Socialist Party had saved capitalism from a proletarian revolution.

In the new parliament social democracy did not have an absolute majority; but it held the chief places in government with its allies, the republican capitalist parties. Its president became president of the German republic; many of its leaders were made chancellors, ministers, state secretaries, provincial governors, town mayors; its members were no longer excluded from offices, dignities, university chairs. Later on, as capitalism felt its power consolidated, they were gradually replaced.

Capitalism, however—or rather: as a matter of course—was not attacked in the least. It acted, conformed to its nature: it made profit, by exploitation of the workers and in every other way. It began by safe-guarding its reserves across the frontiers, in the banks of Amsterdam and London; by selling out the productive forces of the country to foreigners. It rationalized industry to prepare for coming world competition and threw the workers on the street. It robbed and impoverished the middle classes by valuta inflation and wild stock speculation. It concentrated the important branches of production into mighty monopolistic concerns. All under the protection of the Socialist government officials.

For the workers hardly anything had changed. They had the pleasure to see their leaders holding high posts of honor; they were no longer considered a lower class with less rights, as had been the case under the Kaiser; the trade unions were acknowledged as tariff partners. All this was socialism, their president said. But they were either heavily exploited or stricken with unemployment, they were hungry and without hope, while they saw the capitalist class overbearing and growing in riches and power.

The formerly powerful groups, the landowning nobility and the big capitalist owners of the great concerns, kept aloof. They lived on their estates awaiting their turn. The Socialist leaders had not dared to attack them.

The intellectual portion of the capitalist class saw with growing annoyance how those disdained uncultured labor leaders held all the offices and government posts which they wanted for themselves and which they considered as their privilege by virtue of their academic training. Their nationalist feelings, exasperated as they were by the defeat in war and the heavy burden laid upon Germany by the victors, were hurt by the internationality—in words—of the new rulers. What their professors had taught them about the doctrine of Marx: stupid workmen taking the government offices and wrecking society, abasing their fatherland, they saw confirmed by these Socialists in power. An intense hatred grew in them, against the doctrine and the persons, and they waited their turn to drive them out of office.

And when in Germany the nationalist uprising came the Socialist Party was incapable of any fighting and made no appeal to the working class; it knew that no worker would lift a hand for her. It was not defeated in battle; it crumbled to dust, as a molded structure, at the first kick.

That was the test of socialism in power.

But history is not at an end yet. In all countries there are still large socialist parties. What lesson have they learned from this collapse?

Some have learned nothing and continue in the old course, because they cannot learn but have to follow their inner nature. But some have learned a lesson. The lesson that they had not gone far enough yet in renouncing their fundamental principles.

The Belgian Workers Party has adopted and proclaimed a new plan of constructive policy to bring about a kind of organization of society. It consists in state control or state direction of banking, capitalist monopolies and key industries, the lesser capitalist business remaining private enterprises; the former owners, when expropriated, keeping their profits. For the middle classes and petty capitalists better conditions will be secured, and the workers will profit by regular work and social measures. With this platform the party tries to win not only the workers but also the middle classes; it desires not to be, as in the beginning, a workers' party but an all people's party. This platform proclaims the preservation of capitalist exploitation, of capitalist profit, of capitalist competition, of capitalist waste, with only the state more narrowly connected with big business. It tries to unite all classes, capitalists, workers, farmers against big business, against monopolist capital. In these years of crisis, of capitalist breakdown, this Socialist Party presents itself to the capitalist class as the right party to restore to capitalism, by means of a small dose of organization, its former wealth and power.

Certainly this policy will meet with opposition. New groups will arise with socialist ideas, or will split from the old corrupted parties. They will start with the old fundamental principles of class struggle; they say they will avoid the errors committed by their elders. In vain. It was no error; it was the logical outcome of their nature. A political party has to grow, it fights for power, it wants to bring its leaders into parliament where they become big men above the workers, leading, educating, liberating the workers. When it grows it becomes an organ of capitalist society, with instincts of self-preservation having to fear the workers' revolution.

This does not mean that social democracy was a failure. In young capitalism it had its necessary function to wake the workers to class consciousness. Then the working class could be no more than a member of capitalist society, it had to secure its place therein. But now capitalism has grown old, gigantic, it is conquering the whole world, it is shaken by heavy crises, it stands facing revolution, and now the working class is growing large, strong, ripe to fight for its dominion over the world. What was good and right then, is not good and right now that conditions and combatants have changed.

Nor does it mean that now the task of social democracy is finished. But now its task is another than in its youth. When the working class is advancing to revolutionary fight, when a part is gallantly attacking, putting forward new slogans of deliberate fighting, large masses will be hesitating, asking whether there are easier ways, trying to avoid the inexorable hard fight. Then social democracy embodies their hesitations, it promises to liberate them with less sacrifices, by peaceful means, it tries to detain them halfway, to prevent them from rallying with their advanced comrades. It appeals to the fear, the weakness, the lack of self-confidence—which it calls common sense—of the working class, intensifying these by theoretical teachings. It tries to hold the workers back from revolution; when in revolution, it tries to hold them back from radical measures, from taking the whole power in their hands alone; when they are victorious, it tries to hold them from expropriating the capitalists, because buying them out will rouse less resistance. Always it tries to deflect the workers from resolute fighting and action for their supreme ends. In weakening the unity and the fighting spirit of the workers it protects and strengthens capitalism.

When the working class will have won a victory and conquered power, social democracy will have another chance. Of course it joins—provided it has not missed the connection—and takes part in the victory, in order to have its plan of reconstruction of society carried out. This plan is state socialism. Rallying all the "moderate" elements of defeated capitalism it will try to force this plan upon the working class. According to social democratic ideas, the state has the chief function of bringing about socialism. Collective production they understand to be production directed by the state, by the government and its lower organs. The workers are in public service, paid by the state, commanded and supervised by state officials. Of course the leaders of the state are chosen by the working masses themselves; so it is the working people itself that, according to socialist theory, commands itself. This system of state socialism may appear as a kind of intermediary station; in reality it cheats the workers out of their full communist freedom.

CHAPTER 5

THE RUSSIAN REVOLUTION

This chapter is from Pannekoek's handwritten manuscript, and was never published in *International Council Correspondence*. —Ed.

The Russian Revolution was the prominent event in the workers' movement of the last years. It gave an enormous impetus to the revolutionary force of the working class, soon, however, to be followed by decay.

In the enormous Russian Empire 90 percent of the people consisted of peasants, living most miserable lives in their villages, in crass ignorance, tilling the soil with the most primitive tools, oppressed by heavy taxes, having too little land, being at the mercy of the great landowners, who possessed the best land, regularly subjected to famine. The industry was concentrated in the chief towns, large factories, mostly run by foreign capitalists. The workers, originally peasants whom hunger had driven from the villages, also living in misery. They learned the first principles of class consciousness from the illegal socialist propaganda and began to fight for their interests by means of strikes, which were violently repressed. There was no capitalist class of any importance, only a class of small tradesmen in the towns.

The war of 1905 shook the seemingly strong czarist government. Then the working class arose in a series of irregular general strikes, not after a preconceived plan, not with precise aims, but simply as revolts against the employers and against the political despotism. Sometimes they were repressed by military force, but they sprang up again and spread like a running fire. Often the soldiers were carried away; then they revolted, and their delegates joined the strike committees. The government, itself an antiquated half-Asiatic inefficient structure of lazy, cruel and stupid *chinovniks* was paralyzed by these movements,[3] and had to suffer that the workers' councils often became the effective ruling power in the towns. At last, when these revolts concentrated in a gigantic universal strike, the czarist government promised a constitution with a parliament and political rights. Then the inner force of the movement collapsed; the last strikes and revolts were crushed by military force. Czarism was powerful again and tried to introduce some necessary reforms.

The Russian Revolution of 1905 taught a great lesson to the Socialists in Europe. It showed the enormous power a modern proletarian class can exert in spontaneous general strikes. After the first successful strike for universal suffrage in Belgium such strikes had been tried now and then, directed by political and trade union leaders, for special purposes; but usually they failed. Here in Russia it appeared that, if not directed by leaders, but arising out of a resolute fighting spirit of the masses themselves, they can uproot society. Leaders shrink from the extreme consequences of the fight; the masses that have nothing to lose but their chains retain their innermost strength, even in defeat. Because they are directly engaged they feel instinctively how far their forces reach against the enemy.

In the great world war, nine years later, Russia was the weakest member as to its inner structure. A modern war with its big industrial basis and rigid organization puts such a heavy strain on the state organism, that a half-barbaric state as Russia was, could not bear it. When provisions failed in the towns, revolts broke out, and czarism, seemingly mighty but rotten to the core, broke down. In the shape of political party struggles the different classes of Russian society tried to seize the power. After a development of half a year during 1917, the Bolshevik party won.

---

3   [Minor civil or court officials. —Ed.]

The Bolshevik party, officially named the Russian Socialist Party, afterward taking the name of Communist Party, was an organization of well-trained revolutionists, well-versed in Marxian learning as well as in political fighting. They knew that the class struggle of the working class was the basis of social progress, they organized the workers, they had a great influence upon them and refuted every compromise with middle-class parties. They put up three great slogans; firstly: dictatorship of the working class by means of soviets, workers' councils; no parliament therefore where delegates of other classes could become political leaders. Secondly: all the land to the farmers. Thirdly: immediate cessation of the war, because it served capitalist interests only.

So they won. The farmers, taking the land and driving away the great landowners, stood as an unshakable stronghold for the new government. The workers in the great towns and industrial centers, through their strong unity, due to big industry and common fighting, were its solid force. Difficult years ensued, when the powers of all Europe and America attacked them, either directly, or indirectly by providing the white armies with war materials. The Russian workers then showed, and taught to the world, to what height of self-sacrifice, of heroism, of bravery, of endurance and efficiency a class may rise in which the love of newly won freedom and the proletarian feelings of brotherhood are united.

The new government called itself a soviet republic, Union of Soviet Socialist Republics. Soviet congresses actually assembled now and then; but they could not really rule. Rule of the soviets, democratic bodies of delegates from all the working, producing classes meant rule of the farmers as the most numerous class. The farmers, having got the land, wanted, wished to sell its products in free trade to Europe, in order to become wealthy and rich, individually; their rule would have meant the growth of a capitalist society. The workers could prevent this only by setting up a strong government, in which all the state power was centralized, not dependent on soviets. Thus the Bolshevist party, consisting of the vanguard of the working class, concentrated all power in its hands. Now soviet congresses became big shows only with beautiful speeches.

The real parliaments of the new state were the annual party congresses, where the interests and difficulties were discussed, where the different tendencies and groups struggled with one another, and that lines of further development were fixed. The Communist Party provided most of the new state officials, who formed the ruling bureaucracy. The chiefs of this bureaucracy, being at the same time the leaders of the party, were the real rulers of Russia.

It was not the intention of the Bolshevists to carry through communist production; they knew that this can only be achieved as the sequel of highly developed capitalism. At first factory committees were chosen by the workers to supervise and even to manage production; but this system was abolished after half a year; the amount of production under this system being too small and still subjected to an alarming decrease. Directors were appointed by the Central Economic Board, a state organ; the workers had to obey them as well as their staff, the engineers, specialists of the intellectual class. Trade unions were turned into state organs, with compulsory membership for the workers; they had to ensure mainly zeal and a good working tempo. Wages were fixed by the same state organs.

The whole industry was built up on lines of an organized system, directed by central committees, having to determine what products were most needed, where they could be best produced, what plants and factories were to be founded. It was a planned collective production, after projects previously established, the direct reverse of the capitalist production by chance, for personal profit, without a general plan. It was a system of state capitalism; the state being the general director of production and all the workers being its employees. Also for this management of industry a large bureaucracy was needed, taken partly from the ranks of the communist workers, partly from the intellectual specialists.

This huge bureaucracy had to be recruited as much as possible from the working class. It was a heavy drain upon so small a class, numbering only one tenth of the population. Immediately after the revolution all the old party members, all the able men among the workers were dragged into the government posts, where they were badly needed, or enlisted as volunteers and officers in the armies, where they fell in the civil wars for the revolution. And then in the rapidly developing industry a still larger number of new specialists and scientists was needed, which were all taken from the working class, and afterward also in increasing number, from the farmers. All their able young men, all their children with good brains were sent to the high schools, the technical schools, the universities. Out of their numbers, the new intellectual class grew up to fill the ranks of the political and economic bureaucracy of the state.

Thus what before had been one working class was now split up into different classes. One part grew into the state bureaucracy, the new ruling class which held all the social, economic, and political power in its hands. What was left in the factories, supplied by more primitive peasants from the villages, was also differentiated, from the engineers and the skilled technicians, the eager party members and foremen down to the badly paid "black workers," the unskilled laborers. So we can understand, how Russian Bolshevists could consider their rule as rule of the working class, though the real workers in the factories had hardly any influence upon government. Now they could frame the aphorism that the dictatorship of the working class was realized in the dictatorship of the Communist Party, a party consisting for the greater majority of state and other officials! Whenever in party congresses a proposal was made to restore the real workers' democracy, to give the power to the real wage workers, it always was deemed impossible. The ruling bureaucracy did not feel itself as a new ruling class already. Moreover it felt that it had a big task to perform, for which it needed the concentration of all power into its hands.

What in Russia and in Communist Party literature is called the building up of communism is in reality the building up of industrialism. Lenin once said: communism is electrification combined with the soviet system. In other words, less aphoristically: big industry combined with workers' rule. The soviet system, as we have seen, soon disappeared, workers' rule became an empty show. But big industry and electrification were a reality. Communist future was a nice word to harmonize present-day practice with time-honored doctrines. But without these the present-day task was important enough.

Russia was at an extremely low level of development; there was little industry, the productive forces were small and ineffective, the farmers used the most primitive working methods, intellectual culture was lacking, large parts of the population lived in barbarism. To raise Russia to the level of the capitalist countries its productive forces had to be developed, factories built, the natural riches of the country exploited. Big electric power plants were built on the rivers, new railways were constructed, new lands cultivated, universities, technical schools, agricultural academies were founded to procure the intellectual forces and to raise the produce of the soil by scientific methods. To combat the unproductivity of the petty farmers holdings, large state farms were founded, and the peasants were induced by privileges, by persuasion, and by compulsion, to combine their small fields into big cooperative farms (*kolchozes*).

This was the great task of the Bolshevist rulers: to do away with the enormous backwardness of Russia through a rapid development and to bring it in line with the old capitalist countries. Left to the individual enterprise of a capitalist class this would have involved not only a great number of years, but also an enormous waste of energy and enormous sufferings for the working class. Now it was done by state capitalism, by official experts according to a preconceived plan based on the conscious effort of the state power. The Russians are so well aware of the greater efficiency of this system that they speak, in the programs of their five year plan, of not only overtaking but outstripping the old world.

This development was, however, beset with heavy difficulties. The greater, more productive new machines and plants in capitalist countries are built by means of fresh capital, accumulated from former surplus value; big capital is growing continually in the same time as it is wanted. In Russia this big capital was needed right away—for instance to buy American machines—but there had been no time for its accumulation. It must be produced on the spot. In other words: labor spent on railways and electric power stations or on export products could not be spent at the same time on food or clothes; future productivity must be paid for by privation and hardships now. The wages paid to the workers, the prices paid to the farmers for their harvests were kept down as much as possible, to leave a greater surplus for new installations.

Another handicap was the slow tempo of working. The Russian workers, coming from the village with its easygoing, variable, self-determined working tempo, could only gradually adapt themselves to the regular rapid tempo of machine working. The training acquired by the workers in old capitalist countries during several generations, is lacking here, and this too diminishes the surplus.

All this was counterbalanced, however, by the enormous enthusiasm which filled the young people, which inspired them to the greatest exertions, to the utmost of their energy and endurance. The revolution has lifted Russia out of the immobility of barbarism and stagnant misery, has forced her upon the road of rapid, continuous development, has opened unlimited horizons of progress and freedom, has raised energy and culture. Now life is worth living there. It is the awakening of a hundred million people.

To be sure, this is not communism. The workers are not free masters of their work, it is not a society without classes. The workers are exploited wage workers; the surplus of the product exceeding their needs is taken from them and spent by others. As a new ruling class, which sprang up from the working class and the intellectuals, the bureaucracy holds political and economic sway. As a ruling class it feels sufficient to the rulers of other states to make alliances with them and to mingle in their politics.

There is no free press—"the proletarian dictatorship cannot allow the capitalists to undermine the revolution"—nor the right of free speech for contrary opinions. The workers have not the right of organization, nor the right to strike. They have fewer rights than in capitalist countries; a despotic rule imposes its views upon the country and does not allow the workers to feel themselves as a separate exploited class. When workers criticize the government and speak up for real communism, they are persecuted for being "counterrevolutionary."

Considered, however, as a class society, with an exploited and a ruling class, Russia, by its economic system of state capitalism, represents a higher state of development than the private capitalist society of Europe and America. Through the organization of production a higher rate of productivity of labor can be reached. The economic organization also brings about higher intellectual and moral standards, which show some traits of future communism. Spending all one's energy in acquiring personal wealth is despised in Russia just as much as it is admired in America. This strong community feeling is the moral backbone of the new Russian society.

CHAPTER 6

THE COMMUNIST PARTY

This chapter is from Pannekoek's handwritten manuscript. A shorter version was published in *International Council Correspondence* vol. 2, no. 7 (June 1936) under the title "On the Communist Party." —Ed.

During the world war in all countries small groups arose, convinced that out of this ordeal of capitalism a proletarian revolution must ensue, and ready to prepare for it. They once more took the name of Communists, forgotten since the old times of Marx and 1848, to identify themselves from the socialist parties. The Bolshevik party, then having its center in Switzerland, was one of them.

After the war had ceased, they united into communist parties, standing for the proletarian world revolution. In opposition to the socialist parties, who supported the war politics of the capitalist government and represented the submissive fearful tendencies in the working class, the communist parties gathered all the young fighting spirit in its ranks.

In opposition to the socialist theory that not in a ruined, but only in a prosperous capitalism the workers could build up a true commonwealth, the Communists put forth the truth, that it was this very ruin of capitalist production which made a revolution necessary and which would incite the working class to fight for revolution with all its energy.

In opposition to the social-democratic view, that a parliament chosen by general suffrage was a fair representation of society and the basis of socialism, Communists put forth the new truth, stated by Marx and

Engels, that the working class, to attain its aims, had to take the power entirely in its own hands, had to set up its dictatorship, excluding the capitalist class from any share in the government.

In opposition to parliamentarism, they put forth, after the Russian example, the soviets, the workers' councils.

In the defeated Germany, November 1918, a vigorous communist movement sprang up and united the Spartacus group and other groups that had secretly grown up during the war. It was crushed in the following January by the counterrevolutionary forces of the Socialist government.

This prevented in Germany the rise of an independent strong communist power, animated by the spirit of a highly developed modern proletariat. So the Communist Party of Russia dominated entirely the young rising communist groups of the world. They united in the Third International, directed from Moscow. Now Russia remained the only center of world revolution; the interests of the Russian state directed the communist workers all over the world. The ideas of Russian Bolshevism dominated the communist parties in the capitalist countries.

Russia was attacked by the capitalist governments of Europe and America. Russia, in defense, attacked these governments by inciting the working classes to rebellion, by calling them to world revolution. A communist revolution not in the future, but as soon as possible. And if they could not be won for communism, then at least for opposition to the policy of their governments. Hence the communist groups were forced to go into parliament and to go into the trade unions, to drive them as an opposing force against their capitalist governments.

World revolution was the great battle cry. And everywhere in the world, in Europe, in Asia, in America, among the oppressed classes and the oppressed peoples, the call was heard and workers arose. Animated by the Russian example, feeling that now, through the war, capitalism was shaken in its foundations, that it was weakened still more by the economic disorder and crisis. They were small minorities only; but the masses of the workers stood awaiting, looking with sympathy toward

Russia, hesitating still because their leaders said Russians were a backward people and because the capitalist papers spoke of atrocities and predicted an inevitable and rapid breakdown. These very infamies of the capitalist press, however, showed how much the example was hated and feared.

Was a communist revolution possible? Could the working class conquer power and defeat capitalism in England, in France, in America? Certainly not. It had not yet the strength that was needed. Only in Germany perhaps.

What ought to have been done then? The communist revolution, the victory of the working class is not a matter of a few years; it is a whole period of rising and fighting. This crisis of capitalism could only be the starting point for this period. The task of the Communist Party was to build up the power of the working class in this period, step by step. This perhaps was a long way; but there is no other.

The Russian Bolshevik leaders did not understand world revolution in this way. They meant it to come immediately, in a near future. That which had happened in Russia, why could it not happen in other countries? The workers there had only to follow the example of their Russian comrades.

In Russia a firmly organized party of some ten thousands of revolutionists, by means of a working class of hardly a million, within a population of hundred millions, had conquered power, and afterward by the right platforms it stood for and by defending their interests, it won the masses to its side.

In the same way in the rest of the world communist parties, comprising the most eager, class-conscious, able and energetic minorities of the working class, led by capable leaders, could conduct political power, if only the mass of the workers would follow them. Were not the capitalist governments ruling minorities also?

The whole of the working class, which now suffers this minority to rule, has only to back the Communist Party, to vote for it, to follow its call. And the party will do the real work, it is the vanguard, it attacks, it defeats the capitalist government and replaces it, and when in power it will carry through communism, just as in Russia.

And the dictatorship of the working class? It is embodied in the dictatorship of the Communist Party, just as in Russia.

Do as we did—this was the advice, the call, the directive given by the Bolshevik party to the communist parties of the world. It was based upon the idea of equality of Russian conditions with the conditions in capitalist countries.

The conditions were, however, so widely different, that hardly any resemblance was to be seen.

Russia stood on the threshold of capitalism, at the beginning of industrialism. The great capitalist countries stand at the close of industrial capitalism.

Hence the goals were entirely different. Russia had to be raised from primitive barbarism to the high level of productivity reached in America and Europe. This could be done by a party, governing the people, organizing state capitalism. America and Europe, on their high level of capitalist productivity, have to transform themselves to communist production. This can be done only by the common effort of the working class in its entirety.

In Russia the working class was a small minority, and nearly the whole population consisted of primitive peasants. In England, Germany, France, America nearly half, or even the majority of the population consisted of proletarians, wage workers.

In Russia there was a very small, insignificant capitalist class, without much power or influence. In England, Germany, France, America a capitalist class, more powerful than the world had ever seen, dominated society, dominated the whole world.

The Communist Party leaders, by proclaiming that they, that the party should be able to beat the capitalist class, showed by this very assertion that they did not see the real power of this class. By setting Russia as the example to be followed—not only in heroism and fighting spirit, but also in methods and aims—they betrayed their inability to see the difference between the Russian czarist rule and the capitalist rule in Europe and America.

We have already seen what are the elements of power of the capitalist class. With its complete domination of the economic forces, with its money power, its intellectual power, there is not a chance for a minority group to vanquish and destroy it. No party, though led by the ablest leaders, can defeat it.

There is only one power strong enough to vanquish this mighty class. This power is the working class.

The essential basis of capitalist power is its economic power. No political laws issued from above can seriously affect it. It can only be attained by another economic power, by the opposing class, striking at its very root. It is the entirety of the workers who have to come into the field, if capitalism is to be overthrown.

At first sight this appeal to the whole of the working class may appear illusionary. Its mass, its majority is not clearly class conscious, it is ignorant as to social development, indifferent to the revolution, with more egoism for personal interests than solidarity for class interests, submissive and fearful, seeking futile pleasures. Is there much difference between such an indifferent mass and a population as in Russia? Can anything be expected from such a people, rather than from that class-conscious, eager, energetic, self-sacrificing, clear-minded communist minority?

This, however, is only relevant if it should be a question of a revolution of tomorrow, as conceived by the Communist Party.

For the proletarian, revolution, not the superficial chance character of today, is essential, which of course is determined by the present surrounding capitalist world. The real communist revolution depends on the deeper essential class nature of the proletariat.

The working class of Europe and America has qualities in itself that enable it to rise to great force. They are descendants of a middle class of artisans and farmers who for many centuries worked their own soil or their own shop as free people. So they acquired skill and independence, capability and a strong individuality to act for themselves, perseverant industry and the habit of personal energy in work. These qualities the modern workers have inherited from their ancestors. Dominated there-after during one or more generations by capitalism, they were trained by the machine to regular intensity and discipline in collective work. And after the first depression there grew in them, in a continual fight, the new rising virtue of solidarity and class unity.

On these foundations the future greatness of the revolutionary class will be built up.

In Europe and in America there are living hundreds of millions of people possessing these qualities. That as yet they stand before their task, that they have not yet finished it, that they hardly made a begin-ning, does not mean that they are not able to perform it. And no other power can tell them how to act. They have to find their way themselves, by hard suffering and bitter experience. But they have brains and they have hearts to find it out and to do it and to build up that class unity out of which the new mankind will arise.

They are not a neutral indifferent mass that does not count when a revolutionary minority tries to overthrow the ruling capitalist minority. So long as they do not actively take part, the revolution cannot be won. But when they do take part, they are not the people to be led in obedi-ence by a party.

Certainly a party in its ascendance consists of the class's best elements, exceeding the mass of it. And its leaders, usually, are the prominent forces in the party, embodying the great aims in their names, admired, hated, honored. They stand in the front, and when a great fight is lost, its great leaders are destroyed, the party is crushed. Knowing this the lesser leaders, the party officials, will often shrink from the supreme fight, from the boldest aims. The working class itself can be defeated, but it can never be crushed. Its forces are indomitable, it is rooted in the firm earth; as a growing green turf the blooming tops of which are mown, it always comes up anew. The workers can temporarily desist from fighting when weakened, but their forces will increase afterward. A party that then should follow them in their retreat, cannot recover; it must lose its character and repudiate its principles; it is lost forever. A party, a group, leaders have a limited force, which is spent, is sacrificed—in honor, or in dishonor—entirely in the events of class struggle; the class itself draws upon an unlimited store.

Prominent leaders can show the way, parties in their principles and platforms can express the ideas, the aims of the class, temporarily. The class at first follows them, but then it has to pass them, putting up bolder aims, higher ideas, conform to the widening and deepening of the class struggle. The party tries to keep the class at its former lower level, at its more moderate aims, and has to be discarded. The doctrine that a party stands above the class, that it should remain the leader always, being theoretically false, in practice means strangling the class and leading it into defeat.

We will show how in the Communist Party, this doctrine after its first glorious ascendance, led to rapid decay.

* * *

These are the principles leading the Communist Party and deter-mining its practice: the party has to win dictatorship, to conquer power, to make revolution and by this to liberate the workers; the workers have to follow, to back the party and to bring it to power.

Hence its direct aim is to win the masses of the workers as adher-ents, as followers, to bring them to its side. It is not to make them good independent fighters, able to find and to force their own way.

Parliamentary action is one of the means. Though the Communist Party declared that parliamentarism was useless for the revolution, still it went into parliament; this was called "revolutionary parliamentarism," "to demonstrate in parliament the uselessness of parliamentarianism." In reality it was a means to get votes and voters, followers of the party. It served to detract the workers' votes from the socialist parties. Numerous workers, who were disillusioned by the capitalist policy of social democ-racy, who wished to stand for revolution, were won over by the big talk and the furious criticisms of the Communist Party against capitalism. Now this policy opened a new way for them to stick to their old belief that by voting only and following leaders, new and better leaders this time, they would be liberated. These famous revolutionists, who in Russia had founded the state of the workers, told them this easy way was the right way.

Another means was trade unionism. Though the Communist Party declared the unions useless for the revolution, yet the Communists had to become members of them, in order to win the unions for communism. This did not mean the making of the union members into clearly class-conscious revolutionists; it meant the replacing of the "corrupt" old leaders by Communist Party men. It meant the party controlling the ruling machine of the unions; so that it might command the big armies of union members. Of course the old leaders were not willing to give way; they simply excluded the red opposition groups. Then new "red" unions were formed.

Strikes are the schools for communism. When the workers are on strike, are fighting the capitalist class face to face, then they learn the real power of capitalism, they see all its forces directed against themselves. But then they realize more strongly and fully the forces of solidarity, the necessity of unity, they are keen to understand, their spirit is eager to learn. And what they learn as the most important lesson, is that communism is the only salvation.

The Communist Party varied this truth according to its principles. At each strike it was present to take part or, more rightly, to take the lead. The direction must be taken out of the hands of the trade union leaders, who do not have the right fighting spirit. The workers should lead themselves; the meaning of this statement was—because the working class, as you know, is represented by the Communist Party—that the party should lead them. Each success was used to advertise the party. Instead of the communist education, which is a natural outcome of each big fight in capitalism, came the artificial aim: to increase the influence of the party on the masses.

Instead of the natural lesson: communism is the salvation, came the artificial lesson: the Communist Party is the savior. By its revolutionary talk they caught and absorbed all the eager fighting spirit of the strikers, but diverted it to its own aims. Quarrels which were injurious to the workers' cause often were the result.

A continual fight, of course, was made against the Social Democratic Party, to detract its followers from it by criticism of its politics. Their leaders were denounced and called by the most spicy names, as accomplices of capital and traitors of the working class. Doubtlessly a serious, critical exposition showing that social democracy had left the way of class struggle, will open the eyes of many workers. But now, all at once, the scene changed and an alliance was offered to these "traitors" for a common fight against capitalism. This was called solemnly: "the unity of the working class restored." In reality it would have been nothing but the temporary collaboration of two competing groups of leaders, both trying to keep or win obedient followers.

To win followers and votes, it is not necessary to call upon the working class alone. All the poor classes living miserably under capitalism will hail the new and better masters who promise them freedom. So just as the Socialist Party did, the Communist Party addressed its propaganda to all who suffer.

Russia gave the example. The Bolshevist party, though a workers' party, had won power only by their alliance with the peasants. When, once in power, they were threatened by the capitalist tendencies in the wealthy peasants they called upon the poor peasants as the allies of the workers. Then the communist parties in America and Europe, always imitating Russian slogans, directed their appeals to the workers and the poor peasants also. It forgot that in highly developed capitalistic countries there lives in the poor peasants an eager spirit of private ownership, the same as in the big farmers. Could they be won over by promises they would be but unreliable allies, ready to desert at the first contrariety.

The working class in its revolution can only count upon its own force. Other poor classes of society will often join them; but they cannot give additional weight of importance, because the strong innate force, which proletarian solidarity and mastership over the production gives to the working class, is lacking in them. Therefore even in rebellion they are uncertain and fickle. What can be aimed at is that they will not be tools in the capitalists' hands. This cannot be obtained by promises; promises and platforms count with parties; but classes are directed by deeper feelings and passions, founded on interests. It can be reached only when their respect and their confidence is aroused, because they see that the workers bravely and energetically attack the capitalist class.

The matter is different for a Communist Party, wishing to win power for itself. All the poor who suffer under capitalism are equally good as followers of the party. Their despair seeing no sure way out by their own force, makes them the right adherents to a party, that says it will liberate them. They are apt to break out in explosions, but not to climb in continuous fight. In the heavy world crisis of these last few years the increasing masses of the regularly unemployed, in which the need and the idea of a rapid, immediate world revolution became dominant, also turned to the Communist Party. Especially by means of this army the Communist Party hoped to conquer political supremacy for itself.

The Communist Party did not try to increase the power of the working class. It did not educate its adherents to clearness, to wisdom, to unity of all the workers. It educated them into enthusiastic but blind, hence fanatical believers and followers, into obedient subjects of the party in power. Its aim was not to make the working class strong, but to make the party powerful. Because its fundamental ideas originated from primitive Russian, not from highly capitalistic European and American conditions.

When a party wishes to win followers with all means and cannot attract them by arousing their interest in revolution, then it will try to win them by appealing to their reactionary prejudices. The strongest feeling which capitalism awakes and raises with all its might against revolution is nationalism. When in 1923 French troops occupied the Rhineland and everywhere in Germany the waves of nationalism went high, the

Communist Party also played the nationalistic game, trying to compete with the capitalist parties. In the Reichstag it proposed a companionship of the communist armed forces, the "red guards," with the German capitalist army (Reichswehr). Here international politics played a part; Russia, at that time hostile to the victorious Western governments, tried to make an alliance with Germany; hence the German Communist Party had to make friends with its own capitalist government.

This was the chief character of all the communist parties, affiliated to the Third International: they were directed by Moscow, by the Russian Communist leaders; so they were tools of Russian foreign politics. Because Russia was "all the workers' fatherland," the center of communist world revolution, the interests of Russia should be the prominent interest of the communist workers all over the world. It was clearly stated by the Russian leaders, that when a capitalist government should be the ally of Russia against other powers, the workers in that country had to stand by their government; they had to fight their government in the other countries of course. So the class struggle between the capitalist and the workers' class, this fundamental fact of society, had to be made subordinate to the temporary needs and fortunes of Russian foreign politics.

Its dependence on Russia, materially and spiritually, is at the root of all the weakness of the Communist Party. All the ambiguities in the Russian development are reflected in the position of the Communist Party. The Russian leaders have to tell their subjects that their state capitalistic building up of industrialism is the building up of communism. Hence each new factory or electric power plant is hailed in the communist papers as a triumph of communism. In order to encourage the minds of the Russians to persevere, they were told by their papers that the capitalist world was nearly succumbing to a world revolution, and that, envious of Russia, it meditated to make war with Russia. This was repeated in the communist papers all over the world, while at the same time Russia was concluding commercial treaties with those capitalist governments. When Russia made alliances with some capitalist states and took part in their diplomatic quarrels, the communist papers glorified this as a capitulation of the capitalist world before communism. Always it was the advertising of Russian "communism" before the workers of the world.

Russia is the great example; hence the Russian example has to be imitated in the Communist Party. Just as in Russia the party has to dominate the class. In the Russian party the leaders dominate, because they have all the power factors in their hands. In the same way in the Communist Party the leaders dominate, the members have to show "discipline." Moscow, the "Comintern" (Central Committee of the Third International) are the highest leaders; at their command the leaders in every country are dismissed and replaced by others.

It is natural that ever anew in the other countries doubts arose among the members as to the rightness of these Russian methods. But always such opposition was beaten down and excluded from the party. No independent judgment but obedience was demanded.

After the revolution the Russians had built up a "red army" to defend their new freedom against the attacks of the "white armies." In the same way in Germany the Communist Party formed a "red guard," bodies of armed young Communists, to fight against the armed nationalists. If the Communist Party supposed in this way to form the kernel of an army ready to conquer power, it forgot that capitalist violence is much stronger than workers violence, and that the chief power of the working class lies in quite another a direction than that of violence.

Moreover it was not simply a workers' army against capitalism, but also a weapon against all the adversaries of the Communist Party. Wherever in meetings opposition came up and other workers criticized the party politics, the red guards at the command of the leaders had to deal with them and maltreat them. Not opening the brains, but breaking the skulls was the method employed against criticizing fellow workers. Thus young and eager fighters were educated into rowdies instead of into Communists. And when the national revolution came, when nationalist violence proved to be far stronger and more irresistible than Communist violence, numerous young workers, who had learned nothing but to beat their leaders' adversaries, at once changed their colors and became just as zealous National Socialists as before they had been zealous Communists.

Through the glory that radiated from the Russian Revolution, through its own gallant talk the Communist Party assembled year by year all the ardent enthusiasm of young workers under its colors. This it dissipated into idle sham fights, or spilt in useless party politics; all these valuable qualities were lost to the revolution. The best of them, disillusioned, turned their back on the party and tried to find new ground in founding separate groups.

Looking backward we see the world war, as a culmination of capitalist oppression, arouse the revolutionary spirit of the workers, everywhere. Barbarous Russia, as the weakest of the governments, fell at the first stroke, and as a bright meteor the Russian Revolution rose and shone over the earth. But it was another revolution than the workers needed. Its dazzling light first filling them with hope and force, blinded them so that they did not see their own way. Now they have to recover and to turn their eyes to the dawn of their own revolution.

The Communist Party cannot recover. Russia is making its peace with the capitalist powers and taking its place among them, with its own economic system. The Communist Party, inseparably linked to Russia, is doomed to live on sham fighting. Opposition groups split off ascribing the decay to false tactics of some particular leaders, to deviations from the right principles. In vain; the basis of the downfall lies in the principles themselves.

The working class however will come out of this depression wiser and more conscious of its task.

But now capitalist power arises more formidable out of the failings of the working-class parties.

CHAPTER 7

FASCISM

This chapter is from Pannekoek's handwritten manuscript. A shorter version was published in *International Council Correspondence* vol. 2, no. 8 (July 1936) under the title "On the Role of Fascism." —Ed.

Fascism was the capitalist reaction on the deficiency of communism or socialism.

When the working class arises, puts up a strong fight and proclaims its aims to destroy capitalism, at first fear and hatred are roused in the capitalists' hearts. When then it becomes apparent, however, that it is incapable of carrying out its menace, when its force lags far behind its boasting words, then with recovered self-confidence capitalism strikes back. The fear is not forgotten and must be avenged; disdain for the opponent is now mixed with it and leads to a firm determination to destroy its force and block its way for the future.

In Italy after the war there arose a large movement of the syndical-ist trade union workers who were strongly influenced by the Russian communist propaganda. This movement culminated in the occupation of the factories by the workers. But then it became evident that it was a blow in the air. The workers did not know what to do with it.

Occupation of factories can be a strong fighting form in the midst of a great revolutionary uprising, as was shown on a small scale in Germany in 1923. Then the workers find themselves together in their natural grouping, as masters of the apparatus of production, for them the strongholds and centers of resistance. Of course only as an episode of the real fight for power; for this occupation of factories arouses the most resolute hostility in the capitalist class.

In Italy the working class was not prepared for a real revolutionary fight. The occupation was not a result of their power but rather of the weakness and disorganization of capitalist power. They began to work the factories as collective workshops believing that the capitalist class would let them produce and sell in peace. After some weeks they had simply to clear out, utterly disappointed as to the possibilities of a workers' commonwealth.

But the capitalist class had felt the danger. Capitalists and middle-class citizens, intellectuals and military men, all held together against "disorder." If capitalist disorder is not replaced by a new working-class order, then it has to be replaced by a new capitalist order. Young people, disappointed by talkative impotent socialism and bragging communism, imbued with a strong nationalist spirit and educated to brutality in the experience of war, formed the ranks of fascism. In years of street guerilla against the workers, beating them down with brutal force, burning their "People's House," aided by capitalist money power, they grew up into a large and firmly disciplined mass party which grasped the state power from the hands of the old political parties.

The first and chief characteristic of fascism is that of organizing the petty-capitalist and middle class with its narrow-minded spirit of private business into a mass organization, strong enough to beat and check the proletarian organizations. This class, squeezed in between capitalist and working class, unable to fight capitalism, is always ready to turn against the workers' class struggle. Though it hates big capitalism and puts forth anticapitalistic slogans, it is a tool in the hands of capitalism, which pays and directs its political action toward the subduing of the workers.

Its ideas and theories are directed chiefly against the class struggle, against the workers feeling and acting as a separate class. Against this it brings forward a strong nationalist feeling, the idea of the unity of the nation against foreign nations. In this nation the workers have their place, not as a separate class, but combined with the employers as industrial or agrarian groups of production. Representatives of these groups form advisory boards for the government. This is called the corporative state, founded on direct representation of the economic grouping of society, on capitalist labor. It is opposed to the parliamentary system, for which fascism has hardly any use and which it denounces as a power of disruption, a mischievous preaching of internal dissension.

Parliamentarianism is the expression of the supremacy of the people, the citizens, and of the dependence of the government. Fascism puts the state above the citizens; the state as organization of the nation, is the superior objective to which the citizens are subordinate. Not democracy, not the people's rights, but authority, the people's duties stand first. It places the party chief at the head of the state, as a dictator, to rule with his party companions, without interference from parliamentary delegates.

It is clear that this form of government corresponds to the needs of modern capitalism. In a highly developed capitalism economic power is not rooted, as it was in the beginning, in a numerous class of independent producers, but in a small group of big capitalists. Their interests can be served better by influencing a small body of absolute rulers, and their operations seem more safely secured if all opposition of the workers and all public criticism is kept down with an iron fist. Hence a tendency is visible in all countries to increase the power of the central government and of the chieftains of the state. Though this also sometimes is called fascism, it makes some difference whether parliamentary control is maintained, or an open dictatorial rule is established, founded upon the terrorism of a mighty party organization.

In Germany an analogous development of the National Socialist movement took place somewhat later. The revolution of 1918 had brought socialism into power; but this power was made use of to protect capitalism; the Socialists in government let the capitalists operate as they liked. The petty-capitalist classes, seeing their antagonists on both sides now united and Socialist officials involved in foul capitalist affairs, considered

socialist-state concern and capitalist speculation as one common principle of corruption of an international gang of grafters. It opposed to
them the honest small business of petty capitalists and sturdy farmers
of olden times. Young intellectuals of the universities who found their
former monopoly of public offices infringed upon by detested Socialist
leaders, and former officers, jobless through the diminution of the army,
organized the first groups of National Socialism.

They were eager nationalists, because they belonged to the capitalist middle classes and were opposed to the internationalism of the
ruling social democracy. They called themselves socialist, because their
petty-capitalistic feeling was hostile to big business and big finance. They
were strongly antisemitic too. Firstly because Jewish capital played an
important role in Germany, especially in the great stores that caused
the ruin of the small shopkeepers. Secondly because numerous Jewish
intellectuals flooded the universities and the learned professions, and
by their keener wits often—e.g., as lawyers and physicians—left their
German competitors behind them.

Financially these National Socialists were backed by some big capitalist concerns, especially by the armament industry, which felt its interests
endangered by the increasing disarmament conferences. They formed
the illegal fighting groups of capitalism against rising Bolshevism. Then
came the world crisis aggravating the conditions in Germany, exhausted
as it was by the peace treaty indemnities. The revolt of the desperate
middle classes raised National Socialism to the position of the mightiest
party, and enabled it to seize the political power and to make its leader
the dictator of Germany.

Seemingly this dictatorship of middle-class ideas is directed against
big capitalism as well as against the working-class movement. It is clear,
however, that a petty-capitalist program of a return to former times of
small business cannot be carried out. It soon became evident in Germany
that big capitalism and landowning aristocracy are still the real masters
behind the ruling National Socialist Party. In reality this party acts as an
instrument of capitalism to fight and destroy the workers' organizations.

So strong was the power of the new slogans that they drew even a large number of workers with them, who joined the National Socialist Party. They had learned to follow their leaders; but these leaders had disappointed them and were beaten by stronger leaders. The splendor and the spiritual power of the socialist and communist ideals had waned. National Socialism promised the workers a better socialism, by class peace instead of class war. If offered them their appropriate honored place in the nation as members of the united people; not as a separate class. They were not allowed to make a class struggle.

The working class has been thrown back in its regular upward striving for liberation. Its organizations have been wiped out, or, in the case of the trade unions, put directly under the command of capitalist state officials. The workers' papers have been suppressed, free speech is prohibited, socialist or communist propaganda is forbidden and punished with imprisonment in concentration camps or long incarceration. In the enforced uniformity of opinion there is no room for revolutionary teachings. The way of regular progress toward proletarian power, in the development of insight and organization by means of propaganda and discussions, the way to revolution and freedom is blocked by the concrete wall of reaction.

So it seems. But it only means that for the workers the smooth and peaceful way of growing to power is blocked. We said before that the right of free speech, the right of organization, the right of propaganda and of forming political parties were necessary for capitalism. It means that they are necessary to ensure a regular working of capitalist production and capitalist development. It means that once they are gone the class antagonisms must at last explode in heavy uprisings and violent revolutionary movements. The capitalist class has to decide whether it prefers this way; we cannot order them to choose the other way.

It has its reasons. It strongly feels that the heavy world crisis of today is shaking the capitalist system in the heart. It knows that the diminished production is unable to feed the whole working class and at the same time to leave sufficient profits. It is resolved not to bear the losses itself. So it realizes that at last the workers, starved by unemployment, must rise and will rise in revolts. And it tries to forestall them by fortifying its own position, by forging the whole capitalist class into one strong unity, by putting the state power in strong armor, by tying the workers to this state by means of strong fetters, by robbing them of their old means of defense, their Socialist spokesmen and their organizations. This is the reason why in these last years fascism became powerful.

Capitalism at one time seemed to be on the best way of fooling the workers by means of sham democracy and sham reforms. Now it is turning to the other way of heavy oppression. This must drive the workers to resistance and to determined class fighting. Why does capitalism do so? Not of its own free will, but compelled by material economic forces inherent in its innermost nature: by the heavy crisis that endangers its profits and arouses its fears for revolution.

Triumphant fascism boasts that it has blocked the way to communism forever because it has crushed the workers' movement. What it really crushed, were only the ineffective primitive forms. It destroyed the illusions, the old socialist belief, the socialist and communist parties—all obsolete things hampering progress. It destroys at the same time the old party divisions that incited workers against workers. It thereby restores their natural class unity.

Parties are groups of common opinion; organizations depend on membership—both secondary accidentals. Class is the primary reality founded in the nature of capitalism itself. By tradition the workers considered political opinion and organization membership as the real distinctions in society, separating comrades and foes. Now they are thrown back upon the real foundations of their life, the class distinctions between workers and capitalists. They were thinking and feeling in terms of parties and unions—and by tradition may continue to do so for some time; now they are constrained to think and feel in terms of class. Without any walls of partition, they stand one beside the other and they see that they are all comrades, subject to the same capitalist exploitation.

No party discipline can call them to action; they will have to think out and to make their own action, when the burden of fascist capitalism makes itself too heavily felt. The mist of opposing party opinions, of political slogans, of union narrowness, which dimmed the natural class consciousness, has been destroyed. Sharp and relentless the reality of capitalism confronts them; and to fight it they have only themselves, their class unity, to rely upon.

The political parties—we speak of Germany and Italy—have disappeared; only the leaders in exile continue to speak as if they were the parties. This does not mean that they have disappeared forever. If there should come an uprising of the working class, they will come back and present themselves again as leaders. They must be vanquished for the second time, now by the workers themselves, by conscious recognition that they are obsolete.

This does not mean, either, that there will be no more parties in future, that their role is finished. New parties will doubtlessly arise in revolutionary periods, to express in new situations the unavoidable differences of tactical opinions within the working class. Parties in this sense are necessary elements in social development. The working class cannot be given ready-made opinions and platforms from some dictator party, which claims to do the thinking work for it and forbids independent opinion. The working class has to think out and to find its way itself. Then opinions on what is, and what must be, done will differ, because men are different, because what they have seen, heard, read, experienced, learned is different, because their lives—though in the main rather alike—were different in particulars. Groups of common opinion will be formed, to discuss and to propagate their ideas, to fight the scientists of the capitalist class, to wage the spiritual contest with other groups. This is the way of self-education for the working class.

Parties in this sense may be called the scouting groups in the capitalist jungle. They have to investigate the ways, to study science and circumstances, to discuss these in mutual debate, to lay their ideas, their explanations, their advice before their fellow workers. In this way they are the necessary instruments to build up the intellectual power of the working class.

Their task is not to act instead of the workers, to do the real fighting work for the workers and to drag the class behind them. They will not have the power to put themselves in the place of the class. Class unity, class action will be paramount, party opinion subordinate.

* * *

There are points of similarity between fascist Italy and Germany and Bolshevist Russia. They are ruled by dictators, the chiefs of dictator parties—the Communist Party in Russia, the Fascist Party in Italy, the National Socialist Party in Germany. These parties are large strongly organized groups, which by their zeal and enthusiasm, their devotion to the cause, by their discipline and energy are able to dominate state and country and to enforce upon it the stamp of one big hard unity.

This is a similarity in form; the contents are different. In Russia state capitalism builds up the productive forces; private capital is not tolerated. In Italy and Germany state and the ruling party are intimately connected with private big capitalism. But here also a better economic organization is included in the fascist aims.

Big business always means a certain organization of production, transport, and banking in the hands of a small number of directing persons, and thus a certain power of these persons over the mass of the lesser capitalists. Political rulers were connected with these big affairs already before. Now the fascist program proclaims it to be the task of state power to direct and regulate the economic forces. The increase of nationalism in all countries, and the preparing for world war, as expressed in the slogan of autarchy, i.e., the complete self-reliance of each state upon its own resources, imposes upon the political leaders a close cooperation with the leaders of industry. If in the old capitalism the state was a necessary instrument of industry, new industry becomes a necessary instrument of the state too. Ruling the state and ruling industry is being merged into one. Imposing regulations upon private business now means that by the fascist state power the bulk of the lesser capitalists are subjected still more completely to big business.

To be sure, in fascist capitalism the ruling class clings to the principle of private enterprise, if not for others then at least for themselves. The silent contest of big capitalists, monopolists, bankers for supremacy and profit goes on behind the scenes. If, however, the economic crisis lasts, then the increasing misery, the rebellions of workers or middle classes will compel the rulers to more efficient regulations of economic life. Already now capitalist economists look to Russia and study its economics as a possible model and as a way out. "Planned economics" is the talk of politicians in many countries. A development of European and American capitalism in the direction of and into some form of state capitalism may offer itself as a means to prevent, or to thwart, or to turn back a proletarian revolution.

This will be called socialism then. If we compare it to the last program, the "Plan," of the Belgian Social Democratic Party for regulating capitalism the difference is not fundamental. The Belgian plan, indeed, may be called an attempt to compete with fascism in a salvation action for capitalism.

* * *

If now we compare these three parties, the Social Democratic Party, the Communist Party, the Fascist Party, we find that they have their chief aim in common. They want to dominate and rule the working class. Of course in order to save the worker, to make them happy, to make them free. They all say so.

Their means, their platforms are different; they are competitors, and each abuses the others, calling them counterrevolutionaries or criminals.

Social democracy makes an appeal to democracy; the workers shall choose their masters by vote. The Communist Party resorts to revolution; the workers shall rise at the call of the Communist Party, overthrow capitalist rule and put the Communist Party into office. The Fascists make an appeal to national feelings and petty-capitalist instincts. They all aspire to some form of state capitalism or state socialism, where the working class is commanded and exploited by the state, by the community of leaders, directors, and officials, the managers of production.

Their common foundation is the opinion that the working masses are unable to conduct their own affairs themselves. The incapable and stupid many must be led and educated by the capable few.

When the working class fights for its real freedom, in order to take the direction of the production, the rule of society into its own hands, it finds these parties all opposed to it.

CHAPTER 8

THE INTELLECTUAL CLASS

This chapter is from Pannekoek's handwritten manuscript. A shorter version was published in *International Council Correspondence* vol. 1, no. 12 (October 1935) under the title "The Intellectuals." —Ed.

The role of these parties in the workers' movement is not entirely based on tradition and differences of opinion. Economic realities and modern class developments stand behind them too. It is necessary, in this connection, to consider the growing importance of the intellectual middle class in social development.

The intellectual middle class, the engineers, scientists, technical employees are a necessary part of industrial production, quite as indispensable as the workers themselves. Technical progress in replacing workers by machines tends to increase their number. Our statistical data show that while they number only a fraction of the number of the working class, they are increasing at a much stronger rate. So their class interests and their class character must be of increasing importance in the social struggles.

Their growing numbers reflect the growing importance of science and theory in the production of life necessities. In a communist society all will partake of scientific knowledge. In capitalist society it is the privilege and the speciality of a separate class, the intellectual middle class.

The members of this new middle class, contrary to the old independent middle class of small businessmen, live by selling their labor power to the capitalists. In their salaries are paid a higher cost of living and a more expensive education than for common workers. In the socialist press they are called proletarians—indeed they are not owners of instruments of production—who needs must join the workers. But it is only their lower ranks that merge gradually into skilled labor; the higher ranks, by origin and standard of living, by relationship, social standing and culture feel themselves middle-class men, who can rise even to the post of director and then be ranked with the big capitalists. Some of them sympathized with social democracy, but the bulk was filled with the capitalist spirit of striving for a better position for themselves only. In Italy and Germany they form the intellectual backbone of fascism.

What must be the social ideals of this class?

They realize that capitalism is not eternal; they perceive already the signs of its decline, in economic crises, in political revolts and revolutions, in social struggles, in world war. It is not the exploitation of labor, that greatest wrong for the workers, that annoys them in capitalism. It is the disorder in capitalism, the anarchy of production that provokes their criticism. Where they rule, in the factory, the efficiency of labor by means of strict order and conscious regulation is raised to the highest degree. But outside the factory, in society, where capitalists, stock gamblers, politicians rule they see the worst disorder and inefficiency, a scandalous waste of human labor, and the inevitable consequence: poverty and ruin for the whole of society.

What they want, therefore, is organization of production, conscious regulation of labor over the whole of society. They feel themselves the spiritual leaders, the class of intellect and knowledge, destined to take over the lead from the incapable hands of the present rulers. In America the ideas of "technocracy" are the first tokens of such a mode of thinking. By a scientific management of the whole of production, under a central direction which does away with competition and which divests the individual capitalists from their arbitrary power, the amount of product can be raised to such a height that there will be abundance for everybody.

This social ideal of the intellectual middle class is a kind of social-ism. But it is not necessarily directed against the capitalist class. It does not mean to expropriate them or to take their profits away from them. On the contrary, in depriving them of their arbitrary power to damage one another, in abolishing the enormous waste, it will raise the productivity of labor to such a degree that the profits will increase considerably. And at the same time it renders possible an increase and securing of the workers' portion, so that all reason for revolt or revo-lution is taken away.

It is not a socialism of the workers but only a socialism for the work-ers, a socialism made by others, for the benefit also of the workers. The exploitation of the workers will not cease, it will be made more rational. With equal justice this social system may be called organized capitalism.

There is of course no place for democracy in this system. Democracy means, at least formally, rule of the mass, of the whole people. But this socialism is founded upon the rule, the leadership of the few, of the intellectual minority. In present-day capitalism the technical middle class are leaders and directors of the labor process, they command the workers. They can imagine an ideal society only with this leading and commanding function preserved and extended. The intellectual class does not admit class differences founded on noble birth or riches; but it admits differences in brains, in mental capacity, and it considers itself as the class of men with the best brains, selected to lead the great masses of the ungifted common people, destined to be common workers.

Hence the political system belonging to this middle-class social-ism can never be democracy; it must be the dictatorship of a leading bureaucracy.

The socialism once proclaimed as their social goal by the vanguard of the working class, was international. Because they saw production as a worldwide unit process and the class struggle of the workers as the common cause of the working class of the whole world. The intellectual class, however, owing to its middle-class origin, to its close connection with the capitalist class, has a strong national feeling. Moreover the instruments necessary for the regulation of production exist only as power organs of the state. Its socialist goal therefore means a national state socialism. Its rule is the rule of a state bureaucracy, its system of production is state capitalism. International world unity is a faraway dream to them, not a matter of practical ideals.

Some characteristics of the social ideals of the intellectual class are found in social democracy, especially in its state-socialist program, though its relation of leaders to masses has a more democratic stamp. In German national socialism some others of these characteristics are perceptible. The tendencies of a class are never reproduced purely in a political party or a political movement. They are the underlying basis, the underground stream, taking its course and growing after fixed laws, determined by class interests, by needs of social development, by the deepest subconscious feelings which the social conditions produce in a class. They are not adequately represented in the surface phenomena, in the political events, the party platforms, the government's changes, the measures taken, the revolutions, the programs—because in all these the traditions, the existing factors of power, the relative force of contesting or cooperating classes, groups, parties play a role. But then always anew the realities, hidden beneath the surface, break through, upset the old and determine the new ideas and political events. So we have to look into these events for the class forces at work in them, just as for the forces of nature we look into the natural phenomena.

In fascism and national socialism the class spirit of the intellectual middle classes appears in its first germs. We see as yet only a common revolt together with the petty-capitalist and big-capitalist classes against democracy, with only a faint and vague desire for an economically constructive policy. Nevertheless, the spiritual force of the National Socialist slogans of the intellectual class was sufficient to carry away numbers of workers, who saw in it an organizing power against capitalist disorder.

Is it possible that these parties will realize, or try to realize the class ideals of the intellectual class? This class is well-nigh powerless against the capitalist class. The social power of the intellectuals, measured by their number, their class consciousness, their social feeling is still far below the power which formerly the working class had already attained. The capitalist class in Europe and America is so powerful that it need not tolerate any organization or regulation of production beyond its own interests. It is only when capitalism feels itself extremely weakened and endangered, by heavy and long crises, by workers' revolts, by world war, that conditions are different. Then the intellectual class, together with part of the workers, may be called upon to introduce constructive policy leading toward state capitalistic experiments.

When, however, the working class, rising against the unbearable oppression of monopolistic capitalism, by means of revolutionary movements should succeed in beating down capitalist power, what will the intellectual class do? Then the positions will be reversed; the working class by its mighty fighting power carries the other discontented classes along with it in a common assault on capitalism. Then great parts of the intellectual class will join them, won over by the great socialist and communist ideals, and will consider them as their common cause. In every revolutionary movement in history we see great numbers joining it in a common enthusiasm for aims more radical than their own ideals, thereby making the victory more easy. But then afterward it appeared that each of the allies interpreted the slogans and aims in his own way, thus causing dissensions and new fights between the former comrades. The same will doubtlessly be the case in future revolutionary movements.

The slogans: against capitalism, for socialism or communism, will be common to the revolutionary classes. But for each class they mean a different form of social organization. The working class has to build up production from below, by their direct hold over the factories, and to organize them by means of their workers' councils into a democratic commonwealth. The intellectual class will try to install a centrally organized state socialism, directed by a leading bureaucracy.

Is not the intellectual class right in this? Is it not necessary that in these most difficult times of fighting and social reconstruction the ignorant masses should be directed by those who have the best brains? Is it not true that then, for that period this large selected minority class, trained in science, in general and special knowledge, are the natural leaders, up to the time when new generations have been born?

No; this is not true. The organization of society is not a matter of technics, of scientific knowledge. The technics of production are excellent already. Capitalism has developed to a high level the science of the forces of nature and its application. This is the domain of the superior knowledge of the intellectuals. As technical experts in the process of production they may apply their brains for the benefit of the community.

But social organization has to deal with other things, with social forces and with the knowledge of social forces. It is an organization of men. And here the intellectuals have no special capacities. What they bring with them is only the haughty prejudices of the capitalist class. Such as that men will only work when commanded by a boss. In social insight, in knowledge of the real class relations of society, the intellectuals stand below the working class. Because their mind clings to ideas belonging to a passing period. Because outside of their physical machines, in matters of human relations, they are wont to deal not with the realities of social life itself but with their spiritual images, conceptions, theories, abstractions.

Social organization does not depend on qualities of intellect of a minority. It depends on qualities of character of the whole working people. It is only possible by virtue of the enthusiasm, the self-imposed discipline, the moral force of brotherhood and self-sacrifice at work in an all-day practice, by virtue of the utmost exertion of all physical and mental forces, by virtue of the spirit of community in all the workers, animated by the high ideals of communism. It is the consolidation of the workers into one unity through strong moral forces, which cannot be commanded by leaders but must grow up in the masses in their fight for freedom.

Thus the social ideals and aims of the intellectual middle class and of the working class oppose one another. The intellectual class, when it should try to establish some social order, must call upon old instincts of obedience, upon the slave feelings of a bygone humanity. For its state-socialist aims it will find allies in social-democratic and party-communist platforms, in union leaders, in the capitalistic ideas of timid and backward workers, who think communist freedom too high for them, and in the beaten remnants of the capitalist force. Then the working class, finding itself opposed by this block, [which is] trying under the banner of "socialism against anarchy" to preserve the domination of a ruling class over the working masses, will need all its wisdom and all its unity to find and to fight its way to freedom.

CHAPTER 9

THE WORKERS' REVOLUTION

This chapter is from Pannekoek's handwritten manuscript, and was never published in *International Council Correspondence*. —Ed.

The workers' fight for freedom is only in its beginning as yet. We have struggled through the capitalist wilderness, to find ourselves only at the foot of the mountain. What the workers' parties, what trade unions did, was only preliminary action; it was not the real fight. They assured for the workers their place in capitalism. But at the same time, in so doing they made it quite clear that capitalism is no living place for the workers; that they must go on. Now for the first time they can see their real task before them.

The revolutionary movement, obviously, is at a low ebb. Always socialists and communists spoke of the revolution as being near; and now that capitalism is in an economic crisis more deep and long than ever before, and that misery and hopelessness increase beyond measure, now the revolution holds off. On the contrary, reaction came up, capitalist power is taking a stronger grip. The brilliant hopes that first socialism and then communism lit in the hearts of the workers faded. They were reflected lights only, that now led them astray. When the workers seek their new ways and prepare for the real great fight, the illusions awakened by their first uprising become stumbling blocks on their way.

From the insufficiency of the methods used till now, the workers learn that new methods of action have to be followed. Certainly, the old ones were no failures; they were useful in their time. But conditions have changed. They have led the working class so far that it can see the mountain slope to be climbed. They were the experience obtained at the cost of defeat and of the best lives, needed for the putting and the answer of the supreme question: How can the workers win?

The foundation of capitalist power is their economic power, their possession of the factories, their command of production. Here the workers face them directly; and they are many, the others are few. Let them try, however, instead of striking and leaving the factory, to take possession of it. At once the political power of the state will come into action; the courts, the police, the militia are directed, the civil guards, the Pinkertons are protected, by the state. The workers now try to take hold of the state; with their big numbers they go to seize it by voting. In America their representatives would be bought by the capitalists. In Europe they delegated honest and devoted Socialists to conquer the state power. But when these men came into power they were transformed into petty capitalist politicians. On all sides the workers are shut in and bound in the strong webs which the big spider capitalism has woven around them.

Political and economic power is one firm unity in the hands of the capitalists! Workers and Socialists sometimes quarreled about what was their real power, and about their having to fight capitalism in the political or in the economic field. These distinctions have a meaning only for the fight within capitalism. They are futile for the revolutionary fight, where all means of action form a unity against the unity of capitalist power. They are futile still more where a state rule and individual rule are being merged together in the hands of a few leaders.

Is there any way out? To find it we have to go to the root of these power structures.

State power, strictly speaking, is a group of officials and politicians. They form an organized minority, governing the majority as a power above the people, though originating from the people. Its power consists, directly, in its strong organization. A strongly organized minority can always dominate an unorganized majority.

The policeman who clubs a striker knows that he obeys the orders of his superiors; he does his duty, and he is paid for it. The striker knows that it is not a single man who beats him; he knows that the whole government of the US stands behind that man. If he defends himself, more policemen come; if they cannot win, the whole army can be called in; the authority of the state is at stake. The judge in court is not a single man against the strikers he condemns to jail; he represents Uncle Sam, and the whole state power stands behind him. Not only with its physical force but with all its moral force too.

State power is an organization led and commanded by one common will. The decisions and orders of the chiefs of government are obeyed and executed without hesitation, automatically, by every official. A long tradition, fed by the necessity of capitalist rule, has led to it that every official, even without orders, knows what he has to do in daily work as well as in case of emergency. A common feeling of office solidarity, of the necessity of authority and order, a common capitalist mode of thinking directs the will and action of every official in line with the will of the central government. And it is strengthened to a moral force, to a high duty by tradition, by education, by the feeling that for society the obedience of the masses is necessary. State power and authority are sacred, and to attack them is considered the most execrable of crimes, a sacrilege.

If, however, all this should not suffice to withhold those wicked people from revolting, the state has its physical power. It has its army, a heavily armed minority group, bound by the still more rigid bonds of military discipline. By education from childhood onward, by drill, by fear, the soldier has been turned into a will-less tool in the hands of his chiefs, ready even to murder his kindred and comrades.

This is the structure by which political power as a steel framework upholds the society's machine for producing and distributing wealth. Is there any possibility of vanquishing such a strong structure?

There certainly is. A minority organization can be vanquished and destroyed by the organization of the majority. It was able to reign only because the people, the majority, form an unorganized mass of individuals. As soon as this mass becomes an organized mass it must necessarily grow stronger than any minority organization.

It is clear that here organization does not mean simply membership in some union or other body. This is only an outward form. Its essence is the discipline, the inner cement that binds the loose grains to a solid body.

Organization consists in inner qualities of mind and heart, and is defeated only by better organization, by better qualities of mind and heart. Self-confidence and the custom of commanding on the part of superiors, hope of reward, fear of punishment on the side of the inferiors, obedience, duty, faith, these are the moral qualities constituting the discipline of the ruling power. Clear knowledge of society and of class interests, unbreakable unity and solidarity, indomitable courage and self-sacrifice are the intellectual and moral qualities which form the basis of the working-class discipline.

Revolution is the conflict of these two organizations, in which the working class discipline grows to such a degree that it outgrows and destroys the inner coherence of state power.

In each fight these two stand in opposition to one another. In the beginning the workers' coherence had to come into being and to grow up against the oppression of the capitalist class that tried in vain to destroy it. In strikes solidarity grows because the workers perceive that without it they are bound to lose, that it is their only chance to win. This virtue is felt and proclaimed as a high command of proletarian morals, the neglect of which brings shame and dishonor. The protection of scabs by state officials destroys the respect for state authority in increasing numbers of workers. Grudgingly, the state must allow the workers' unions to fight the capitalist class by means of this new force of proletarian solidarity.

Now the fights grow larger and lead to big class conflicts. Great strikes by their extension become public, they become state affairs. Each strike is a bit of rebellion against the existing order, though with legal means, and is treated as such. The state tries to overawe the workers by a display of its powers and at the same time to conciliate them by arbitration and small concessions. If the workers do not let themselves be overawed, the state power must come into action. The aim is always to loosen the coherence of the workers, to dissolve them into single individuals with different opinions and character. Therefore the common legal rights are actually, if not legally, suspended. The ordinary means of understanding, discussing, persuading are repressed by brutal methods. If the strikers want to keep and show their unity and assemble in forbidden meetings, they have to stand up against police attacks. If then their thousands make a stand with firm determination and do not yield, the now inadequate police force is powerless. The state power is obliged to bring its stronger forces into the field and to send soldiers.

The same case occurs when in a fight for political rights, the working class, carrying through a forbidden demonstration, overflows the streets in endless numbers. A strong conviction and a firm readiness to suffer and to make sacrifices for the cause is necessary to bring about such a demonstration of unity. Then in its turn it exalts the spirit of unity and the enthusiasm of the workers to a higher level, the police forces are powerless to cope with the fearless masses, and stronger forces of repression, the strongest power of the state, the army is needed.

With the army, however, the same conditions repeat themselves. Revolutions in European history may serve to demonstrate the psychical forces and the reactions involved. Against a rebellion on a limited scale it is a successful weapon; but over against the mass of the people fighting for its life necessities, matters are different. The armed force may shoot at masses filling the streets or assembling in large meetings; but it cannot exterminate them. The shooting means frightening the masses by killing some of them. If, however, the masses have such a great unity in their common determined will, such a firm conviction of their great aims, that they do not disperse, that they do not run away panic-stricken, or that, if they do, they always reassemble, anew, then the aim of the rulers is missed. Then, on the contrary, the coherence of their army is shaken. Military discipline can be put to no harder test than to be ordered against peaceful masses standing up for a just cause.

Once or twice the soldiers may obey, then they cannot be relied upon anymore. They hesitate, they begin to think for themselves, they begin to feel uneasy, seeing the firm courage on the other side; still more if they are informed about the workers' cause.

Thus, when measuring swords with one another, the strongest discipline dissolves the weaker discipline. The free spontaneous organization of the working masses, if it be strong enough, is able to destroy the enforced discipline of the state's armed organs. This is the weak spot of these sharpest power factors of the state: if really they are compelled to come into action against the new rising power of the working class, they become blunted.

So these great class conflicts acquire a revolutionary character. State power, the steel frame of capitalist domination, is beginning to dissolve. In Europe, where some dozens of nations are jammed together on a small continent, with immense hatreds and impending wars, political conflicts may most easily lead to revolution. Because the working class has to make this revolution, big strike movements, universal strikes,[4] political strikes, will be its prominent form.

In America, where the richest and most arrogant capitalist class dominates a one-state continent, big strikes in the first place may be expected to lead to revolutionary class conflicts. The state may try to conciliate the workers by small concessions; but they cannot be conciliated forever, and the fight will break out again. The state may try to repress a strike by force; then the workers in defense will try to extend it, and in this way to augment their pressure upon capitalist society. They will try to make it more general, to make a universal strike in the end.[5] In

---

4   [It is clear in Pannekoek's handwritten manuscript that he initially wrote "general strikes" but later changed every mention of them (except one he seemingly missed) to "universal strikes." Perhaps he thought this stylistic edit would appeal more to American workers? It may also be the case that he felt "universal" implied a larger scale than "general." —Ed.]

5   [This sentence was followed by the following, though Pannekoek crossed it out: "When the workers fighting by trades, separately and alone against the whole capitalist class and its State Power, of course are defeated one trade after another, then

these general fights of class against class, all distinction between political and economic fights has disappeared.

A universal strike usually breaks out for some special aim: to win a strike for one trade, or to defend or to obtain an important political right. This aim may or may not be reached; this fades into the background when compared to the unintentional effects. Just as in the world war, the special object of contentions were forgotten in the great power contest in general. In the same way, a universal strike immediately becomes primarily a measuring of strength of the classes.

Like other fighting methods of the workers, a universal strike by its very nature makes use of legal rights only, and yet it has stronger effects than an illegal rebellion. Hence it cannot be suppressed by legal actions of the rulers. They can only try to weaken the force that enabled the strike, the fighting spirit, the unity, the clear-sighted determination of the workers. The state mobilizes all its forces against it as against a rebellion. By exhibiting its military forces, its machine guns, it tries to break the courage; by prohibiting meetings it tries to isolate the individuals, and to break up their unity; by publishing false rumors of defeats of the workers in other towns, it tries to instill uncertainty and doubt into their hearts; by publishing calumnies about atrocities, it tries to detract part of the fighters. Hence the strike can only be won, if the unity, the clear insight, the courage, the independence of the workers rise to such a height, that all these means cannot reach them.

A universal strike means firstly a demonstration of the whole working class in an attitude of fight. In ordinary times all their energy is absorbed by their work, and only during a few hours of the night weary heads may be occupied with general interests. Now they quit work; all their energy is devoted to the public cause, and their utmost attention is directed to the interests of their class. This mobilization of forces alone already means a serious warning to the ruling class. It means at

---

naturally must come the idea to unite the forces of all the trades, and all at the same time strike against the capitalist class as a whole." —Ed.]

the same time a heavy blow to state power; for it shows that the state cannot ensure capitalist order.

More efficient still than this demonstration is its effect on production. When the production apparatus is stopped the whole of society becomes paralyzed. If the workers refuse to work, society cannot exist. A universal strike demonstrates to all classes that the workers are the direct masters of production.

Now the workers constitute the chief part of society; so they cannot allow society to be paralyzed for a long time. They themselves must live. The aim of a universal strike is never to starve society, but only to put a heavy constraint upon the capitalist class and its central organ, the state power. A capitalist government unable to check a general strike is like a government of olden times that was not able to crush a rebellion. It loses its authority, its self-confidence, its inner solidarity. Especially through the moral effects of the workers' fight. Their demands, the motive of the fight, must appear just and right, even to many members of the capitalist class. Politicians and intellectuals will raise their voice to proclaim that the granting of these demands is to be preferred to the risk of civil war. The unity of the ruling class is broken.

To this are added the direct effects of the strike on the functioning of government. A general traffic strike prevents the transport of soldiers, it cuts off local authorities from regular intercourse with the central resorts, it paralyzes several functions of government. Emergency methods, aircraft, scabbing by capitalist volunteers may give some relief but cannot entirely neutralize these effects. Local and provincial officials standing face to face with the difficulties, reduced to their own resources, acting on their own responsibilities will try to compromise here, will use the heaviest violence at another place. The lower functionaries lose faith in the power they represent, they lose their self-confidence. The political power of the state is breaking up into fragments, its organization is loosened, its rigid discipline begins to dissolve.

Here is presupposed a strike, where the working class develops such complete unity, discipline, insight, and firmness that it comes out victorious; we are considering here its effects, the mechanism through which it could win. Of course a universal strike can be lost as well as won; history shows instances of both. There have been universal strikes, proclaimed by the leaders to satisfy the fighting spirit of the masses, and meant to cease after some meddling with the capitalist class. There have been universal strikes where the workers, trying to attain what was beyond their powers, had to break off the strike, in complete exhaustion.

If we discuss universal strikes we can only make use of the experiences of the past, what they teach us about conditions and effects. They will doubtlessly play a much more important role in future; but of the form they will assume in the future, when they are larger and more powerful, we can have only uncertain notions. The working class has always created its new methods of action itself, finding them according to its needs and its feeling of power. Theorists and writers could do no more than transfer the experience of warfare in the past, summarizing them and explaining them, to the later generations.

A few remarks must yet be added. A universal strike is not an event to happen once and as one tremendous upheaval destroying state power and capitalist rule. It is not revolution itself but only an episode in a long process of revolution. It raises the power of the workers, because it is owing to these strong appeals to unity of action and wisdom of decision that their unity and their wisdom are increased. And at the same time, it diminishes the power of capitalism. Then, however, new "socialistic" governments, embodying their victory, but at the same time intending to stop the fighting to arouse inner dissensions and to break the unity, may temporarily restore the capitalist power. So over and over again the fight has to recur, always mightier, alternated or combined with other modes of mass action. Capitalist power cannot fall at one blow, however heavy.

The capitalist class will not leave its state in the lurch. When the state, using its ordinary powers, cannot withstand the working class in universal strike, using its strict striking rights, then the deeper sources of capitalist power are brought into the field. If the army cannot be trusted, groups of young capitalists, eager to fight the "reds," will replace them as a volunteer army, and with their money power they will organize armies of hooligans. With all brutal means of terrorism and with the most horrible modern war contrivances, they will attack the workers. Their appearance tends to turn a peaceful strike movement into a civil war.

When, however, such forces come into the field, it confirms this very decay of the state power as a separate supreme power factor that, through its authority, its embodying law and order, acts as protector of the capitalist class. It needs to be protected itself; the new forces become independent powers, directly rooted in the capitalist class. The stronghold is crumbling; the defendants must rely on their own fighting force. This force is still big enough; but its former power factors are reduced chiefly to money power and to spiritual influence, the capitalist spirit of personal greed, of brutal oppression, of law servility, living in large parts of the people still. These forces are strong enough to bring hard fighting and heavy losses for the working class; but they are not sufficient to win in the long run against the idealism,[6] the growing unity, the radiant goal of the revolutionary masses. The capitalist class will build up new political organizations, new forms of government, usurping the power and proclaiming that they stand for law and order. In reality, their inmost character is already that of organizations for disorder and lawlessness.

Indeed, during this period of revolutionary class struggles, the picture has changed continuously. The working class, forming one united whole in these struggles, is growing into the position of the real society, the collectivity of working people ruling itself and ruling society. Whereas the fighting forces of the capitalist class are growing into the position of

---

6   [It should go without saying, but many are prone to jump to conclusions, that the "idealism" Pannekoek encourages is not philosophical idealism, the notion that ideas are predominant over the material world. Because of such words, including "spiritual" and "wisdom," some American council communists hesitated to publish some of his works during the 1930s. See Pannekoek's letter to Paul Mattick dated February 2, 1936, in the Association Archives Antonie Pannekoek, https://www.aaap.be. For philosophical writings that clearly show his adherence to historical materialism, see his article "Society and Mind in Marxian Philosophy," chapter 13 of this volume, as well as his book *Lenin as Philosopher* in which he criticises Lenin's mechanical, bourgeois materialism. —Ed.]

lawless troops of rebels, trying to disturb the new proletarian order by violence and murder. The forms of organization which the working class has been building in its fight, now develop into the form of organization of the new society.

* * *

Social revolution is the transferring of supremacy in society from an old ruling class to a new class. Its characteristic feature is the breakdown of the power institutions of the old class. Its political organization is crumbling to nothing, is dissolved and disappears. The people stand as the masters of society.

In European history, something similar happened several times in capitalist revolutions; the working masses stood as masters after having dispersed the government power in street fights or strikes. But they could not always remain in the streets or on strike; after the victory they had to go to work again. So their momentary fighting unity, their mass power, vanished; they changed back into a number of isolated groups or persons. Then a new ascending capitalist group could easily form a new government, in line with the needs of production. The difference with the coming communist revolution is that then the workers will hold the power firmly in their hands. This is only possible by means of the new forms of organization which the working class built up during its fight. They are the constructive side of the revolution.

Revolutions were always the constructive moments in human history. Contrary to the legend, which frightened reactionaries try to make us believe, that revolutions are only destructive, history shows that all great progress in political and social institutions is made or started in revolutions. Firstly because the power of resistance of the old class that profited from the old institutions has been removed. Then also because the constructive force of men has grown.

In revolution mankind seems to be changed into different beings. The extreme demands of the fight, where mental and moral qualities turn the scales between victory and annihilation, raise those qualities to the highest pitch. With mind and heart in the utmost tension, man is capable of brilliant deeds of high courage. New ideas arise in the minds; with daring spirit, men create their new material and mental world, thinking thoughts they never had dared to dream, shedding old traditions as dead scales, building up new social institutions. The workers' revolution in all these points exceeds former revolutions, moreover binds men into the strongest unity, enlightens them to the utmost clarity of mind, and builds up a new organization of society, the expression and the warrant of its lasting freedom and unity.

It is to these forms of organization that we must now turn our eyes.

CHAPTER 10

THE WORKERS' COUNCILS

This chapter is from Pannekoek's handwritten manuscript. A shorter version was published in *International Council Correspondence* vol. 2, no. 5 (April 1936) under the title "Workers' Councils." —Ed.

In these revolutionary fights the working class needs organization. Not only in the sense, now, of a spiritual force, the spirit of organized action, but in the sense of a visible form, a form of organization. When great masses have to act as a unit after one common will, a mechanism is needed for understanding and discussion, for the taking and issuing of decisions, for the proclaiming of actions and aims.

This does not mean, of course, that all great actions and universal strikes are carried out with soldierlike discipline after the decisions of a central board. Such cases will occur, certainly. But more often through their eager fighting spirit, their solidarity and passion, masses will break out in strikes, to help their comrades or to protest against some capitalist atrocity, with no general plan, in passionate revolt; and then such a strike will spread like a prairie fire all over the country. In the Russian Revolution of 1905 the strike waves went up and down. Often the most successful were those that had not been decided in advance, while the strikes that had been proclaimed by the central committees often failed. Nevertheless, also in such cases the strikers, once they are fighting, want mutual contact and understanding, in order to unite in an organized force what sprung up spontaneously.

Here a difficulty presents itself. Without strong organization, without joining forces and binding their will into one solid body, without uniting their action into one common deed, they cannot win against the strong organization of capitalist power. But when thousands and millions of workers are united in one body, this can only be managed by functionaries acting as representatives of the members. And we have seen that then these officials become masters of the organization, with interests different from the revolutionary interests of the workers.

How can the working class in revolutionary fight unite its force into a big organization without falling into the pit of officialdom?

The answer is given by putting another question: If all that the workers do is to pay their fees and to obey when their leaders order them out and order them in, are they themselves then really fighting the fight for freedom?

Fighting for freedom is not letting your leaders think for you and decide, and following obediently behind them, or from time to time scolding them. Fighting for freedom is partaking to the full of one's capacity, thinking and deciding for oneself, taking all responsibilities as a self-reliant individual, amid equal comrades.

It is true that to think for oneself, to think out what is true and right, with a head dulled by fatigue, is the hardest, the most difficult task; it is much harder than to pay and to obey. But it is the only way to freedom. To be liberated by others, whose leadership is the essential part of the liberation, means the getting of new masters instead of the old ones.

Freedom, the goal of the workers, means that they shall be able, man for man, to manage the world, to use and deal with the treasures of the earth so as to make it a happy home for all. How can they ensure this if they are not able to conquer and defend this themselves?

The proletarian revolution is not simply the vanquishing of capitalist power. It is the rise of the whole working people out of dependence and ignorance into independence and clear consciousness of how to make their life. It is by this that they are able to crush capitalist power.

True organization, as the workers need it in the revolution, implies that everyone takes part in it, body and soul and brains, that everyone takes part in leadership as well as in action, and has to think out, to decide and to perform to the full of his capacities. Such an organization is a body of self-determining people. There is no place for professional leaders. Certainly there is obeying; everybody has to follow the decisions, which he himself has taken part in making. But the full power always rests with the workers themselves.

Can such a form of organization be realized? What must be its structure? It is not necessary to construct it or think it out. History has already produced it. It sprang into life out of the practice of the class struggle.

Its prototype, its first trace is found in the strike committees. In a big strike all the workers cannot assemble in one meeting. They choose delegates to act as a committee. Such a committee is only the executive organ of the strikers; it is continually in touch with them, and has to carry out the decisions of the strikers. Each delegate at every moment can be replaced by others; such a committee never becomes an independent power. In such a way common action as one body can be secured, and yet the workers have all decisions in their own hands. Usually in strikes the uppermost lead is taken out of the hands of these committees by the trade unions and their leaders.

In the Russian Revolution, when strikes broke out irregularly in the factories, the strikers chose delegates which, for the whole town, or for an industry or railway over the whole state or province, assembled to bring unity into the fight. They had at once to discuss political matters and to assume political functions, because the strikes were directed against czarism. They were called soviets, councils. In these soviets all the details of the situation, all the workers' interests, all political events were discussed. Continually the delegates went to and fro between the assembly and their factories; in the factories and shops the workers in general meetings discussed the same matters, took their decisions and often sent new delegates: Able Socialists were appointed as secretaries, to give advice based on their wider knowledge. Often these soviets had to act as political powers, as a kind of primitive government when the czarist power was paralysed, when officials and officers did not know what to do and left the field to them.

Thus these soviets became the permanent center of the revolution; they were constituted by delegates of all the factories, striking or working. They could not think of becoming an independent power; the members were often changed, and sometimes the whole soviet was arrested and had to be replaced by new delegates. Moreover they knew that all their force was rooted in the workers' will to strike or not to strike; often their calls were not followed, when they did not concur with the workers' instinctive feelings of power or weakness, of passion or prudence.

So the soviet system proved to be the appropriate form of organization for a revolutionary working class. In 1917 it was at once adopted in Russia, and everywhere workers' and soldiers' soviets came into being and were the driving force of the revolution.

The complementary proof was given in Germany. In 1918, after the breakdown of the military power, workers' and soldiers' councils, in imitation of Russia, were founded. But the German workers, educated in party and union discipline, full of social-democratic ideas of republic and reform as the next political aims, chose their party and union officials as delegates to these councils. When fighting and acting themselves they acted and fought in the right way; but from lack of self-confidence they chose leaders filled with capitalist ideas, and these always spoiled matters. It is natural that a "council congress" such as this then resolved to abdicate for a new parliament to be chosen as soon as possible.

Here it became evident that the council system is the appropriate form of organization only for a revolutionary working class. If the workers do not intend to go on with the revolution they have no use for soviets.

If the workers are not far enough advanced yet to see the way of revolution, if they are content with the leaders doing all the work of speechifying and mediating and bargaining for reforms within capitalism, then parliaments and party and union congresses—called workers' parliaments, because they work after the same principle—are all they need. If however, they fight with all their energy for revolution, if with intense eagerness and passion they take part in every event, if they think over and decide for themselves all details of fighting, because they have to do the fighting, then workers' councils are the organization they need.

This implies that workers' councils cannot be formed by revolutionary groups. Such groups can only propagate the idea, by explaining to their fellow workers the necessity of council organization, when the working class as a self-determining power fights for freedom. Councils are the form of organization only for fighting masses, for the working class as a whole, not for revolutionary groups.

They originate and grow up along with the first action of a revolutionary character. With the development of revolution their importance and their functions increase.

At first they may appear as simple strike committees, in opposition to the labor leaders when the strikes go beyond the intentions of the leaders and rebel against the unions and their leaders.

In a universal strike the functions of these committees are enlarged. Now delegates of all the factories and plants have to discuss and to decide about all the conditions of the fight; they will try to regulate into consciously devised action all the fighting power of the workers; they must see how they will react upon the governments' measures, the doings of soldiers or capitalist gangs. It is from the workers that the actual decisions come, by means of this very strike action. So they cannot but consider the matters with all attention; in the councils only the summary, the facet is taken of all these decisions. But the councils are the place where the opinions, the will, the readiness, the hesitation or the eagerness, the energy and the obstacles of all these masses concentrate and combine into a common line of action. They are the symbols, the exponents of the workers' power; but at the same time only the spokesmen, which can be replaced at any moment. At one moment they are outlaws to the capitalist world, and at the next they have to treat as equal parties with the high functionaries of government.

When the revolution develops to such power that the state power is seriously affected, then the workers' councils have to assume political functions. In a political revolution this is their first and chief function. They are the central bodies of the workers' power; they have to take all possible measures to weaken and defeat the adversary. Like a power at war they have to stand guard over the whole country controlling the efforts of the capitalist class to collect and restore its forces and to subdue the workers. They have to look after a number of public affairs, which otherwise were state affairs: public health, public security, the uninterrupted course of social life. They have to take care of the production itself, the most important and difficult task and concern of the working class in revolution. They are the new political organs of the workers' class, substituting the crumbling political organs of the capitalist class.

A social revolution in history never began as a simple change of political rulers, who then, after having acquired political power, carried out the necessary social changes by means of new laws. Already before and during the fight the rising class built up its new social organs, as new sprouting branches within the dead husk of the former organism. In the French Revolution the new capitalist class, the citizens, the businessmen, the artisans built up in each town and village their communal boards, their new courts of justice, illegal at the time, usurping simply the functions of the powerless functionaries of royalty. While their delegates in Paris discussed and made the new constitution, the actual constitution was made all over the country by the citizens holding their political meetings, building up their political organs, afterward legalized by law.

In the same way during the proletarian revolution the new rising class creates its new forms of organization which step by step in the process of revolution, supersede, the old state organization. The workers' councils as the new form of political organization take the place of parliamentarism, the political form of capitalist rule.

Parliamentary democracy is considered by capitalist theorists as well as by social democrats as the perfect democracy, conforming to justice and equality. In reality it is only a disguise for capitalist domination, and contrary to justice and equality. It is the council system that is the true workers' democracy.

Parliamentary democracy is a foul democracy. The people are allowed to vote once in four or five years and to choose their delegates; woe to them if then they do not choose the right man. Only at the polls the voters can exert their power, thereafter they are powerless. The chosen delegates are now the rulers of the people: they make laws and constitute governments, and the people have to obey. Usually, by the election mechanism, only the big capitalist parties with their powerful apparatus, with their papers, their noisy advertising have a chance to win. Real trustees of discontented groups seldom have a chance to win some few seats.

In the soviet system each delegate can be repealed at any moment. Not only do the workers continually remain in touch with the delegate, discussing and deciding for themselves, but the delegate is only a temporary messenger to the council assemblies. Capitalist politicians denounce this "characterless" role of a delegate, in that he may have to speak against his personal opinion. They forget, that just because there are no fixed delegates only those will be sent whose opinions conform to the workers' opinion.

The principle of parliamentary representation is that the delegate in parliament shall act and vote according to his own conscience and conviction. If on some question he should ask the opinion of his voters, it is only his own prudence. He has to decide on his own responsibility, not the people. The principle of the soviet system is just the reverse; the delegates express the opinion of the workers.

In the elections for parliament the citizens are grouped according to voting districts and counties, that is to say according to their dwelling place. Persons of different trades or classes, having nothing in common, accidentally living near to each other, are combined into an artificial group which has to be represented by one delegate.

In the councils the workers are represented in their natural groups, according to factories, shops, and plants. The workers of one factory or one big plant form a unit of production; they belong together by their collective work. In revolutionary epochs they are in immediate contact to interchange opinions, they live under the same conditions and have the same interests. They must act together; the factory is the unit, which as a unit has to strike or to work, and its workers must decide what they collectively have to do. So the organization and delegation after factories and workshops is necessary.

It is at the same time the principle of representation of the communist order growing up in the revolution. Production is the basis of society or, more rightly, it is the contents, the essence of society; hence the order of production is at the same time the order of society. Factories are the working units, the cells of which the organism of society consists. The main task of the political organs, which mean nothing else but the organs managing the totality of society, concerns the productive work of society. Hence it goes without saying that the working people, in their councils, discuss these matters and choose their delegates collected in their production units.

We should not believe, though, that parliamentarism, as the political form of capitalism, was not founded on production. Always the political organization is adapted to the character of production as the basis of society. Representation according to dwelling place, belongs to the system of petty capitalist production, where each man is supposed to be possessor of his own small business. Then there is a mutual connection between all these businessmen at one place, dealing with one another, living as neighbors, knowing one another and therefore sending one common delegate to parliament. This was the basis of parliamentarism. We have seen that later on this parliamentary delegation system proved to be the right system for representing the growing and changing class interests within capitalism.

At the same time, it is clear now why the delegates in parliament had to take political power in their hands. Their political task was only a small part of the task of society. The most important part, the productive work, was the personal task of all the separate producers, the citizens as businessmen; it required nearly all their energy and care. When every individual took care of his own small lot, then society as their totality went right. The general regulations by law, necessary conditions, doubtlessly, but of minor extent, could be left to the care of a special group or trade, the politicians.

With communist production the reverse is true. Here the all-important thing, the collective productive work is the task of society as a whole; it concerns all the workers collectively. Their personal work does not claim their whole energy and care; their mind is turned to the collective task of their factory, to the still more collective task of society. The general regulation of this collective work cannot be left to a special group of persons; it is the vital interest of the whole working people.

There is another difference between parliamentarism and the soviet system. In parliamentary democracy one vote is given to every adult man (and sometimes woman) on the strength of their supreme, inborn right of belonging to mankind, as is so beautifully expressed in celebration speeches. In the soviets, on the other hand, only the workers are represented. Can the council system then be said to be truly democratic, if it excludes the other classes of society?

The council system embodies the dictatorship of the proletariat. Marx and Engels more than half a century ago explained that the social revolution was to lead to the dictatorship of the working class as the next political form, and that this was essential in order to bring about the necessary changes in society. Socialists, thinking in terms of parliamentary representation only, tried either to excuse, or to criticize the violation of democracy and the injustice of arbitrarily excluding persons from the polls because they belong to certain classes. Now we see how the development of the proletarian class struggle in a natural way produces the organs of this dictatorship, the soviets.

It is certainly no violation of justice that the councils, as the fighting centers of a revolutionary working class, do not include representatives of the opposing class. And thereafter the matter is not different. In a rising communist society there is no place for capitalists; they have to disappear, and they will disappear. Whoever takes part in the collective work is a member of the collectivity and takes part in the decisions. Persons, however, who stand outside the process of collective production, by the structure of the council system are automatically excluded from influence upon it. Whatever remains of the former exploiters and robbers has no vote in the regulation of a production in which they take no part.

There are other classes in society that do not directly belong to the two chief opposite classes: small farmers, independent artisans, intellectuals. In the revolutionary fight they may waver to and fro, but on the whole they are not very important, because they have less fighting power.

Mostly their forms of organization and their aims are different. To make friends with them or to neutralize them, if this is possible without impeding the proper aims, or to fight them resolutely if necessary, to decide upon the way of dealing with them with equity and firmness, will be the concern, often a matter of difficult tactics, of the fighting working class. In the production system, insofar as their work is useful and necessary, they will find their place, and they will exert their influence after the principle that whoever does the work has a chief vote in regulating the work.

More than half a century ago Engels said that through the proletarian revolution the state would disappear; instead of the ruling over men comes the managing of affairs. This was said at a time when there could not be any clear idea about how the working class would come into power. Now we see the truth of this statement confirmed; in the process of revolution the old state power will be destroyed. And the organs that take its place, the workers' councils, for the time being will certainly have important political functions still, to repress the remnants of capitalist power. Their political function of governing, however, will be gradually turned into nothing but the economic function of managing the collective process of production of goods for the needs of society.

* * *

By gradual steps mankind rose out of the animal state, where it was dependent entirely on nature. The construction and improvement of tools was the basis of a steady increase of the product of its labor.

Before civilization, in the barbaric stage, agriculture and cattle breeding secured them a modest living. But men were still at the mercy of the forces of nature, entirely bound to their small tribal communities, always at war. The world was full of supreme powers and enemies.

Civilization begins when with commerce, industry, and richer agriculture the productivity of labor increases, so that a ruling class can live on the surplus product. The exploitation of the laboring masses by the ruling few constitutes the history of civilization.

Through commerce and industry, men as artisans and merchants, rise as independent individuals, free from the old tribal bonds, as self-determining, self-reliant citizens. Art and science begin to grow.

Capitalism arises, the earth is discovered and its treasures are exploited. The forces of nature are disclosed, and they are applied in the technical process of labor, in the increasing perfection of the tools, the machines, the working methods. And now, at an ever increasing rate, with the ever more rapid development of science and technics, the productivity of labor increases by leaps and bounds, shoots up, ever steeper, in a tremendous expansion. The whole world is conquered and uprooted by capitalist industrialism. Mankind has built up a mechanism of production which is ready to melt into one world unit. But it cannot do so, because the capitalist rulers, directed by unrestrained individualism and blind greed, are incapable of handling it. And so it threatens to wreck the world in one general destruction.

Until the working masses, the exploited class, grown up with capitalism, conscious at last of their strength and their needs of existence, take the mechanism of production into their own hands and turn it into the foundation of abundance and freedom for mankind, then for the first time man becomes master of his own fate.

Capitalism brought man to the threshold of the new era, because it made him the master of nature and its forces—a promise, but not more than a promise, of unlimited wealth. But he could not dominate the psychical forces in himself. His independent individualism was in contradiction to the community of society. With his greed and his fear, his egoism and his passions, he destroyed his fellow creatures and kept the world in a state of misery.

Capitalism raised man from his primitive state to a high level. But only his intellectual state. It left his moral quality weak and low. Because egoism was a condition to success, a hard egoism was bred and raised by capitalism, manifesting itself in a war of all against all.

Communism raises the moral quality of man to the highest degree. Because this is an absolute condition to success in the class fight against capitalism. Because this is bred and fostered in the daily practice of communist production.

Communism means man is master of his own nature. All his faculties and energies are now consciously directed toward one common aim. He has learned to dominate the psychical forces in himself, in binding his strong individualism into a stronger community feeling. So his domination of nature becomes complete.

The original production on a small scale, the work with small tools, divided mankind into isolated individuals. Big industry, the work in large groups with developed machinery unites them to collective action and collective feeling. Communist world production welds them into one large brotherhood.

Then the way of unlimited progress lies open before them.

PART II

OTHER COUNCIL COMMUNIST WRITINGS (1936–54)

CHAPTER 11

THE PARTY AND THE WORKING CLASS

This chapter was published in *International Council Correspondence* vol. 2, no. 9–10 (September 1936). It appears to be an edited translation of Pannekoek's article "Partij en arbeidersklasse" published in *Persdienst van de groep van Internationale Communisten* vol. 9, no. 1 (January 1936). —Ed.

The first traces of a new labor movement are just becoming visible. The old movement is organized in parties. The belief in parties is the main reason for the impotence of the working class; therefore we avoid forming a new party—not because we are too few, but because a party is an organization that aims to lead and control the working class.

In opposition to this, we maintain the working class can rise to victory only when it independently attacks its problems and decides its own fate. The workers should not unquestioningly accept the slogans of others, nor of our own groups, but must think, act, and decide for themselves. This conception is in sharp contradiction to the tradition of the party as the most important means of educating the proletariat. Therefore many, though repudiating the socialist and communist parties, resist and oppose us. This is partly due to their traditional concepts; after viewing the class struggle as a struggle of parties, it becomes difficult to consider it as purely the struggle of the working class, as a class struggle.

But partly this concept is based on the idea that the party nevertheless plays an essential and important part in the struggle of the proletariat. Let us investigate this latter idea more closely.

Essentially, the party is a grouping according to views, conceptions; the classes are groupings according to economic interests. Class membership is determined by one's part in the process of production; party membership is the joining of persons who agree in their conceptions of the social problems. Formerly it was thought this contradiction would disappear in the class party, the "workers' party." During the rise of the social democracy, it seemed that it would gradually embrace the whole working class, partly as members, partly as supporters. Because Marxian theory declared that similar interests beget similar viewpoints and aims, the contradiction between party and class was expected gradually to disappear. History proved otherwise. The social democracy remained a minority, other working-class groups organized against it, sections split away from it, and its own character changed. Its own program was revised or reinterpreted.

The evolution of society does not proceed along a smooth even line, but in conflicts and contradictions.

With the intensification of the workers' struggle, the might of the enemy also increases and besets the workers with renewed doubts and fears as to which road is the best. And every doubt brings on splits, contradictions, and fractional battles within the labor movement. It is futile to bewail these conflicts and splits as harmful in dividing and weakening the working class. The working class is not weak because it is split up—it is split up because it is weak. Because the enemy is powerful and the old methods of warfare prove unavailing, the working class must seek new methods. Its task will not become clear as the result of enlightenment from above, it must discover it through hard work, through thought and conflict of opinions. It must find its own way; therefore the internal struggles. It must relinquish old ideas and illusions and adopt new ones, and because this is difficult, therefore the magnitude and severity of the splits.

Nor can we delude ourselves into believing that this period of party and ideological strife is only temporary and will make way to renewed harmony. True, in the course of the class struggle there are occasions when all forces unite on a great achievable objective and the revolution is carried on with the might of a united working class. But after that, as after every victory, come the differences on the question: What next? And even if the working class is victorious, it is always confronted by the most difficult task of subduing the enemy further, reorganizing production, creating new order. It is impossible that all workers, all strata and groups, with their ofttimes still diverse interests should, at this stage, agree on all matters and be ready for united rapid and decisive further action. They will find the true course only after the sharpest controversies and conflicts and only thus will achieve clarity.

If, in this situation, persons with the same fundamental conceptions unite for the discussion of practical steps and seek clarification through discussions, and propagandize their conclusions, such groups might be called parties, but they would be parties in an entirely different sense from those of today. Action, the actual struggle, is the task of the working masses themselves, in their entirety, in their natural groupings as factory and millhands, or other natural productive groups, because history and economy have placed them in the position where they must and they only can fight the working class struggle. It would be insane if the supporters of one party were to go on strike while those of another continue to work. But both tendencies will defend their position on strike or no strike in the factory meetings, thus affording an opportunity to arrive at a well-founded decision. The struggle is so great, the enemy so powerful that only the masses as a whole can achieve a victory—the result of the material and moral power of action, unity and enthusiasm, but also the result of the mental force of thought, of clarity. In this lies the great importance of such parties or groups based on opinions, that they bring clarity in their conflicts, discussions and propaganda. They are the organs of the self-enlightenment of the working class by means of which the workers find their way to freedom.

Naturally *such* parties are not static and unchangeable. Every new situation, every new problem will find minds diverging and uniting in new groups with new programs. They have a fluctuating character and constantly readjust themselves to new situations.

Compared to such groups, the present workers' parties have an entirely different character, for they have a different objective; they want to seize power for themselves. They aim not at being an aid to the working class in its struggle for emancipation, but to rule it themselves and proclaim that constitutes the emancipation of the proletariat. The social democracy which rose in the era of parliamentarism conceives of this rule as a parliamentary government. The Communist Party carries the idea of party rule through to its furthest extreme in the party dictatorship.

Such parties, in distinction to the groups described above, must be rigid structures with clear lines of demarcation through membership card, statutes, party discipline and admission and expulsion procedures. For they are instruments of power, fight for power, bridle their members by force, and constantly seek to extend the scope of their power. It is not their task to develop the initiative of the workers; rather they aim at training loyal and unquestioning members of their faith. While the working class in its struggle for power and victory needs unlimited intellectual freedom, the party rule must suppress all opinions except its own. In "democratic" parties, the suppression is veiled; in the dictatorship parties, it is open, brutal suppression.

Many workers already realize that the rule of the socialist or communist parties will be but the concealed form of the rule of a bourgeois class in which the exploitation and suppression of the working class remains. Instead of these parties, they urge the formation of a "revolutionary party" that will really aim at the rule of the workers and the realization of communism. Not a party in the new sense of those described above, but a party as those of today, that fights for power as the vanguard of the class, as the organization of conscious, revolutionary minority that seizes power in order to use it for the emancipation of the class.

We claim there is an internal contradiction in the term: "revolutionary party." Such a party cannot be revolutionary. It is no more revolutionary than the creators of the Third Reich. When we speak of revolution, we naturally speak of the proletarian revolution, the seizure of power by the working class itself.

The "revolutionary party" is based on the idea that the working class needs a group of leaders who vanquish the bourgeoisie for the workers and to construct a new government (note that the working class is not yet considered fit to reorganize and regulate production). But is not this as it should be? As the working class does not yet seem capable of revolution, is it not necessary that the revolutionary vanguard, the party, make the revolution for it? And is this not true as long as the masses willingly endure capitalism?

Against this, we raise the question: What forces can such a party raise for the revolution? How is it able to defeat the capitalist class? Only if the masses stand behind it. Only if the masses rise and through mass attacks, mass struggle, and mass strikes, overthrow the old regime. Without the action of the masses, there can be no revolution.

Two things can follow. The masses remain in action, they do not go home and leave the government to the new party. They organize their power in factory and workshop, prepare for the further conflict to the complete defeat of capital; through the workers' councils they establish a firm union to take over the complete direction of all society—in other words, they prove they are not as incapable of revolution as it seemed. Of necessity, then, conflicts will arise with the party which itself wants to take over power and which sees only disorder and anarchy in the self-action of the working class. Possibly the workers will develop their movement and sweep out the party. Or, the party, with the help of bourgeois elements defeats the workers. In either case, the party is an obstacle to the revolution, because it wants to be more than a means of propaganda and enlightenment; because it feels itself called upon to lead and rule as a party.

On the other hand, the masses may follow the party faith, and leave to it the further direction of affairs. They follow the slogans from above, have confidence in the new government (as in Germany in 1918) that is to realize communism, and go back home and to work. Immediately the bourgeoisie exerts its whole class power, the roots of which are unbroken; its financial forces, its great intellectual resources, and its economic power in factories and great enterprises. Against this the government party is too weak. Only through moderation, concessions, and yielding can it maintain itself. The excuse is given then, that more cannot be secured at the moment, that it is insanity for the workers to try to force impossible demands. Thus the party, deprived of class power becomes the instrument for maintaining bourgeois power.

We stated before that the term "revolutionary party" was contradictory in the proletarian sense. We can state it otherwise: In the term "revolutionary party," "revolutionary" always means a bourgeois revolution. Always, when the masses overthrow a government and then allow a new party to take power we have a bourgeois revolution—the substitution of a ruling caste by a new ruling caste. It was so in Paris in 1830, when the finance bourgeoisie supplanted the landed proprietors, in 1848, when the industrial bourgeoisie supplanted the financiers, and in 1870, the combined petty and large bourgeoisie took over the reins.

In the Russian Revolution the party bureaucracy came to power as the ruling caste. But in Western Europe and America the bourgeoisie is much more powerfully entrenched in plants and banks, so that a party bureaucracy cannot push them aside. The bourgeoisie in these countries can be vanquished only by repeated and united action of the masses in which they seize the mills and factories and build up their councils.

Those who speak of "revolutionary parties" draw incomplete, limited conclusions from history. When the socialist and communist parties became organs of bourgeois rule for the perpetuation of exploitation, these well-meaning people merely concluded that they would have to do better. They cannot realize that the failure of these parties is due to the fundamental conflict between the self-emancipation of the working class through its own power and the pacifying of the revolution through a new sympathetic ruling clique. They think they are the revolutionary vanguard because they see the masses as indifferent and inactive. But the masses are inactive only because they cannot yet comprehend the course of the struggle and the unity of class interests, although they instinctively sense the great power of the enemy and the enormity of their task. Once conditions force them into action they will attack the task of self-organization and the conquest of the economic power of capital.

CHAPTER 12

STATE CAPITALISM AND DICTATORSHIP

This article was published in *International Council Correspondence* vol. 3, no. 1 (January 1937). It appears to be an edited translation of Pannekoek's article "Staatskapitalismus und Diktatur" published in *Internationale Rätekorrespondenz*, no.16/17 (May 1936). —Ed.

I

The term "state capitalism" is frequently used in two different ways: first, as an economic form in which the state performs the role of the capitalist employer, exploiting the workers in the interest of the state. The federal mail system or a state-owned railway are examples of this kind of state capitalism. In Russia, this form of state capitalism predominates in industry: the work is planned, financed, and managed by the state; the directors of industry are appointed by the state and profits are considered the income of the state. Second, we find that a condition is defined as state capitalism (or state socialism) under which capitalist enterprises are controlled by the state. This definition is misleading, however, as there still exists under these conditions capitalism in the form of private ownership, although the owner of an enterprise is no longer the sole master, his power being restricted so long as some sort of social insurance system for the workers is accepted.

It depends now on the degree of state interference in private enterprises. If the state passes certain laws affecting employment conditions, such as the hiring and firing of workers, if enterprises are being financed by a federal banking system, or subventions are being granted to support the export trade, or if by law the limit of dividends for the large corporations is fixed—then a condition will be reached under which state control will regulate the entire economic life. This will vary from the strict state capitalism in certain degrees. Considering the present economic situation in Germany we could consider a sort of state capitalism prevailing there. The rulers of big industry in Germany are not subordinated subjects of the state but are the ruling power in Germany through the fascist officials in the governing offices. The National Socialist Party developed as a tool of these rulers. In Russia, on the other hand, the bourgeoisie was destroyed by the October Revolution and has disappeared completely as a ruling power. The bureaucracy of the Russian government took control of the growing industry. Russian state capitalism could be developed as there was no powerful bourgeoisie in existence. In Germany, as in Western Europe and in America, the bourgeoisie is in complete power, the owner of capital and the means of production. This is essential for the character of capitalism. The decisive factor is the character of that class which are the owners in full control of capital and not the inner form of administration or the degree of state interference in the economic life of the population. Should this class consider it a necessity to bind itself by stricter regulation—a step that would also make the smaller private capitalists more dependent upon the will of the big capitalists—the character of private capitalism would still remain. We must therefore distinguish the difference between state capitalism and such private capitalism that may be regulated to the highest degree by the state.

Strict regulations are not simply to be looked upon as an attempt to find a way out of the crisis. Political considerations also play a part. Examples of state regulation point to one general aim: preparation for war. The war industry is regulated, as well as the farmers' production of food—in order to be prepared for war. Impoverished by the results of the last war—robbed of provinces, raw materials, colonies, capital, the German bourgeoisie must try to rehabilitate its remaining forces by rigorous concentration. Foreseeing war as a last resort, it puts as much of its resources as is necessary into the hands of state control. When faced with the common aim for new world power, the private interests of the various sections of the bourgeoisie are put into the background. All the capitalist powers are confronted with this question: To what extent the state, as the representative of the common interests of the national bourgeoisie, should be entrusted with powers over persons, finances, and industry in the international struggle for power? This explains why in those nations of a poor but rapidly increasing population, without any or with but few colonies (such as Italy, Germany, Japan) the state has assumed the greatest power.

One can raise the question: Is not state capitalism the only "way out" for the bourgeoisie? Obviously state capitalism would be feasible, if only the whole productive process could be managed and planned centrally from above in order to meet the needs of the population and eliminate crises. If such conditions were brought about, the bourgeoisie would then cease being a *real* bourgeoisie. In bourgeois society, not only exploitation of the working class exists but there must also exist the constant struggle of the various sections of the capitalist class for markets and for sources of capital investment. This struggle among the capitalists is quite different from the old free competition on the market. Under cover of cooperation of capital within the nation there exists a continuous struggle between huge monopolies. Capitalists cannot act as mere dividend collectors, leaving initiative to state officials to attend to the exploitation of the working class. Capitalists struggle among themselves for profits and for the control of the state in order to protect their sectional interests and their field of action extends beyond the limits of the state. Although during the present crisis a strong concentration took place within each capitalist nation, there still remains powerful international interlacements (of big capital). In the form of the struggle between nations, the struggle of capitalists continues, whereby a severe political crisis in war and defeat has the effect of an economic crisis.

When, therefore, the question arises whether or not state capitalism—in the sense in which it has been used above—is a necessary intermediate stage before the proletariat seizes power, whether it would be the highest and last form of capitalism established by the bourgeoisie, the answer is *no*. On the other hand, if by state capitalism one means the strict control and regulation of private capital by the state, the answer is *yes*, the degree of state control varying within a country according to time and conditions, the preservation and increase of profits brought about in different ways, depending upon the historical and political conditions and the relationship of the classes.

II

Nevertheless it is possible and quite probable that state capitalism will be an intermediary stage, until the proletariat succeeds in establishing communism. This, however, could not happen for economic but for political reasons. State capitalism would not be the result of economic crises but of the class struggle. In the final stage of capitalism, the class struggle is the most significant force that determines the actions of the bourgeoisie and shapes state economy.

It is to be expected that, as a result of great economic tension and conflict, the class struggle of the future proletariat will flare up into mass action—whether this mass action be the cause of wage conflicts, wars, or economic crises, whether the shape it takes be that of mass strikes, street riots, or armed struggle—the proletariat will establish council organizations, organs of self-determination and uniform execution of action. This will particularly be the case in Germany. There the old political organs of the class struggle have been destroyed; workers stand side by side as individuals with no other allegiance but to that of their class. Should far-reaching political movements develop in Germany, the workers could function only as a class, fight only as a class, when they oppose the capitalist principle of one-man dictatorship with the proletarian principle of self-determination of the masses. In other parliamentary countries, on the other hand, the workers are severely handicapped in their development of independent class action by the activities of the political parties. These parties promise the working class safer fighting methods, force upon the workers their leadership, and make the majority of the population their unthinking followers, with the aid of their propaganda machinery. In Germany these handicaps are a dying tradition.

Such primary mass struggles are only the beginning of a period of revolutionary development. Let us assume a situation favorable to the proletariat; that proletarian action is so powerful as to paralyze and overthrow the bourgeois state. In spite of unanimous action in this respect, the degree of maturity of the masses may vary. A clear conception of aims, ways, and means will be acquired only during the process of revolution and after the first victory differences as to further tactics will assert themselves. Socialist or Communist Party spokesmen appear; they are not dead, at least their ideas are alive among the "moderate" section of the workers. Now their time has come to put into practice their program of "state socialism."

The most progressive workers whose aim must be to put the leadership of the struggle into the control of the working class by means of the council organization, (thereby weakening the enemy power of the state force) will be encountered by "socialist" propaganda in which will be stressed the necessity of speedily building the socialist order by means of a "socialistic" government. There will be warnings against extreme demands, appeals to the timidity of those individuals to whom the thought of proletarian communism is yet inconceivable, compromises with bourgeois reformists will be advised, as well as the buying-out of the bourgeoisie rather than forcing it through expropriation to embittered resistance. Attempts will be made to hold back the workers from revolutionary aims—from the determined class struggle. Around this type of propaganda will rally those who feel called upon to be at the head of the party or to assume leadership among the workers. Among these leaders will be a great portion of the intelligentsia who easily adapt themselves to "state socialism" but not to council communism and other sections of the bourgeoisie who see in the workers' struggles a new class position from which they can successfully combat communism. "Socialism against anarchy," such will be the battle cry of those who will want to save of capitalism what there can be saved.

The outcome of this struggle depends on the maturity of the revolutionary working class. Those who now believe that all one has to do is to wait for revolutionary action, because then economic necessity will teach the workers how to act correctly, are victims of an illusion. Certainly workers will learn quickly and act forcefully in revolutionary times. Meanwhile heavy defeats are likely to be experienced, resulting in the loss of countless victims. The more thorough the work of enlightenment of the proletariat, the more firm will be the attack of the masses against the attempt of "leaders" to direct their actions into the channels of state socialism. Considering the difficulties with which the task of enlightenment now encounters, it seems improbable that there lies open for the workers a road to freedom without setbacks. In this situation are to be found the possibilities for state capitalism as an intermediary stage before the coming of communism.

Thus the capitalist class will not adopt state capitalism because of its own economic difficulties. Monopoly capitalism, particularly when using the state as a fascist dictatorship, can secure for itself most of the advantages of a single organization without giving up its own rule over production. There will be a different situation, however, when it feels itself so hard-pressed by the working class that the old form of private capitalism can no longer be saved. Then state capitalism will be the way out: the preservation of exploitation in the form of a "socialistic" society, where the "most capable leaders," the "best brains," and the "great men of action" will direct production and the masses will work obediently under their command. Whether or not this condition is called state capitalism or state socialism makes no difference in principle. Whether one refers to the first term "state capitalism" as being a ruling and exploiting state bureaucracy or to the second term "state socialism" as a necessary staff of officials who as dutiful and obedient servants of the community share the work with the laborers, the difference in the final analysis lies in the amount of the salaries and the qualitative measure of influence in the party connections.

Such a form of society cannot be stable, it is a form of retrogression, against which the working class will again rise. Under it a certain amount of order can be brought about but production remains restricted. Social development remains hindered. Russia was able, through this form of organization, to change from semibarbarism to a developed capitalism, to surpass even the achievements of the Western countries' private capitalism. In this process figures the enthusiasm apparent among the "upstart" bourgeois classes, wherever capitalism begins its course. But such state capitalism cannot progress. In Western Europe and in America the same form of economic organization would not be progressive, since it would hinder the coming of communism. It would obstruct the necessary revolution in production; that is, it would be reactionary in character and assume the political form of a dictatorship.

III

Some Marxists maintain that Marx and Engels foresaw this development of society to state capitalism. But we know of no statement by Marx concerning state capitalism from which we could deduce that he looked upon the state when it assumes the role of sole capitalist, as being the last phase of capitalist society. He saw in the state the organ of suppression, which bourgeois society uses against the working class. For Engels, "The Proletariat seizes the power of the state and then changes the ownership of the means of production to state ownership."

This means that the change of ownership to state ownership did not occur previously. Any attempt to make this sentence of Engels responsible for the theory of state capitalism, brings Engels into contradiction with himself. Also, there is no confirmation of it to be found in actual occurrences. The railroads in highly developed capitalist countries, like England and America, are still in the private possession of capitalistic corporations. Only the postal and telegraphic services are owned by the states in most countries, but for other reasons than their high state of development. The German railroads were owned by the state mostly for military reasons. The only state capitalism which was enabled to transfer the means of production to state ownership is the Russian, but not on account of their state of high development, rather on account of their low degree of development. There is nothing, however, to be found in Engels which could be applied to conditions as they exist in Germany and Italy today, these are strong supervision, regulation, and limitation of liberty of private capitalism by an all-powerful state.

This is quite natural, as Engels was no prophet; he was only a scientist who was well aware of the process of social development. What he expounds are the fundamental tendencies in this development and their significance. Theories of development are best expressed when spoken of in connection with the future; it is therefore not harmful to use caution in expressing them. Less cautious expression, as is often the case with Engels, does not diminish the value of the prognostications in the least, although occurrences do not exactly correspond to predictions. A man of his caliber has a right to expect that even his suppositions be treated with care, although they were arrived at under certain definite conditions. The work of deducing the tendencies of capitalism and their development, and shaping them into consistent and comprehensive theories assures to Marx and Engels a prominent position among the most outstanding thinkers and scientists of the nineteenth century, but the exact description of the social structure of half a century in advance in all its details was an impossibility even for them.

Dictatorships, as those in Italy and Germany, became necessary as means of coercion to force upon the unwilling mass of small capitalists the new order and the regulating limitations. For this reason such dictatorship is often looked upon as the future political form of society of a developed capitalism the world over.

During forty years the socialist press pointed out that military monarchy was the political form of society belonging to a concentrated capitalistic society. For the bourgeois is in need of a kaiser, the Junkers, and the army in defense against a revolutionary working class on one side and the neighboring countries on the other side. For ten years the belief prevailed that the republic was the true form of government for a developed capitalism, because under this form of state the bourgeoisie were the masters. Now the dictatorship is considered to be the needed form of government. Whatever the form may be, the most fitting reasons for it are always found. While at the same time countries like England, France, America, and Belgium with a highly concentrated and developed capitalism, retain the same form of parliamentary government, be it under a republic or kingdom. This proves that capitalism chooses many roads leading to the same destination, and it also proves that there should be no haste in drawing conclusions from the experiences in one country to apply to the world at large.

In every country great capital accomplishes its rule by means of the existing political institutions, developed through history and traditions, whose functions are then being changed expressly. England offers an instance. There the parliamentary system in conjunction with a high measure of personal liberty and autonomy are so successful that there is no trace whatever of socialism, communism or revolutionary thought among the working classes. There also monopolistic capitalism grew and developed. There, too, capitalism dominates the government. There, too, the government takes measures to overcome the results of the depression, but they manage to succeed without the aid of a dictatorship. This does not make England a democracy, because already a half a century ago two aristocratic cliques of politicians held the government alternately, and the same conditions prevail today. But they are ruling by different means; in the long run these means may be more effective than the brutal dictatorship. Compared with Germany, the even and forceful rule of English capitalism looks to be the more normal one. In Germany the pressure of a police government forced the workers into radical movements, subsequently the workers obtained external political power, not through the efforts of a great inner force within themselves, but through the military debacle of their rulers, and eventually they saw that power destroyed by a sharp dictatorship, the result of a petty bourgeois revolution which was financed by monopolistic capital. This should not be interpreted to mean that the English form of government is really the normal one, and the German the abnormal one; just as it would be wrong to assume the reverse. Each case must be judged separately, each country has the kind of government which grew out of its own course of political development.

Observing America, we find in this land of greatest concentration of monopolistic capital as little desire to change to a dictatorship as we find in England. Under the Roosevelt administration certain regulations and actions were effected in order to relieve the results of the depression, some were complete innovations. Among these there was also the beginning of a social policy, which was hitherto entirely absent from American politics. But private capital is already rebelling and is already feeling strong enough to pursue its own course in the political struggle for power. Seen from America, the dictatorships in several European countries appear like a heavy armor, destructive of liberty, which the closely pressed-in nations of Europe must bear, because inherited feuds whip them on to mutual destruction, but not as what they really are, purposeful forms of organization of a most highly developed capitalism.

The arguments for a new labor movement, which we designate with the name of council communism, do not find their basis in state capitalism and fascist dictatorship. This movement represents a vital need of the working classes and is bound to develop everywhere. It becomes a necessity because of the colossal rise of the power of capital, because against a power of this magnitude the old forms of labor movement become powerless, therefore labor must find new means of combat. For this reason any program principles for the new labor movement can be based on neither state capitalism, fascism, nor dictatorship as their causes, but only the constantly growing power of capital and the impotence of the old labor movement to cope with this power.

For the working classes in fascist countries both conditions prevail, for there the risen power of capital is the power holding the political as well as the economic dictatorship of the country. When there the propaganda for new forms of action connects with the existence of the dictatorship, it is as it should be. But it would be folly to base an international program on such principles, forgetting that conditions in other countries differ widely from those in fascist countries.

CHAPTER 13

SOCIETY AND MIND IN MARXIAN PHILOSOPHY

This chapter was published in *Science and Society* vol. 1, no. 4 (Summer 1937). —Ed.

I

Marx's theory of social development is known as the "materialistic conception of history" or "historical materialism." Before Marx the word "materialism" had long been used in opposition to idealism, for whereas idealistic philosophical systems assumed some spiritual principle, some "Absolute Idea" as the primary basis of the world, the materialistic philosophies proceeded from the real material world. In the middle of the nineteenth century, another kind of materialism was current which considered physical matter as the primary basis from which all spiritual and mental phenomena must be derived. Most of the objections that have been raised against Marxism are due to the fact that it has not been sufficiently distinguished from this mechanical materialism.

Philosophy is condensed in the well-known quotation "it is not the consciousness of men that determines their existence, but, on the contrary, their social existence determines their consciousness." Marxism is not concerned with the antithesis matter-mind; it deals with the real world and the ideas derived therefrom. This real world comprises everything observable—that is, all that by observation may be declared an objective fact. The wage relations between workman and employer, the constitution of the United States, the science of mathematics, although not consisting of physical matter, are quite as real and objective as the factory machine, the Capitol or the Ohio River. Even ideas themselves in their turn act as real, observable facts. Mechanical materialism assumes that our thoughts are determined by the motions of atoms in the cells of our brains. Marxism considers our thoughts to be determined by our social experience observed through the senses or felt as direct bodily needs.

The world for man is society. Of course, the wider world is nature, and society is nature transformed by man. But in the course of history this transformation was so thorough that now society is the most important part of our world. Society is not simply an aggregate of men; men are connected by definite relations not chosen by them at will, but imposed upon them by the economic system under which they live and in which each has his place.

The relations which the productive system establishes between men have the same stringency as biological facts; but this does not mean that men think only of their food. It means that the manner in which man earns his living—that is, the economic organization of production—places every individual in determinate relations with his fellow men, thus determining his thinking and feeling. It is true, of course, that even up to the present nearly all the thoughts of men have been orientated around the getting of food, because a livelihood has never been assured for everybody. The fear of want and hunger has weighed like a nightmare on the minds of men. But, in a socialist system, when this fear will have been removed, when mankind will be master of the means of subsistence, and thinking will be free and creative, the system of production will also continue to determine ideas and institutions.

The mode of production (*Produktionsweise*), which forms the mind of man, is, at the same time, a product of man. It has been built up by mankind during the course of centuries, everyone participating in its development. At any given moment, its structure is determined by given conditions, the most important of which are technics and law. Modern capitalism is not simply production by large scale machinery; it is production by such machines under the rule of private property. The growth of capitalism was not only a change from an economy utilizing small tools to large scale industry, but at the same time, a development of the guild-bound craftsmen into wage laborers and businessmen. A system of production is a determinate system of technics regulated for the benefit of the owners by a system of juridical rules.

The oft-quoted thesis of the German jurist, Stammler, that law determines the economic system ("das Rechtbestimmt die Wirtschaft"), is based upon this circumstance. Stammler thought that by this sentence he had refuted Marxism, which proclaimed the dominance of economics over juridical ideas. By proclaiming that the material element, the technical side of the labor process, is ruled and dominated by ideological elements, the juridical rules by which men regulate their relations at their own will, Stammler felt convinced that he had established the predominance of mind over matter. But the antithesis technics-law does not coincide at all with the antithesis matter-mind. Law is not only spiritual rule but also hard constraint, not only an article on the statute books, but also the club of the policeman and the walls of the jail. And technics is not only the material machines but also the power to construct them, including the science of physics.

The two conditions, technics and law, play different roles in determining the system of production. The will of those who control technics cannot by itself create these technics, but it can, and does, make the laws. They are voluntary, but not capricious. They do not determine productive relations, but take advantage of these relations for the benefit of the owners and they are altered to meet advances in the modes of production. Manufacture using the technics of small tools led to a system of craft production, thus making the juridical institution of private property necessary. The development of big industry made the growth of large scale machinery possible and necessary, and induced people to remove the juridical obstacles to its development and to establish laissez-faire trade legislation. In this way technics determines law; it is the underlying force, whereas law belongs to the superstructure resting on it. Thus Stammler, while correct in his thesis in a restricted sense, is wrong in the general sense. Just because law rules economics, people seek to make such laws as are required by a given productive equipment; in this way technics determines law. There is no rigid, mechanical, one-to-one dependence. Law does not automatically adjust itself to every new change of technics. The economic need must be felt and then man must change and adjust his laws accordingly. To achieve this adjustment is the difficult and painful purpose of social struggles. It is the quintessence and aim of all political strife and of all great revolutions in history. The fight for new juridical principles is necessary to form a new system of production adapted to the enormous modern development of technics.

Technics as the productive force is the basis of society. In primitive society, the natural conditions play the chief role in determining the system of production. In the course of history technical implements are gradually improved by almost imperceptible steps. Natural science, by investigating the forces of nature, develops into the important productive force. All the technicalities in developing and applying science, including the most abstract mathematics, which is to all appearances an exercise in pure reason, may therefore be reckoned as belonging to the technical basis of the system of production, to what Marx called the "productive forces." In this way material (in a physical sense) and mental elements are combined in what Marxists call the material basis of society.

The Marxian conception of history puts living man in the center of its scheme of development, with all his needs and all his powers, both physical and mental. His needs are not only the needs of his stomach (though these are the most imperative), but also the needs of head and heart. In human labor, the material, physical side and the mental side are inseparable; even the most primitive work of the savage is brain work as much as muscle work. Only because under capitalism the division of labor separated these two parts into functions of different classes, thereby maiming the capacities of both, did intellectuals come to overlook their organic and social unity. In this way, we may understand their erroneous view of Marxism as a theory dealing exclusively with the material side of life.

II

Marx's historical materialism is a method of interpretation of history. History consists of the deeds, the actions of men. What induces these actions? What determines the activity of man?

Man, as an organism with certain needs which must be satisfied as conditional to his existence, stands within a surrounding nature, which offers the means to satisfy them. His needs and the impressions of the surrounding world are the impulses, the stimuli to which his actions are the responses, just as with all living beings. In the case of man, consciousness is interposed between stimulus and action. The need as it is directly felt, and the surrounding world as observed through the senses, work upon the mind, produce thoughts, ideas, and aims, stimulate the will and put the body in action.

The thoughts and aims of an active man are considered by him as the cause of his deeds; he does not ask where these thoughts come from. This is especially true because thoughts, ideas, and aims are not as a rule derived from the impressions by conscious reasoning, but are the product of subconscious spontaneous processes in our minds. For the members of a social class, life's daily experiences condition, and the needs of the class mold, the mind into a definite line of feeling and thinking, to produce definite ideas about what is useful and what is good or bad. The conditions of a class are life necessities to its members, and they consider what is good or bad for them to be good or bad in general. When conditions are ripe men go into action and shape society according to their ideas. The rising French bourgeoisie in the eighteenth century, feeling the necessity of laissez-faire laws, of personal freedom for the citizens, proclaimed freedom as a slogan, and in the French Revolution conquered power and transformed society.

The idealistic conception of history explains the events of history as caused by the ideas of men. This is wrong, in that it confuses the abstract formula with a special concrete meaning, overlooking the fact that, for example, the French bourgeoisie wanted only that freedom that was good for itself. Moreover, it omits the real problem, the origin of these ideas. The materialistic conception of history explains these ideas as caused by the social needs arising from the conditions of the existing system of production. According to this view, the events of history are determined by forces arising out of the existing economic system. The historical materialist's interpretation of the French Revolution in terms of a rising capitalism which required a modern state with legislation adapted to its needs does not contradict the conception that the revolution was brought about by the desire of the citizen for freedom from restraint; it merely goes further to the root of the problem. For historical materialism contends that rising capitalism produced in the bourgeoisie the conviction that economic and political freedom was necessary, and thus awakened the passion and enthusiasm that enabled the bourgeoisie to conquer political power and to transform the state.

In this way Marx established causality in the development of human society. It is not a causality outside of man, for history is at the same time the product of human action. Man is a link in the chain of cause and effect; necessity in social development is a necessity achieved by means of human action. The material world acts upon man, determines his consciousness, his ideas, his will, his actions, and so he reacts upon the world and changes it. To the traditional middle-class mode of thinking this is a contradiction—the source of endless misrepresentations of Marxism. Either the actions of man determine history, they say, and then there is no necessary causality because man is free; or if, as Marxism contends, there is causal necessity, it can only work as a fatality to which man has to submit without being able to change. For the materialistic mode of thinking, on the contrary, the human mind is bound by a strict causal dependence to the whole of the surrounding world.

The thoughts, the theories, the ideas, that former systems of society have thus wrought in the human mind, have been preserved for posterity, first in material form in subsequent historical activity. But they have also been preserved in a spiritual form. The ideas, sentiments, passions, and ideals that incited former generations to action were laid down in literature, in science, in art, in religion and in philosophy. We come into direct contact with them in the study of the humanities. These sciences belong to the most important fields of research for Marxian scholars; the differences between the philosophies, the literatures, the religions of different peoples in the course of centuries can only be understood in terms of the molding of men's minds through their societies, that is, through their systems of production. It has been said above that the effects of society upon the human mind have been deposited in material form in subsequent historical events. The chain of cause and effect of past events which proceeds from economic needs to new ideas, from new ideas to social action, from social action to new institutions, and from new institutions to new economic systems is complete and ever reenacted. Both original cause and the final effect are economic and we may reduce the process to a short formula by omitting the intermediate terms which involve the activity of the human mind. We can then illustrate the truth of Marxian principles by showing how, in actual history, effect follows cause. In analyzing the present, however, we see numerous causal chains which are not finished. When society works upon the minds of men, it often produces ideas, ideals, and theories which do not succeed in arousing men to social or class-motivated action, or fail to bring about the necessary political, juridical, and economic changes. Frequently too, we find that new conditions do not at once impress themselves upon the mind. Behind apparent simplicities lurk complexities so unexpected that only a special instrument of interpretation can uncover them at the moment. Marxian analysis enables us to see things more clearly. We begin to see that we are inside of a process fraught with converging influences, in the midst of the slow ripening of new ideas and tendencies which constitute the gradual preparation of revolution. This is why it is important to the present generation, which today has to frame the society of tomorrow, to know how Marxian theory may be of use to them, in understanding the events and in determining their own conduct. Hence a more thorough consideration of how society acts upon the mind will be necessary here.

III

The human mind is entirely determined by the surrounding real world. We have already said that this world is not restricted to physical matter only, but comprises everything that is objectively observable. The thoughts and ideas of our fellow men, which we observe by means of their conversation or by our reading are included in this real world. Although fanciful objects of these thoughts such as angels, spirits, or an Absolute Idea do not belong to it, the belief in such ideas is a real phenomenon, and may have a notable influence on historical events.

The impressions of the world penetrate the human mind as a continuous stream. All our observations of the surrounding world, all experiences of our lives are continually enriching the contents of our memories and our subconscious minds.

The recurrence of nearly the same situation and the same experience leads to definite habits of action; these are accompanied by definite habits of thought. The frequent repetition of the same observed sequence of phenomena is retained in the mind and produces an expectation of the sequence. The rule that these phenomena are always connected in this way is then acted upon. But this rule—sometimes elevated to a law of nature—is a mental abstraction of a multitude of analogous phenomena, in which differences are neglected and agreement emphasized. The names by which we denote definite similar parts of the world of phenomena indicate conceptions which likewise are formed by taking their common traits, the general character of the totality of these phenomena, and abstracting them from their differences. The endless diversity, the infinite plurality of all the unimportant, accidental traits, are neglected and the important, essential characteristics are preserved. Through their origin as habits of thought these concepts become fixed, crystallized, invariable; each advance in clarity of thinking consists in more exactly defining the concepts in terms of their properties, and in more exactly formulating the rules. The world of experience, however, is continually expanding and changing; our habits are disturbed and must be modified, and new concepts substituted for old ones. Meanings, definitions, scopes of concepts all shift and vary.

When the world does not change very much, when the same phenomena and the same experiences always return, the habits of acting and thinking become fixed with great rigidity; the new impressions of the mind fit into the image formed by former experience and intensify it. These habits and these concepts are not personal but collective property; they are not lost with the death of the individual. They are intensified by the mutual intercourse of the members of the community, who all are living in the same world, and they are transferred to the next generation as a system of ideas and beliefs, an ideology—the mental store of the community. Where for many centuries the system of production does not change perceptibly, as for example in old agricultural societies, the relations between men, their habits of life, their experience of the world remain practically the same. In every new generation living under such a static productive system the existing ideas, concepts, and habits of thinking will petrify more and more into a dogmatic, unassailable ideology of eternal truth.

When, however, in consequence of the development of the productive forces, the world is changing, new and different impressions enter the mind which do not fit in with the old image. There then begins a process of rebuilding, out of parts of old ideas and new experiences. Old concepts are replaced by new ones, former rules and judgments are upset, new ideas emerge. Not every member of a class or group is affected in the same way and at the same time. Ideological strife arises in connection with the class struggles and is eagerly pursued, because all the different individual lives are linked in diverse ways with the problem of how to pattern society and its system of production. Under modern capitalism, economic and political changes take place so rapidly that the human mind can hardly keep pace with them. In fierce internal struggles, ideas are revolutionized, sometimes rapidly, by spectacular events, sometimes slowly, by continuous warfare against the weight of the old ideology. In such a process of unceasing transformation, human consciousness adapts itself to society, to the real world.

Hence Marx's thesis that the real world determines consciousness does not mean that contemporary ideas are determined solely by contemporary society. Our ideas and concepts are the crystallization, the comprehensive essence of the whole of our experience, present and past. What was already fixed in the past in abstract mental forms must be included with such adaptations of the present as are necessary. New ideas thus appear to arise from two sources: present reality and the system of ideas transmitted from the past. Out of this distinction arises one of the most common objections against Marxism. The objection, namely, that not only the real material world, but in no less degree, the ideological elements—ideas, beliefs and ideals—determine man's mind and thus his deeds, and therefore the future of the world. This would be a correct criticism if ideas originated by themselves, without cause, or from the innate nature of man, or from some supernatural spiritual source. Marxism, however, says that these ideas also must have their origin in the real world under social conditions.

As forces in modern social development, these traditional ideas hamper the spread of new ideas that express new necessities. In taking these traditions into account we need not leave the realm of Marxism. For every tradition is a piece of reality, just as every idea is itself a part of the real world, living in the mind of men; it is often a very powerful reality as a determinant of men's actions. It is a reality of an ideological nature that has lost its material roots because the former conditions of life which produced them have since disappeared. That these traditions could persist after their material roots have disappeared is not simply a consequence of the nature of the human mind, which is capable of preserving in memory or subconsciously the impressions of the past. Much more important is what may be termed the social memory, the perpetuation of collective ideas, systematized in the form of prevailing beliefs and ideologies, and transferred to future generations in oral communications, in books, in literature, in art, and in education. The surrounding world which determines the mind consists not only of the contemporary economic world, but also of all the ideological influences derived from continuous intercourse with our fellow men. Hence comes the power of tradition, which in a rapidly developing society causes the development of the ideas to lag behind the development of society. In the end tradition must yield to the power of the incessant battering of new realities. Its effect upon social development is that instead of permitting a regular gradual adjustment of ideas and institutions in line with the changing necessities, these necessities when too strongly in contradiction with the old institutions, lead to explosions, to revolutionary transformations, by which lagging minds are drawn along and are themselves revolutionized.

CHAPTER 14

GENERAL REMARKS ON THE QUESTION OF ORGANIZATION

This chapter was published in *Living Marxism* vol. 4, no. 5 (November 1938). —Ed.

Organization is the chief principle in the working-class fight for emancipation. Hence the forms of this organization constitute the most important problem in the practice of the working-class movement. It is clear that these forms depend on the conditions of society and the aims of the fight. They cannot be the invention of theory, but have to be built up, spontaneously, by the working class itself, guided by its immediate necessities.

With expanding capitalism the workers first built their trade unions. The isolated worker was powerless against the capitalist; so he had to unite with his fellows in bargaining and fighting over the price of his labor power and the hours of labor. Capitalists and workers have opposite interests in capitalistic production; their class struggle is over the partition of the total product between them. In normal capitalism the share of the workers is the value of their labor power, i.e., what is necessary to sustain and to restore continually their capacities to work. The remaining part of the product is the surplus value, the share of the capitalist class. The capitalists, in order to increase their profit, try to lower wages and increase the hours of labor. Where the workers were powerless wages were depressed below the existence minimum; the hours of labor were lengthened until the bodily and mental health of the working class deteriorated so as to endanger the future of society. The formation of unions and of laws regulating working conditions—features rising out of the bitter fight of workers for their very life conditions—were necessary to restore normal conditions of work in capitalism. The capitalist class itself recognizes that trade unions are necessary to direct the revolt of the workers into regular channels to prevent them from breaking out in sudden explosions.

Similarly, political organizations have grown up, though not every-where in exactly the same way, because the political conditions are different in different countries. In America, where a population of farm-ers, artisans, and merchants free from feudal bonds could expand over a continent with endless possibilities, conquering the natural resources, the workers did not feel themselves a separate class. They were imbued, as were the whole of the people, with the middle-class spirit of indi-vidual and collective fight for personal welfare, and the conditions made it possible to succeed to a certain extent. Except at rare historic moments or among recent immigrant groups, no necessity was felt for a separate working-class party. In the European countries, on the other hand, the workers were dragged into the political struggle by the fight of the rising bourgeoisie against feudalism. They soon had to form their working-class parties and, together with part of the middle class had to fight for political rights, for the right to form unions, for free press and speech, for universal suffrage, for democratic institutions. A polit-ical party needs general principles for its propaganda; for its fight with other parties it wants a theory having definite views about the future of society. The working class of Europe, in which communistic ideas had already developed, found its theory in the scientific work of Marx and Engels, explaining the development of society through capitalism toward communism by means of the class struggle. This theory was accepted in the programs of the social-democratic parties of most European coun-tries; in England, the Labour Party formed by the trade unions, professed analogous but more vague ideas about a kind of socialist commonwealth as the aim of the workers.

In their programs and propaganda the proletarian revolution was the final result of the class struggle; the victory of the working class over its oppressors was to be the beginning of a communistic or socialist system of production. But so long as capitalism lasted, the practical fight had to center on immediate needs and the preservation of standards in capitalism. Under parliamentary government parliament is the battlefield where the interests of the different classes of society meet; big and small capitalists, land owners, farmers, artisans, merchants, industrialists, workers, all have their special interests that are defended by their spokesmen in parliament, all participate in the struggle for power and for their part in the total product. The workers have to take part in this struggle. Socialist or labor parties have the special task of fighting by political means for the immediate needs and interests of the workers within capitalism. In this way they get the votes of the workers and grow in political influence.

II

With the modern development of capitalism conditions have changed. The small workshops have been superseded by large factories and plants with thousands and tens of thousands of workers. With this growth of capitalism and of the working class, its organizations also had to expand. From local groups the trade unions grew to big national federations with hundreds of thousands of members. They had to collect large funds for support in big strikes, and still larger ones for social insurance. A large staff of managers, administrators, presidents, secretaries, editors of their papers, an entire bureaucracy of organization leaders developed. They had to haggle and bargain with the bosses; they became the specialists acquainted with methods and circumstances. Eventually they became the real leaders, the masters of the organizations, masters of the money as well as of the press, against the members, who lost much of their power. This development of the organizations of the workers into instruments of power over them has many examples in history; when organizations grow too large, the masses lose control of them.

The same change takes place in the political organizations, when from small propaganda groups they grow into big political parties. The parliamentary representatives are the leading politicians of the party. They have to do the real fighting in the representative bodies, they are the specialists in that field, they make up the editorial, propaganda, and executive personnel; their influence determines the politics and tactical line of the party. The members may send delegates to debate at party congresses, but their power is nominal and illusionary. The character of the organization resembles that of the other political parties—of organizations of politicians who try to win votes for their slogans and power for themselves. Once a Socialist Party has a large number of delegates in parliament it makes alliances with others against reactionary parties to form a working majority. Soon Socialists become ministers, state officials, mayors and aldermen. Of course, in this position they cannot act as delegates of the working class, governing for the workers against the capitalist class. The real political power and even the parliamentary majority remain in the hands of the capitalist class. Socialist ministers have to represent the interests of the present capitalist society, i.e., of the capitalist class. They can attempt to initiate measures for the immediate interests of the workers and try to induce the capitalist parties to acquiesce. They become middlemen—mediators—pleading with the capitalist class to consent to small reforms in the interests of the workers, and then try to convince the workers that these are important reforms which they should accept. And then the Socialist Party, as an instrument in the hands of these leaders, has to support them and also, instead of calling upon the workers to fight for their interests, to pacify them and deflect them from the class struggle.

Indeed, fighting conditions have grown worse for the workers. With their capital the power of the capitalist class has increased enormously. The concentration of capital in the hands of some few captains of finance and industry, the coalition of the bosses themselves, confronts the trade unions with a much stronger and often nearly unassailable power. The fierce competition of the capitalists of all countries over markets, raw materials, and world power, the necessity of using increasing parts of the surplus value for this competition, for armaments, and welfare; the falling of the profit rate compel the capitalists to increase the rate of exploitation, i.e., to lower the working conditions for the workers. Thus the trade unions meet increasing resistance, the old methods of struggle grow useless. In their bargaining with the bosses the leaders of the organization have less success; because they know the power of the capitalists, and because they themselves do not want to fight—since in such fights the funds and the whole existence of the organization might be lost—they must accept what the bosses offer. So their chief task is to assuage the discontent of the workers, and to defend the proposals of the bosses as important gains. Here also the leaders of the workers' organizations become mediators between the opposing classes. And when the workers do not accept the conditions and strike, the leaders either must oppose them or allow a sham fight, to be broken off as soon as possible.

The fight itself, however, cannot be stopped or minimized; the class antagonism and the depressing forces of capitalism are increasing, so that the class struggle must go on, the workers must fight. Time and again they break loose spontaneously without asking the unions and often against their decisions. Sometimes the union leaders succeed in regaining control of these actions. This means that the fight will be gradually smothered in some new arrangement between the capitalists and labor leaders. This does not mean that without this interference such wildcat strikes would be won. They are too restricted to the directly interested groups. Only indirectly the fear of such explosions tends to foster caution by the capitalists. But these strikes prove that the class fight between capital and labor cannot cease, and that when the old forms are not practicable any more, the workers spontaneously try out and develop new forms of action. In these actions revolt against capital is also revolt against the old organizational forms.

III

The aim and task of the working class is the abolition of capitalism. Capitalism in its highest development, with its ever deeper economic crises, its imperialism, its armaments, its world wars, threatens the workers with misery and destruction. The proletarian class fight, the resistance and revolt against these conditions, must go on till capitalist domination is overthrown and capitalism is destroyed.

Capitalism means that the productive apparatus is in the hands of the capitalists because they are the masters of the means of production, and hence of the products, they can seize the surplus value and exploit the working class. Only when the working class itself is master of the means of production does exploitation cease. Then the workers control entirely their conditions of life. The production of everything necessary for life is the common task of the community of workers, which is then the community of mankind. This production is a collective process. First each factory, each large plant is a collective of workers, combining their efforts in an organized way. Moreover, the totality of world production is a collective process; all the separate factories have to be combined into a totality of production. Hence, when the working class takes possession of the means of production, it has at the same time to create an organization of production.

There are many who think of the proletarian revolution in terms of the former revolutions of the middle class, as a series of consecutive phases: first, conquest of government and installment of a new government, then expropriation of the capitalist class by law, and then a new organization of the process of production. But such events could lead only to some kind of state capitalism. As the proletariat rises to dominance it develops simultaneously its own organization and the forms of the new economic order. These two developments are inseparable and form the process of social revolution. Working-class organization into a strong unity capable of united mass actions already means revolution, because capitalism can rule only unorganized individuals. When these organized masses stand up in mass fights and revolutionary actions, and the existing powers are paralyzed and disintegrated, then, simultaneously, the leading and regulating functions of former governments fall to the workers' organizations, and the immediate task is to carry on production, to continue the basic process of social life. Since the revolutionary class fight against the bourgeoisie and its organs is inseparable from the seizure of the productive apparatus by the workers and its application to production, the same organization that unites the class for its fight also acts as the organization of the new productive process.

It is clear that the organizational forms of trade union and political party, inherited from the period of expanding capitalism, are useless here. They developed into instruments in the hands of leaders unable and unwilling to engage in revolutionary fight. Leaders cannot make revolutions: labor leaders abhor a proletarian revolution. For the revolutionary fights the workers need new forms of organization in which they keep the powers of action in their own hands. It is not necessary to try to construct or to imagine these new forms; they can originate only in the practical fight of the workers themselves. They have already originated there; we have only to look into practice to find its beginnings everywhere where the workers are rebelling against the old powers.

In a wildcat strike the workers decide all matters themselves through regular meetings. They choose strike committees as central bodies, but the members of these committees can be recalled and replaced at any moment. If the strike extends over a large number of shops, they achieve unity of action by larger committees consisting of delegates of all the separate shops. Such committees are not bodies to make decisions according to their own opinion, and over the workers; they are simply messengers, communicating the opinions and wishes of the groups they represent, and conversely, bringing to the shop meetings, for discussion and decision, the opinion and arguments of the other groups. They cannot play the roles of leaders, because they can be momentarily replaced by others. The workers themselves must choose their way, decide their actions; they keep the entire action, with all its difficulties, its risks, its responsibilities, in their own hands. And when the strike is over the committees disappear.

The only examples of a modern industrial working class as the moving force of a political revolution were the Russian Revolutions of 1905 and 1917. Here the workers of each factory chose delegates, and the delegates of all the factories together formed the "soviet," the council where the political situation and necessary actions were discussed. Here the opinions of the factories were collected, their desires harmonized, their decisions formulated. But the councils, though a strong direct-ing influence for revolutionary education through action, were not commanding bodies. Sometimes a whole council was arrested and reor-ganized with new delegates; at times, when the authorities were paralyzed by a general strike, the soviets acted as a local government, and delegates of free professions joined them to represent their field of work. Here we have the organization of the workers in revolutionary action, though of course only imperfectly, groping and trying for new methods. This is possible only when all the workers with all their forces participate in the action, when their very existence is at stake, when they actually take part in the decisions and are entirely devoted to the revolutionary fight.

After the revolution this council organization disappeared. The proletarian centers of big industry were small islands in an ocean of primitive agricultural society where capitalist development had not yet begun. The task of initiating capitalism fell to the Communist Party. Simultaneously, political power centered in its hands and the soviets were reduced to subordinate organs with only nominal powers.

The old forms of organization, the trade union and political party and the new form of councils (soviets), belong to different phases in the development of society and have different functions. The first has to secure the position of the working class among the other classes within capitalism and belongs to the period of expanding capitalism. The latter has to conquer complete dominance for the workers, to destroy capitalism and its class divisions, and belongs to the period of declining capitalism. In a rising and prosperous capitalism council organization is impossible

because the workers are entirely occupied in ameliorating their condition
of life, which is possible at that time through trade unions and political
action. In a decaying crisis-ridden capitalism these are useless and faith
in them can only hamper the increase of self-action by the masses. In
such times of heavy tension and growing revolt against misery, when
strike movements spread over whole countries and strike at the roots
of capitalist power, or when following wars or political catastrophes the
government authority crumbles and the masses act, the old organizational forms fail against the new forms of self-activity of the masses.

IV

Spokesmen for socialist or communist parties often admit that, in revolution, organs of self-action by the masses are useful in destroying the
old domination; but then they say these have to yield to parliamentary
democracy in order to organize the new society. Let us compare the basic
principles of both forms of political organization of society.

Original democracy in small towns and districts was exercised by the
assembly of all the citizens. With the big population of modern towns
and countries this is impossible. The people can express their will only
by choosing delegates to some central body that represents them all. The
delegates for parliamentary bodies are free to act, to decide, to vote, to
govern after their own opinion; by "honor and conscience" as it is often
called in solemn terms.

The council delegates, however, are bound by mandate; they are sent
simply to express the opinions of the workers' groups who sent them.
They may be called back and replaced at any moment. Thus the workers
who gave them the mandate keep the power in their own hands.

On the other hand, members of parliament are chosen for a fixed
number of years; only at the polls are the citizens masters—on this one
day when they choose their delegates. Once this day has passed, their
power has gone and the delegates are independent, free to act for a
term of years according to their own "conscience," restricted only by
the knowledge that after this period they have to face the voters anew;

but then they count on catching their votes in a noisy election campaign, bombing the confused voters with slogans and demagogic phrases. Thus not the voters but the parliamentarians are the real masters who decide politics. And the voters do not even send persons of their own choice as delegates; they are presented to them by the political parties. And then, if we suppose that people could select and send persons of their own choice, these persons would not form the government; in parliamentary democracy the legislative and the executive powers are separated. The real government dominating the people is formed by a bureaucracy of officials so far removed from the people's vote as to be practically independent. That is how it is possible that capitalistic dominance is maintained through general suffrage and parliamentary democracy. This is why in capitalistic countries, where the majority of the people belongs to the working class, this democracy cannot lead to a conquest of political power. For the working class, parliamentary democracy is a sham democracy, whereas council representation is real democracy: the direct rule of the workers over their own affairs.

Parliamentary democracy is the political form in which the different important interests in a capitalist society exert their influence upon government. The delegates represent certain classes: farmers, merchants, industrialists, workers; but they do not represent the common will of their voters. Indeed, the voters of a district have no common will; they are an assembly of individuals, capitalists, workers, shopkeepers, by chance living at the same place, having partly opposing interests.

Council delegates, on the other hand, are sent out by a homogeneous group to express its common will. Councils are not only made up of workers, having common class interests; they are a natural group, working together as the personnel of one factory or section of a large plant, and are in close daily contact with each other, having the same adversary, having to decide their common actions as fellow workers in which they have to act in united fashion; not only on the questions of strike and fight, but also in the new organization of production. Council representation is not founded upon the meaningless grouping of adjacent villages or districts, but upon the natural groupings of workers in the process of production, the real basis of society.

However, councils must not be confused with the so-called corporative representation which is propagated in fascist countries. This is a representation of the different professions or trades (masters and workers combined), considered as fixed constituents of society. This form belongs to a medieval society with fixed classes and guilds, and in its tendency to petrify interest groups it is even worse than parliamentarism, where new groups and new interests, rising up in the development of capitalism soon find their expression in parliament and government.

Council representation is entirely different because it is the representation of a fighting revolutionary class. It represents working-class interests only, and prevents capitalist delegates and capitalist interests from participation. It denies the right of existence to the capitalist class in society and tries to eliminate them as capitalists by taking the means of production away from them. When in the progress of revolution the workers must take up the functions of organizing society the same council organization is their instrument. This means that the workers' councils then are the organs of the dictatorship of the proletariat. This dictatorship of the proletariat is not a shrewdly devised voting system artificially excluding capitalists and middle-class members from the polls. It is the exercise of power in society by the natural organs of the workers, building up the productive apparatus as the basis of society. In these organs of the workers, consisting of delegates of their various branches in the process of production, there is no place for robbers or exploiters standing outside productive work. Thus the dictatorship of the working class is at the same time the most perfect democracy, the real workers' democracy, excluding the vanishing class of exploiters.

V

The adherents of the old forms of organization exalt democracy as the only right and just political form, as against dictatorship, an unjust form.

Marxism knows nothing of abstract right or justice; it explains the political forms in which mankind expresses its feelings of political right, as consequences of the economic structure of society. By the Marxian theory we can find also the basis of the difference between parliamentary democracy and council organization. As middle-class democracy and proletarian democracy they reflect the different character of these two classes and their economic systems.

Middle-class democracy is founded upon a society consisting of a large number of independent small producers. They want a government to take care of their common interests: public security and order, protection of commerce, uniform systems of weight and money, administering of law and justice. All these things are necessary in order that everybody can do his business in his own way. Private business takes the whole attention, forms the life interests of everybody, and those political factors are, though necessary, only secondary and demand only a small part of their attention. The chief content of social life, the basis of existence of society, the production of all the goods necessary for life, is divided up into the private business of the separate citizens, hence it is natural that it takes nearly all their time, and that politics, their collective affair, providing only for auxiliary conditions, is a subordinate matter. Only in middle-class revolutionary movements do people take to the streets. But in ordinary times politics are left to a small group of specialists, politicians, whose lifework consists just of taking care of these general, political conditions of middle-class business.

The same holds true for the workers, as long as they think only of their direct interests. In capitalism they work long hours, all their energy is exhausted in the process of exploitation, and but little mental power and fresh thought is left them. Wage earning is the most immediate necessity of life; their political interests, their common interest in safeguarding their interests as wage earners may be important but are still an accessory. So they leave this part of their interests also to specialists, to their party politicians and their trade union leaders. By voting as citizens or members the workers may give some general directions, just as middle-class voters may influence their politicians, but only partially, because their chief attention must remain concentrated upon their work.

Proletarian democracy, under communism, depends upon just the opposite economic conditions. It is founded not on private but on collective production. Production of the life necessities is no longer a personal business, but a collective affair. The collective affairs, formerly called political affairs, are no longer secondary, but the chief object of thought and action for everybody. What was called politics in former society, a domain for specialists, has become the life interest of every worker. It is not the securing of some necessary conditions of production, it is the process and the regulation of production itself. The separation of private and collective affairs and interests has ceased. A separate group or class of specialists taking care of the collective affairs is no longer necessary. Through their council delegates which link them together the producers themselves are managing their own productive work.

The two forms of organization are not distinguished in that the one is founded upon a traditional and ideological basis, and the other on the material productive basis of society. Both are founded upon the material basis of the system of production; one on the declining system of the past, the other on the growing system of the future. Right now we are in the period of transition, the time of big capitalism and the beginnings of the proletarian revolution. In big capitalism the old system of production has already been destroyed in its foundations; the large class of independent producers has disappeared. The main part of production is collective work of large groups of workers; but the control and ownership have remained in a few private hands. This contradictory state is maintained by the strong power factors of the capitalists, especially the state power exerted by the governments. The task of the proletarian revolution is to destroy this state power; its real content is the seizure of the means of production by the workers. The process of revolution is, in an alternation of actions and defeats, the building up of the organization of the proletarian dictatorship, which at the same time is the dissolution, step by step, of the capitalist state power. Hence it is the process of the replacement of the organization system of the past by the organization system of the future.

We are only in the beginnings of this revolution. The century of class fight behind us cannot be considered as such a beginning, only as a preamble. It developed invaluable theoretical knowledge, it found gallant revolutionary words in defiance of the capitalist claim of being a final social system; it awakened the workers from the hopelessness of misery. But its actual fight remained bound within the confines of capitalism, it was action through the medium of leaders and sought only to set easy masters in the place of hard ones. Only a sudden flickering of revolt, such as political or mass strikes breaking out against the will of the politicians, now and then announced the future of self-determined mass action. Every wildcat strike, not taking its leaders and catchwords from the offices of parties and unions, is an indication of this development, and at the same time a small step in its direction. All the existing powers in the proletarian movement, the socialist and communist parties, the trade unions, all the leaders whose activity is bound to the middle-class democracy of the past, denounce these mass actions as anarchistic disturbances. Because their field of vision is limited to their old forms of organization, they cannot see that the spontaneous actions of the workers bear in them the germs of higher forms of organization. In fascist countries, where the old middle-class democracy has been destroyed, such spontaneous mass actions will be the only form of future proletarian revolt. Their tendency will not be a restoration of the former middle-class democracy but an advance in the direction of the proletarian democracy, i.e., the dictatorship of the working class.

CHAPTER 15

MARX AND UTOPIA— PARTY AND CLASS

This undated piece went unpublished. It may have been written in the 1940s, as there is a reference to "two world wars." It has been transcribed from Pannekoek's handwritten manuscript. —Ed.

What has been generally recognized as the great performance of Marx is the substitution of scientific socialism for utopian socialism. Socialism before his time consisted in fantastic descriptions of an imagined better society, which after Thomas More's brilliant sketch were designated by the general name of utopias. Marx made socialism an object of scientific prediction, as the natural outcome of the process of social development. This prediction was based on his theory summarized, as far as it concerns us here, in the thesis that the history of civilization was a history of class struggles. Social classes are the groups of human society differing and opposed by through their different functions and opposing interests in the process of production. The conflict of these interests affords the main contents of political strife. Thus economy, the economic structure of society, the system of production, constitutes the basis of all political dealings and events. In a still wider philosophical conception, developed in his criticism of Hegelian and post-Hegelian philosophy, called by him historical materialism, he proclaimed the economic structure of society the basis of all ideas and ideologies.

This theory explained, for the history of the last centuries, the rise of capitalism as the dominant economic system and the rise of the bourgeoisie as the ruling class. But at the same time, applied to the present and the future, it enabled him to foresee their decline and downfall. Behind the new proud masters he detected the proletarian class, product of capitalist industry, suppressed and detested, and now and then breaking loose in vain rebellions. These were the first indications of a new class struggle waged by the working class against the capitalist class, the start of a revolutionary fight of the workers for mastery over the production, which in the end will elevate mankind to a higher stage of freedom. In his analysis of capital, his lifework, he investigated its elements as the basis of all its visible phenomena, its progress over the world, its concentration in fewer hands, its accumulation of riches and misery, its crises, its violence, its wars and its inevitable collapse when the working class driven to revolution conquers power over society.

A century has passed since. And now we hear that Marx's prediction has failed. The working class has failed to destroy capitalism and to establish socialism. In the last part of the nineteenth century, the Socialist Party developed as the political organization of the working class; and in the years after 1900 it seemed to be well on the way to conquer political supremacy, most decidedly in Germany but also, in less radical forms, in other countries of Western Europe. But then two world wars destroyed all this semblance of power and revealed capitalist supremacy in blazing terror. And nowadays the working class lies more strongly fettered than before, with socialist freedom a distant phantom, Marx's prediction an illusion and socialism a utopia again.

What has failed is the doctrine of the Socialist Party as an instrument for liberation of the working class. It was a useful instrument for asserting the workers their place in the capitalist society, so that they could maintain themselves against the depressing power of capital. They wanted reforms, civil rights, franchise, to build up their unions. But to give them a background of possibility, to give enthusiasm and confidence, the vision of another future than capitalism had to be added.

Marx never identified the working class with the Socialist Party; even the name social democracy did not come from him (he always spoke of communism) but from Lassalle. Marx's theory did not deal with parties but with classes; his prediction does not speak of conquest of political power by a Socialist Party, but of conquest of economic and social mastery by the working class.

This does not mean that the fervent party activity of the workers was a mistake. It was an inevitable, necessary form of action against the heavy pressure of rising capitalism.

The past hundred years were the century of the socialist parties, at first (during the second half of the nineteenth century) in rising influence and power, but then (after 1900) declining by reformism, transforming themselves into middle-class parties ruling for capitalism, or (in Russia as the so-called Communist Party) growing into a state bureaucracy enslaving and exploiting the working class. Where new socialist parties were formed to uphold the revolutionary traditions and aims they remained insignificant little groups.

This development was not a chance happening. We have to recognize a deeper meaning in it. Socialist parties taking the lead of the working class, aspiring at political power to abolish capitalism and to introduce socialism, must be seen as the first primitive form of proletarian class struggle, at a time when the just awakening working class was not yet able to take its fight for liberation entirely into its own hands. Its fight was a fight through leaders. The workers, surely, had their part in the task; they had to vote Socialists into the parliaments, and in special cases, at the call of the party, had to break through mass actions the resistance of the ruling class. To this present-day division of functions belongs a theory of the future. Once political power was conquered, the constructive work, the new organization of production on a socialist basis should be the legislative work of the new government, the Socialist rulers, parliamentarians and officials; the workers had to obey the leaders. The basic idea is that the new world of socialism must develop through continuous progressive reforms of capitalism. The outcome is a reformed modernized capitalism represented by Socialist ministers hovering more powerfully above the masses than ever before. This [was] made easy by socialism [being] defined as identical to planned production.

It is quite natural that in the present period of heavy world transformations groups come forward proposing to establish a new and better party, a really revolutionary party, based on true scientific, i.e., Marxian, principles and strictly cutting off all reformist tendencies; a party of selected, honest, devoted, and capable leaders, to direct the rebellious but unintelligent masses. Tradition shows admirable examples of successful action in the past. And then guided by the superiority feeling of intellectuals convinced that for the heavy task of defeating capitalism a deep insight and knowledge of social conditions will be necessary, which is inaccessible to the working masses.

There is a difficulty. There are already, in different countries, half a dozen of groups all pretending that they are the true Marxian revolutionaries. Who shall decide between them? And what, when the Communist Party, bigger than all of them, comes forward and brushes them all aside saying that it is the true genuine Marxian party?

It is an illusion to think that a Socialist Party can be an instrument for liberation of the working class, for two connected reasons. Firstly, as to its program for the future; it intends to establish a socialist government, directing production through state officials; this means that new masters instead of the old ones will rule the workers and their work; and a ruling class by necessity becomes an exploiting class. Secondly, as to its way of fighting capitalism, *its ideas for the future society correspond to their practical behavior today*, it finds its function in directing the class struggle of the working class, formulating the programs and platforms, carrying out propaganda, giving out the catchwords, and, in critical situations, calling up [workers] to actions. This, however, finds its limitations in the narrow possibilities of a responsible board of leaders, and cannot bring into action the boundless possibilities of a fighting class which draws its force from out the depths of society.

Such showed itself, e.g., in 1907 in Germany in the campaign for extension of the franchise for the Prussian diet; a first mass demonstration of the workers, taking place against prohibition by the police, made such an impression, that it was not repeated or continued in bigger actions; the party leaders feared that in a more violent collision with state power their organizations could be damaged or destroyed. Something analogous occurred in England in the big strike of 1927, where the three largest trade unions took up a strong fight for better working conditions; when the state authorities mobilized all their forces the union leaders lost their stomach and called off the strike to the great disappointment of the workers. Surely it was not only the fear of the leaders for the effects of a collision of their earthenware pot with the government's iron pot; they surely were frightened themselves by the strong impact of the working masses threatening their own instinctive feelings of leadership.

A Socialist Party, however skillfully constructed and conducted, cannot destroy capitalist power and annihilate capitalism (neither can trade unionism); it can be done only by the working class itself, developing all its potential forces. Where party leaders are restrained by responsibilities, only the class can have the persistence and tenacity because they ever anew are stirred up by capitalist pressure.

Replacement of the existing government by a government of Socialists is not the liberation of the working class. Surely, by a shrewd play of words, it may be argued that the party represents and embodies the class, and that a government based on a majority vote is identical with self-rule of the people. In reality party rule is the rule of a new minority of party officials and politicians over the working masses. We may take it for sure that the English workers of today feel this intuitively, though they are not yet able to break through the network of organization statutes and political slogans in which they are captured. They are not capable to break through it because as yet they do not have a clear conception of the meaning and essence of their deepest ideals, of freedom and mastery over production.

II

From the surface phenomena of political program and strife we have to turn to the depths of society, the economic structure, the economic functions and struggle of the class. Economic power, power over the production apparatus, is the foundation of political power, which is its executive agency. Under private capitalism the capitalist is owner and has the disposal of the production apparatus; so he is master politically; and the workers can by stubborn fight defend their life conditions only. Under state capitalism, state power, i.e., the body of rulers and officials, has the disposal of the production apparatus and has the command over its use and over the workers using it. Under common ownership, the disposal of the workers themselves over the production apparatus will be the basis of their social and political freedom.

We often read that there is a fundamental difference between the rise of the bourgeoisie in the past and the rise of the working class in the future in that the bourgeoisie could win political domination because, and after, it had acquired economic dominance, whereas, conversely, the working class will acquire economic dominance because, and after, it will have won political dominance. The fallacy of this judgment, due to the misidentification of party rule and workers' mastery, became visible, e.g., when in 1918 in Germany the dominating Socialist Party immediately set to work to restore the political power of the capitalist owners of the shops and the machines. England too under a Labour government may serve as an instance how Socialist Party rule without mastery of the workers in the shops secures capitalist exploitation. So the essential task of the fighting workers will be to make themselves masters of the production apparatus, the shop. Since the power of the state tries to preclude and hinder it, they will have to crush its power.

Just as the rise of the bourgeoisie consisted in a series of political revolutions and economic transformations extending over many centuries, the rise of the working class will *be a historical process of economic and political fights combined, in different successive forms.* Thus, what appeared to some Socialists as a decline or collapse of socialism after 1900, now presents itself as the close of its first phase, that chiefly was the defense against the crushing impact of private capitalism, in order to ascertain its existence within it.

When in the coming times it will have to rebel against the heavier pressure of an organized capitalism backed by a mightier state power, the socialist movement will have to develop new forms of fight, stronger in aims and methods. In their spontaneous big actions and mass strikes, the workers cannot avoid to take possession of the shops, so as to make them centers of resistance; and when state organs try to turn them out, they must try to paralyze the action of these organs and the state machinery itself.

Two great problems stand before the working class, the organization of production and the organization of their fight. Practically the two tasks coalesce, because organization of production can start only after successes in their fight, and success in their fight is only fixed by concurrent organization of production. But they have to be treated separately in order to understand their character as two different proceedings.

When the commanding capitalist or his manager—or at least his commanding power—has been expelled, the organization of production in the shop is the task of the workers, i.e., of the entire personnel that took part in the productive work, manual workers, technicians, scientists, with the exclusion of all profit interests. They had run the shop before, they can run it, even better, thereafter. Though now on an entirely new basis, self-rule in equality, it will give no difficulty. The organization of the separate shops into an entirety of social production, formerly the result of capitalist profit manipulations, must be established now by common planning.

It is clear that for production under such entirely new principles new forms of administration, regulation and decision will be needed, that we cannot make out, ascertain or even think out beforehand; they will be established by the workers according to practical necessities when the need presents itself; we can only surmise something of their general character. When a collectivity too large to gather in one assembly has to discuss and decide on its work, it does so by means of delegates, sent out and returning and reporting as messengers of the opinions and will of the separate groups. For such delegates the name workers' councils has come into use. It means that all initiative and all decision rests in the hands of the working communities, the working personnel themselves.

Whereas the organization of production by the workers is a thing of the future—only imperfect glimpses and temporary attempts could be seen during revolutionary events—the organization of their fight is a thing of the present.

The most immediate and most genuine form of fight of the workers is the strike, the refusal to work. Here they are acting themselves, according to their own spontaneous impulse and their own deliberate decision. As to the parliamentary struggle of a Socialist Party, it is only metaphorically that it may be called a working-class fight; it is their political leaders that fight by speeches and votes. The workers have only to cast a ballot, in secret; this is all their "fighting." There is no risk in it; no self-sacrifice is needed. In the strike however, they take the risks themselves, and only by developing a strong unity these risks can be alleviated. Thus solidarity grows as a new class character; only by this growth the working class acquires the capability of winning and exerting power over society. Whereas by taking part in the party fight knowledge of political and social relations may increase, it is the direct action of the workers in strikes that molds their inner character and transforms them into the new men needed for organizing a new world.

This holds still more for modern times when they stand over against the combined force of big capitalist concerns, state power, and the trade union leaders. Modern development of capitalism, notwithstanding the increasing productivity of labor, presses ever more heavily upon the conditions of work and life. The old forms of resistance, parliamentary opposition and restricted strikes led by trade unions now become inefficient. Wildcat strikes flame up, ever again, spontaneously. They indicate that the workers, instinctively, are developing new and stronger forms of struggle; the unofficial "wild" strike is their first weapon. To be truly efficient these must extend themselves and involve ever wider masses. Shop occupation adds to the forms of contest. When state power tries to beat them down, the action must expand into mass strikes of a political character, trying to paralyze the hostile state power. In this way, in a series of future struggles, of which we cannot now foresee the details, the entire working class of the world will become involved in the process of annihilating capitalist and state power, the liberation of mankind from exploitation. The organs by means of which it establishes its unity of purpose and action, at first simple strike committees, gradually with bigger tasks extending their functions, then develop into some form of workers' councils organizing social production.

Considered in this way, the rise of the working class to freedom and social mastery appears as a great historical process occupying the near future.

It will be intermingled with great contests and world wars of the huge old and new capitalist powers, sometimes stimulated and sometimes repressed by them, sometimes also as the sole efficient peace power thwarting them. Then we see that which till now was called the workers' movement or socialism to have been only a first preliminary skirmish of the classes. And that our task does not consist in reviving former and obsolete forms of fighting, such as party movement, but in studying the new aspects of class struggle.

CHAPTER 16

THE FAILURE OF THE WORKING CLASS

This chapter was published in *Politics* vol. 3, no. 8 (September 1946).
—Ed.

In former issues of *Politics* the problem has been posed: why did the working class fail in its historical task? Why did it not offer resistance to national socialism in Germany? Why is there no trace of any revolutionary movement among the workers of America? "What has happened to the social vitality of the world working class? Why do the masses all over the globe no longer seem capable of initiating anything new aimed at their own self-liberation?" (November 1945, p. 349). Some light may be thrown upon this problem by the following considerations.

It is easy to ask: why did not the workers rise against threatening fascism? To fight you must have a positive aim. Opposed to fascism there were two alternatives: either maintaining, or returning to, the old capitalism, with its unemployment, its crises, its corruption, its misery—whereas national socialism preserved itself as an anticapitalist reign of labor, without unemployment, a reign of national greatness, of community politics; or proceeding to a socialist revolution. Thus, indeed, the deeper question is: why did not the German workers make their revolution?

Well, they had experienced a revolution: 1918. But it had taught them the lesson that neither the Social Democratic Party, nor the trade unions were instruments of their liberation; both turned out to be instruments for restoring capitalism. So what were they to do? The Communist Party did not show a way either; it propagated the Russian system of state capitalism, with its still worse lack of freedom.

Could it have been otherwise? The avowed aim of the Socialist Party in Germany—and then in all countries—was state socialism. According to its program the working class had to conquer political dominance, and then by its power over the state had to organize production into a state-directed planned economic system. Its instrument was to be the Socialist Party, developed already into a huge body of 300,000 members, with a million trade union members and three million voters behind them, led by a big apparatus of politicians, agitators, editors, eager to take the place of the former rulers. According to program then, they should expropriate by law the capitalist class and organize production in a centrally directed planned system.

It is clear that in such a system the workers, though their daily bread may seem to be secured, are only imperfectly liberated. The upper stories of society have been changed then, but the foundations bearing the entire building remain the old ones: factories with wage-earning workers under the command of directors and managers. So we find it described by the English Socialist G.D.H. Cole, who after the First World War by his studies on guild socialism and other reforms of the industrial system strongly influenced the trade unions in the direction of socialism. He says: "The whole people would be no more able than the whole body of shareholders in a great enterprise to manage an industry. . . . It would be necessary, under Socialism as much as under large scale capitalism, to entrust the actual management of industrial enterprise to salaried experts, chosen for their specialized knowledge and ability in particular branches of work. . . . There is no reason to suppose that the methods of appointing the actual managers in socialised industries would differ widely from those already in force in large scale capitalist enterprise. . . . There is no reason to suppose that socialisation of any industry would mean a great change in its managerial personnel."

Thus the workers will have got new masters instead of the old ones. Good humane masters instead of the bad rapacious masters of today. Appointed by a Socialist government or at best chosen by themselves. But, once chosen, they must be obeyed. The workers are not master over their shops, they are not master of the means of production. Above them stands the commanding power of a state bureaucracy of leaders and managers. Such a state of things can attract the workers as long as they feel powerless over against the power of the capitalists; so in their first rise during the nineteenth century this was put up as the goal. They were not strong enough to drive the capitalists out of the command over the production installations; so their way out was state socialism, a government of socialists expropriating the capitalists.

Now that the workers begin to realize that state socialism means new fetters they stand before the difficult task of finding and opening new roads. This is not possible without a deep revolution of ideas, accompanied by much inner strife. No wonder that the vigor of the fight slackens, that they hesitate, divided and uncertain, and seem to have lost their energy.

Capitalism, indeed, cannot be annihilated by a change in the commanding persons; but only by the abolition of commanding. The real freedom of the workers consists in their direct mastery over the means of production. The essence of the future free world community is not that the working masses get enough food, but that they direct their work themselves, collectively. For the real content of their life is their productive work; the fundamental change is not a change in the passive realm of consumption, but in the active realm of production. Before them now the problem arises how to unite freedom and organization; how to combine mastery of the workers over the work with the binding up of all this work into a well-planned social entirety. How to organize production, in every shop as well as over the whole of world economy, in such a way that they themselves as parts of a collaborating community regulate their work. Mastery over production means that the personnel, the bodies of workers, technicians, and experts that by their collective effort run the shop and put into action the technical apparatus are at the same time the managers themselves. The organization into a social entirety is then performed by delegates of the separate plants, by so-called workers' councils, discussing and deciding on the common affairs. The development of such a council organization will afford the solution of the problem; but this development is a historical process, taking time and demanding a deep transformation of outlook and character.

This new vision of a free communism is only beginning to take hold of the minds of the workers. And so now we begin to understand why former promising workers' movements could not succeed. When the aims are too narrow there can be no real liberation. When the aim is a semi- or a mock liberation, the inner forces aroused are insufficient to bring about fundamental results. So the German socialist movement, unable to provide the workers with arms powerful enough to successfully fight the powerful monopolistic capital, had to succumb. The working class had to search for new roads. But the difficulty of disentangling itself from the net of socialist teachings imposed by old parties and old slogans, made it powerless against aggressive capitalism, and brought about a period of continuous decline, indicative of the need for a new orientation.

Thus what is called the failure of the working class is the failure of its narrow socialist aims. The real fight for liberation has still to begin; what is known as the workers' movement in the century behind us, seen in this way, was only a series of skirmishes of advance guards. Intellectuals, who are wont to reduce the social struggle to the most abstract and simple formulae, are inclined to underrate the tremendous scope of the social transformation before us. They think how easy it would be to put the right name into the ballot box. They forget what deep inner revolution must take place in the working masses; what an amount of clear insight, of solidarity, of perseverance and courage, of proud fighting spirit is needed to vanquish the immense physical and spiritual power of capitalism.

The workers of the world nowadays, have two mighty foes, two hostile and suppressing capitalist powers over against them: the monopolistic capitalism of America and England, and the Russian state capitalism. The former is drifting toward social dictatorship camouflaged in democratic forms, the latter proclaims dictatorship openly, formerly with the addition "of the proletariat," which, however, nobody now believes any more. The former by the aid of the socialist program of socialist parties, the latter by the sounding slogans and wily tricks of the Communist Party, try to keep the workers in a state of obedient well-drilled followers, acting only at the command of the party leaders. The tradition of glorious fights in the past is helpful to keep them in spiritual dependence on obsolete ideas. In the competition for world domination, each tries to keep the workers in its fold, by shouting against capitalism here, against dictatorship there.

In the awakening resistance to both, the workers are beginning to perceive that they can fight successfully only by adhering to and proclaiming the exactly opposite principle. The principle of devoted collaboration of free and equal personalities. Theirs is the task of finding out the way in which this principle can be effectuated in their practical action.

II

The paramount question presenting itself here is whether there are indications of an existing or awakening fighting spirit among the working class. So we must leave the field of political party strife, now chiefly intended to fool the masses, and turn to the field of economic interests, where they fight intuitively their bitter struggle for living conditions. Here we see that with the development of small business into big business the trade unions cease to be fighting instruments of the workers. In modern times these organizations ever more turn into the organs by which monopoly capital dictates its terms to the working class.

When the workers begin to realize that the trade unions cannot direct their fight against capital they stand before the task of finding and practicing new forms of struggle. These new forms are the wildcat strikes. Here they shake off direction by the old leaders and the old organizations; here they take the initiative in their own hands; here they have to think out time and ways, to take the decisions, to do all the work of propaganda, of extension, of directing their action themselves. Wildcat strikes are spontaneous outbursts, the genuine practical expression of class struggle against capitalism though without wider aims as yet; but they embody a new character already in the rebellious masses: self-determination instead of determination by leaders, self-reliance instead of obedience, fighting spirit instead of accepting the dictates from above, unbreakable solidarity and unity with the comrades instead of duty imposed by membership. The unit in action and strike is of course the same as the unit of daily productive work, the personnel of the shop, the plant, the docks; it is the common work, the common interest against the common capitalist master that compels them to act as one solid body. In these discussions and decisions all the individual capabilities, all the forces of character and mind of all the workers, exalted and strained to the utmost, are cooperating toward the common goal.

In the wildcat strikes we may see the beginnings of a new practical orientation of the working class, a new tactics, the method of direct action. They represent the only actual rebellion of man against the deadening suppressing weight of world-dominating world capital. Surely, on a small scale such strikes mostly have to be broken off without success—warning signs only. Their efficiency depends on their extension over ever larger masses; only fear for such indefinite extension can compel capital to make concessions. If the pressure by capitalist exploitation grows heavier—and we may be sure it will—resistance will be aroused ever anew and will comprise larger masses. When, then, it takes such dimensions as to seriously disturb the social order, when they assail capitalism in its inner essence, the mastery of the shops, the workers will have to face state power with all its resources. Then their strikes must assume a political character; then they have to broaden their social outlook; then their strike committees, embodying their class community, assume wider social functions, taking the character of workers' councils. Then the social revolution, the breakdown of capitalism, comes in sight.

Is there any reason to expect such a revolutionary development in coming times, through conditions that were lacking in the past and till now? It seems that we can, with some probability, indicate such conditions. In Marx's writings we find the sentence: a production system does not perish before all its innate possibilities have developed. In the persistence of capitalism, we now begin to detect some deeper truth in this sentence than was suspected before. As long as the capitalist system can feed and keep alive the masses of the population, they feel no stringent necessity to do away with it. And it is able to do so as long as it can grow and expand its realm over wider parts of the world. Hence, as long as half the population of the earth stands outside capitalism its task is not finished. The many hundreds of millions thronged in the fertile plains of Eastern and Southern Asia are living in precapitalistic conditions still. As long as they can afford a market to be provided with rails and locomotives, with trucks, machines, and factories, capitalist enterprise, especially in America, may prosper and expand. And it is on the working class of America that henceforth world revolution depends.

This means that the necessity of revolutionary struggle will impose itself once capitalism comprises the bulk of mankind, once a further significant expansion is hampered. The threat of wholesale destruction in this last phase of capitalism makes this fight a necessity for all the producing classes of society, the farmers and intellectuals as well as the workers. What is condensed here in these short sentences means an extremely complicated historical process filling a period of revolution, prepared and accompanied by spiritual fights and fundamental changes in basic ideas. These developments should be an object of careful study to all those to whom communism without dictatorship, social organization on the basis of community-minded freedom, represents the future of mankind.

CHAPTER 17

PUBLIC OWNERSHIP AND COMMON OWNERSHIP

This chapter was published in *Western Socialist* vol. 14, no. 132 (November 1947). —Ed.

The acknowledged aim of socialism is to take the means of production out of the hands of the capitalist class and place them into the hands of the community of the workers. This aim is sometimes spoken of as public ownership, sometimes as common ownership of the production apparatus. There is, however, a marked and fundamental difference.

Public ownership is the ownership, i.e., the right of disposal, by a public body representing society, by government, state power or some other political body. The persons forming this body, the politicians, officials, leaders, secretaries, managers, are the direct masters of the production apparatus; they direct and regulate the process of production; they command the workers. Common ownership is the right of disposal by the workers themselves; the working class itself—taken in the widest sense of all that partake in really productive work, including employees, farmers, scientists—is direct master of the production apparatus, managing, directing, and regulating the process of production which is, indeed, their common work.

Under public ownership the workers are not masters of their work; they may be better treated and their wages may be higher than under private ownership; but they are still exploited. Exploitation does not mean simply that the workers do not receive the full produce of their labor; a considerable part must always be spent on the production apparatus and for unproductive though necessary departments of society. Exploitation consists in that others, forming another class, dispose of the produce and its distribution; that they decide what part shall be assigned to the workers as wages, what part they retain for themselves and for other purposes. Under public ownership this belongs to the regulation of the process of production, which is the function of the bureaucracy. Thus in Russia bureaucracy as the ruling class is master of production and produce, and the Russian workers are an exploited class. In Western countries we know only of public ownership (in some branches) of the capitalist state. Here we may quote the well-known English "Socialist" writer G.D.H. Cole, for whom socialism is identical with public ownership. He wrote: "The whole people would be no more able than the whole body of shareholders in a great modern enterprise to manage an industry. . . . It would be necessary, under socialism as much as under large scale capitalism, to entrust the actual management of industrial enterprise to salaried experts, chosen for their specialized knowledge and ability in particular branches of the work" (p. 674). There is no reason to suppose that socialisation of any industry would mean a great change in its managerial personnel" (p. 676 in "An Outline of Modern Knowledge," ed. by Dr. W. Rose, 1931). In other words: the structure of productive work remains as it is under capitalism; workers subservient to commanding directors. It clearly does not occur to the "Socialist" author that "the whole people" chiefly consists of workers, who are quite able, being producing personnel, to manage the industry, that consists in their own work.

As a correction to state-managed production, sometimes workers' control is demanded. Now, to ask control, supervision, from a superior indicates the submissive mood of helpless objects of exploitation. And then you can control another man's business; what is your own business you do not want controlled, you do it. Productive work, social production, is the genuine business of the working class. It is the content of their life, their own activity. They themselves can take care if there is no police or state power to keep them off. They have the tools, the machines in their hands, they use and manage them. They do not need masters to command them, nor finances to control the masters.

Public ownership is the program of "friends" of the workers who for the hard exploitation of private capitalism wish to substitute a milder modernized exploitation. Common ownership is the program of the working class itself, fighting for self-liberation.

We do not speak here, of course, of a socialist or communist society in a later stage of development, when production will be organized so far as to be no problem any more, when out of the abundance of produce everybody takes according to his wishes, and the entire concept of "ownership" has disappeared. We speak of the time that the working class has conquered political and social power, and stands before the task of organizing production and distribution under most difficult conditions. The class fight of the workers in the present days and the near future will be strongly determined by their ideas on the immediate aims, whether public or common ownership, to be realized at that time.

If the working class rejects public ownership with its servitude and exploitation, and demands common ownership with its freedom and self-rule, it cannot do so without fulfilling conditions and shouldering duties. Common ownership of the workers implies, first, that the entirety of producers is master of the means of production and works them in a well-planned system of social production. It implies secondly that in all shops, factories, enterprises the personnel regulate their own collective work as part of the whole. So they have to create the organs by means of which they direct their own work, as personnel, as well as social production at large. The institute of state and government cannot serve for this purpose because it is essentially an organ of domination, and concentrates the general affairs in the hands of a group of rulers. But under socialism the general affairs consist in social production; so they are the concern of all, of each personnel, of every worker, to be discussed and decided at every moment by themselves. Their organs must consist of delegates sent out as the bearers of their opinion, and will be, continually returning and reporting on the results arrived at in the assemblies of delegates. By means of such delegates that at any moment can be changed and called back the connection of the working masses into smaller and larger groups can be established and organization of production secured.

Such bodies of delegates, for which the name of workers' councils has come into use, form what may be called the political organization appropriate to a working class liberating itself from exploitation. They cannot be devised beforehand, they must be shaped by the practical activity of the workers themselves when they are needed. Such delegates are no parliamentarians, no rulers, no leaders, but mediators, expert messengers, forming the connection between the separate personnel of the enterprises, combining their separate opinions into one common resolution. Common ownership demands common management of the work as well as common productive activity; it can only be realized if all the workers take part in this self-management of what is the basis and content of social life; and if they go to create the organs that unite their separate wills into one common action.

Since such workers' councils doubtlessly are to play a considerable role in the future organization of the workers' fights and aims, they deserve keen attention and study from all who stand for uncompromising fight and freedom of the working class.

CHAPTER 18

MARX AND BAKUNIN

This chapter is an extract of a letter (dated May 26, 1949) to
Australian anarchist Kenneth Joseph Kenafick, who helped
Pannekoek publish *Workers' Councils* in English and had sent a copy
of his own book, *Michael Bakunin and Karl Marx*, to Pannekoek to
read and critique on February 12, 1949. It went unpublished, but
appears to have been prepared by Pannekoek for publication as
an article. What is here has been transcribed from Pannekoek's
handwritten copy. —Ed.

I think that we are now in a mood, determined by the present conditions
produced by social development, to look more objectively, without taking
sides, at that contest between two great revolutionaries that dominated
the revolutionary movement in the nineteenth century; to appreciate that
we have both of them, and to understand their difference and opposition.
Both took part in the revolution of 1848, as co-militants; but then their
ways parted; they were indeed products of entirely diverse social milieus.
Bakunin came from Russia where czarist absolutism kept down all social
and spiritual progress; Marx was formed by the rising Western industrial
capitalism. For Bakunin therefore liberty was the great idea; he saw in
state power the basis of the slavery and poverty of the masses. Marx
saw in capitalist exploitation the cause of misery and slavery; political
freedom he saw present in England, where, however, the workers' misery
was greatest; and since at that time capitalism was a mass of separate

competing small business, unorganized, he considered organization as the chief demand, which could only be ascertained by a central dominating power, democratic state power, dominated by the working class. So their basic ideas stood against one another; Marx saw that Bakunin's political freedom was not sufficient (vide England); Bakunin saw that Marx's organized state power would bring worst slavery. Bakunin had studied and assimilated, as many Russians, Western science and knowledge, and, different from other Russians, applied them to take part in the struggle of the exploited masses in Western Europe, thinking that their grievances were the same as his. Marx revolutionized Western science and put in this way, by his historical materialism and his economic theory of capitalism, a new basis to all further class struggle.

Their clash in the First International has been treated from both sides, by socialists and anarchists, each defending their great forerunners, repeating mostly all the old arguments and accusations.[7] You know the work of the Swiss author Brupbacher on Marx and Bakunin;[8] when the well-known German historian and Socialist Franz Mehring then confirmed to his point of view and expressed his own critical attitude to many of Marx's assertions, he found much reproach among his Socialist Party comrades; I think I remember that Rjasanoff,[9] certainly one of the best experts in Socialist history, criticized Mehring thereon.

---

7   [It is ironic that Pannekoek mentions socialists (by which he means Marxists) and anarchists defending their respective theorists with old arguments right after he reduced Bakunin to freedom and antistatism due to his Russian background and likewise Marx to organization and anticapitalism due to his German background. Pannekoek never seemed to have a solid grasp on anarchism; his social-democratic education on the subject stained his understanding all his life, though here we see him easing up somewhat by conceptualising council communism as a sort of synthesis of Marxist and anarchist views. —Ed.]

8   [Fritz Brupbacher, *Marx und Bakunin: Ein Beitrag zur Geschichte der Internationalen Arbeiterassoziation* (1913). —Ed.]

9   [Russian émigré as well as founder and director of the Marx-Engels Institute in Moscow, N. Rjasanoff (the pen name of David B. Goldendach, also known as David Riazanov). In 1913–14 he wrote a furious article series in *Die Neue Ziet* titled "Sozialdemokratische Flagge und anarchistische Ware" in which he fanatically lashed out at Mehring's sympathetic review of Brupbacher's book. —Ed.]

It was not simply the clash of two opposite characters, here the fiery spirit who appealed to the rebellious feelings to fight for freedom, there the fundamental scientist trying to organize the awakening working class. It was the problem how to unite organization and freedom into one form and method of revolutionary action. It could not be solved at that time, because its solution demands a higher stage of proletarian consciousness than was present in the nineteenth century. Capitalist development has since changed these conditions. Organization has become a weapon of capitalism, and in its hands state power became, in Germany and in Russia, a crushing instrument of despotic suppression of all freedom. Now that Socialists calling themselves followers of Marx, in unilateral distortion of his views, act as agents of state capitalism, now it is natural that the attention turns, in wide circles, to the writing of Bakunin. And so I think that a book explaining his views will find much interest among the workers.[10]

We should not forget, however, that thereby the problem is not solved. This solution can only proceed from the action of the working class, when it has to fight against worsening conditions under a more powerful state dictatorship.

I think it must be clear that council organization forms the synthesis of the views that in the preceding century seemed to stand in complete antagonism.[11] Therein the goals of organization and freedom are combined into a harmonious unit. It first appeared spontaneously in the soviets of the Russian Revolution, but was there soon suppressed and distorted by state capitalism. Then in Germany 1918–19 it sprang up as Arbeiterräte, and here and in Holland, in the splinter groups opposing the development of the Communist Party, the idea of workers' councils found ever more a clear expression. By this new point of view I think we will be able to understand better the work of our great predecessors.

---

10   [Kenneth Joseph Kenafick's book *Michael Bakunin and Karl Marx* was published the year prior. It goes through Bakunin's life and ideas, pointing out where he and Marx agreed and differed. —Ed.]

11   [Kenafick noted in his February 12, 1949, letter to Pannekoek that he felt "a synthesis of Marxian and Anarchist ideas on a higher plane is the only feasible line for the working class movement to take today." —Ed.]

CHAPTER 19

SOME REMARKS ON PARLIAMENTARISM

This chapter was published in *Left*, no. 149 (May 1949). —Ed.

I

In the second half of the nineteenth century the opinion spread widely among the workers that socialism can and must be won by a parliamentary conquest of political power; and it seemed well on the way. In the twentieth century disappointment brought skepticism; reformist, so-called socialist parties rose to power but deteriorated into agencies of capitalism. Many of the most sincere militant groups lost confidence in parliamentary action, and the masses stand aloof, indifferent. What can be the reason?

Socialist propaganda can clearly demonstrate the advantages of socialist order above capitalist disorder and exploitation. The working masses constitute the majority of the population, and they have the ballot. As soon as they see the necessity of socialism they can by their vote establish a majority in parliament that installs a socialist government. Acts of parliament and measures of the government can then bring about the necessary changes in social structure. Thus the working class will have won mastery over society, will have gained socialism without anything of a violent revolution. It is quite easy.

That is just the difficulty. It is too easy. If in attacking a strong fortress you find the gate open, inviting you to enter, you suspect traps, or at least you know that the real fight has to come elsewhere. Everybody knows that the conquest of power by the working class, its conquest of mastery over society, the annihilation of capitalism, can only be the result of a long and heavy class war, of the utmost exertion, of stubborn fight and great sacrifice. There must be a flaw in the argument.

The working class stands over against a foe more powerful than ever was the ruling class. The bourgeoisie is not simply master because it has the majority in parliament. The entire fabric of political institutions, of administration and bureaucracy, of higher and lower officials, is in its hands. The practice of the present government is highly instructive in showing how these powers are able to follow their own old ways in policy independent of parliament. Though state power is its mightiest instrument to keep the masses down, the power of the bourgeoisie has deeper roots in society, material and spiritual roots. Its material power consists in its ownership of all the riches of the earth, of the entire production apparatus on which the working people are dependent for life. Its spiritual power consists in that its mode of thinking, the middle-class worldview, dominates the mind of the masses, who by tradition, by education, by the press, by literature and art, by film and broadcasting, in a continual effective propaganda, are kept in spiritual dependence.

To vanquish this all-embracing power the working class has to develop a superior power. Through the growth of capitalism itself it ever more constitutes the majority of the people. Since the decline of small trade it holds the most important function in society; on its productive work, its handling of the productive apparatus, depends the life of society. By the very practice of work and life it learns class consciousness; the knowledge of the real character of capitalist exploitation, thus acquired, undermines the middle-class ideas and teachings. Through the practice of its unceasing enforced fight to improve or uphold its working and living conditions it acquires the strong unity, the solidarity, the devotion to common class interests, that makes the separate individuals into a solid unbreakable bloc able to withstand and at last to break the power of the foe.

The belief that the working class can win mastery by parliamentary majority means that it is sufficient if only one of its factors of power is used, namely the large number, possessing only a first trace of class consciousness. But more than number counts social importance. A majority class without an important function in social economy cannot win a ruling place, cannot even keep it when it had it before; thus the proletarian class in ancient Rome. The social importance of the modern proletarian class is the chief warrant that it will be able to win; and this is entirely left out of play in the election of a parliament. In its most direct coercive force it comes forward in a political strike, such as in 1893 in Belgium, by which universal suffrage was conquered from an unwilling ruling class. Moreover, in the voting for a Socialist candidate class consciousness is needed in its most primitive form only, not in its necessary, more developed character of broad knowledge among the workers about social structure, involving their capability of managing their own work, social production. What forms their special class character, what constitutes the chief strength of the working class, their strong unity and community feeling, the most essential condition for defeating the power of bourgeoisie and state, remains entirely unused.

The conquest of mastery and freedom by the working class will be a hard and difficult fight. It is by means of the exigencies of this fight, through its sacrifices, its hardships, its dangers, in defeat and victory, that the working class must acquire those qualities that make it strong and capable for self-rule, for ruling society. Can simply putting secretly a name into a ballot box be called a fight at all? What sacrifices, what hardships, what dangers does it impose? Parliamentary elections may afford some propaganda increasing social knowledge, and may awaken confidence; that is all. German social democracy in its great time succeeded in combining this with a broad organization and instruction of the masses; but the real force to withstand capitalist and state power was lacking; so it had to submit when called up for war, and after that the decline went on. According to the abstract doctrine of parliamentarism a Socialist majority in parliament could be elected by masses submissive, ignorant, and selfish, as they were in the first rise of capitalism. Practically, to be sure, this does not happen; on the reverse it might be surmised that just an instinctive feeling of the workers that in this way freedom and mastery cannot be won, deters them from voting for socialist revolution and directs their vote to immediate reforms of capitalism.

Thus our first remark can be summarized: in parliamentary action the least essential only of the power factors of the working class are used.

II

Socialism or communism, in their original sense, means that the workers take their lot entirely in their own hands. In the conception of parliamentary conquest of power they put their lot into the hands of a parliament and a government; these have to transform society and abolish capitalism by means of parliamentary acts and governmental regulations. Parliament and government do the essential work; the workers after having voted play a mostly passive role. That is the reason why no qualities were needed in the working class. The conquest of power could look so easy because it is no conquest at all: new better rulers have replaced the old bad rulers. The workers are no masters of the means of production; production is organized and regulated by the state, the community as it is called, i.e., in reality by the state organs, the officials; the workers can exert their influence only indirectly. Those who do the essential work, needs command the work. So the outcome of a parliamentary conquest cannot be other than state socialism, based on public ownership of the production apparatus. State organs and officials practically having the direction, the disposal over production, over the product, over its distribution between workers, officials, reparation funds, etc., by necessity develop into a new ruling and exploiting class.

The conception of parliamentary conquest of socialism was natural, and came up by necessity, in the nineteenth century when the working class was a powerless mass of sufferers. The only way to liberate them from exploitation and to annihilate capitalism under such conditions was the legislative action of state power in the hands of clear-sighted Socialists. This liberation was to be the glorious task of social democracy, as an array of leaders, intellectuals, politicians, and revolutionists, backed by the host of followers and adherents. The decline, afterward, of social democracy, visible in socialist and communist parties standing or governing for one or another form of capitalism, indicates that this conception now is obsolete. The working class is entering into another period of its fight. It is another class now than it was a century ago; it is growing into a social power by its mere presence determining all politics; it begins to feel confident that it will be able to win social ascendancy. Now the belief that they have only to vote and that others will liberate them, can only have a paralyzing effect on the exertion of their own forces. They have to face the hard but promising truth that they have to do it all themselves, alone.

State power, government, when organizing and directing production, does it by command, from above. The working class organizing and directing production, i.e., their own work, the contents of their life, does it from below, by means of mutual understanding, based on community feeling. For this purpose they have to build up a social organization of production expressing and ascertaining the self-action of mankind in its productive work, different, hence, from political organs embodying foreign command. Such an organization of self-action completely under control of the workers, is usually denoted by the name of council organization. In the future fight for social dominance this form of organization is likely to replace parliament—the genuine instrument of the middle class—as an instrument of the revolutionary working class.

Even when in a country with so mighty parliamentary traditions as England, in the turmoil of heavy social contests parliaments are elected with genuine Socialist majorities, the essential work of new organization must be done in the shops by the workers themselves. The transformation of society cannot be accomplished by decrees from above; it consists in the establishment of new working conditions, of new mutual relations in the enterprises, the units of practical life. In the French Revolution the farmers had already taken the land and burned the feudal titles, the urban citizens had already taken administration and jurisdiction in their own hands before legislation formulated and enacted the new conditions.

Our second remark may be summarized: parliamentarism cannot bring freedom and mastery to the working class, but only new masters instead of the old ones.

III

While on the parliamentary field in all countries the parties are fighting which of them shall, in its special way, rule and direct the working masses, these themselves are involved in a heavy fight against the masters, ever again exploding in strikes. It is a continual struggle for life itself, the only actual class struggle. Declining, devastated and impoverished capitalism can keep itself up only by pressing down the life and working conditions of the working class to the utmost. It is not that the capitalists have grown more greedy than before; it is the simple fact that the production apparatus has greatly been destroyed by world war. To rebuild it capitalism has to spend more of the total social labor on the means of production, less on the articles of consumption; this means, since the former are the property of the capitalists, that their share in the total product must increase, the share of the working class has to diminish. This is the meaning of "reconstruction." Thus, all powers of capitalism are put to work to intensify the exploitation, to press down the standard of living, to hurry up the tempo of the work, to squeeze labor power to the utmost. Since the single capitalists are not able to do that sufficiently their common organ, the state, supplies its physical and moral power toward this noble aim of saving the capitalist world. So the workers have to resist in an embittered struggle; they are fighting for their very life, against all the powers dominating them, the capitalists, the state, the unions, the political parties. They break forth in spontaneous wild strikes, ever again, because every just won increase of nominal wage lags behind the rising costs of living. In these strikes they stand single-handed, over against an entire hostile world. Here they can only have success by developing those moral and spiritual qualities: boldness, solidarity, devotion, endurance, that once will enable them to win freedom.

Whereas in all its other actions the working class acts in the role of followers directed and led by others, in the wild strikes we see them resume their own liberty of action, direct their action themselves. That means a fundamental jump forward. But these actions as yet are too limited to bring important results. They are spontaneous outbursts against unbearable conditions, but they are lacking in consciousness of wider scopes. As separate little squads the striking groups are defeated one by one. Once this consciousness arises and the strikes grow into a mass character they are by necessity directed against the state organs as their most powerful and direct foe. The constraining power of the state trying to crush them has to be attacked and defeated in mass actions by the superior firmly welded power of the united working class.

This is the significance of the strike movements flaring up again and again in different countries. They should be attentively followed, studied and supported by every Socialist. We cannot determine in advance what forms of action will be serviceable in future; the creative power of a fighting class will devise them in future as it did in the past. But the essential thing is that in the present struggles those capabilities and powers are engendered that will form the basic conditions of the workers' revolution.

Thus our third remark: the most heavy and genuine class fight of the workers against the capitalist class going on at present and preparing them for revolution stands outside the realm of parliamentarism.

CHAPTER 20

ON WORKERS' COUNCILS

This chapter was published as "Über Arbeiterräte" in *Funken* vol. 3, no. 1 (1952). This English translation comes from the Kurasje Council Communist Archive (https://www.kurasje.org), with only a few minor grammatical tweaks to better match the original. It reads quite accurately when compared to the original, available in the German section of the Marxists Internet Archive (https://www.marxists.org). —Ed.

I would like to make some critical and complementary remarks about Comrade Kondor's observations on *Bourgeois or Socialist Organisation* in the issue of *Funken* for December 1951.

When firstly he criticizes the present-day role of the trade unions (and parties), he is completely right. With the changes in the economic structure the function of the different social structures must also change. The trade unions were and are indispensable as organs of struggle for the working class under private capitalism. Under monopoly and state capitalism, toward which capitalism increasingly develops, they turn into a part of the ruling bureaucratic apparatus, which has to integrate the working class into the whole. As organizations maintained and developed by the workers themselves they are better than any apparatus of compulsion for installing the working class as a section within the social structure as smoothly as possible. In today's transitional period this new character comes to the fore ever more strongly. This realization shows that it would be wasted effort to repair the old relationship. But at the same time it can be used to give the workers greater freedom in choosing the forms of struggle against capitalism.

The development toward state capitalism—often propagated under the name socialism in Western Europe—does not mean the liberation of the working class but greater servitude. What the working class strives for in its struggle, liberty and security, to be master of its own life, is only possible through control of the means of production. State socialism is not control of the means of production by the workers, but control by the organs of the state. If it is democratic at the same time, this means that workers themselves may select their masters. By contrast, direct control of production by workers means that the employees direct the enterprises and construct the higher and central organizations from below. This is what is called the system of workers' councils. The author is thus perfectly correct when he emphasizes this as the new and future principle of organization of the working class. Organized autonomy of the productive masses stands in sharp contrast to the organization from above in state socialism. But one must keep the following in mind.

"Workers' councils" do not designate a form of organization whose lines are fixed once and for all, and which only requires a subsequent elaboration of the details. It means a principle—the principle of the workers' self-management of enterprises and of production. This principle can in no way be implemented by a theoretical discussion about the best practical forms it should take. It concerns a practical struggle against the apparatus of capitalist domination. In our day, the slogan of workers' councils does not mean assembling fraternally to work in cooperation; it means class struggle—in which fraternity plays its part—it means revolutionary action by the masses against state power. Revolutions cannot, of course, be summoned up at will; they arise spontaneously in moments of crisis, when the situation becomes intolerable. They occur only if this sense of the intolerable lives in the masses, and if at the same time there exists a certain generally accepted consciousness of what ought to be done. It is at this level that propaganda and public discussion play their part. And these actions cannot secure a lasting success unless large sections of the working class have a clear understanding of the nature and goal of their struggle. Hence the necessity for making workers' councils a theme for discussion.

So, the idea of workers' councils does not involve a program of practical objectives to be realized—either tomorrow or in a few years—it serves solely as a guide for the long and heavy fight for freedom, which still lies ahead for the working class. Marx once put it in these words: the hour of capitalism has sounded; however he left no doubt about the fact that this hour would mean an entire historical epoch.

CHAPTER 21

THE NEED FOR THE WORKERS TO LEAD THEMSELVES

This chapter consists of three letters Pannekoek wrote to "Pierre Chaulieu" (a pen name used by Cornelius Castoriadis) of *Socialisme ou barbarie*. The first was published in *Socialisme ou barbarie* vol. 4, no. 14 (April–June 1954) along with a reply by Castoriadis. Additional letters followed, but were not published in *Socialisme ou barbarie*. One of Pannekoek's follow-up letters, from August 10, 1954, is not included here since it merely consists of a single paragraph giving context to an article he attached and hoped *Socialisme ou barbarie* would potentially publish.

The replies by Castoriadis, which can be found online at the Cornelius Castoriadis/Agora International website (https://agorainternational.org), are not included here since they add little to Pannekoek's ideas, which are the focus of this book. Pannekoek is quite clear which specific points of Castoraidis's he is addressing, so the reader should have no issues.

Finally, it should be noted that the first letter is an English translation of the French translation that appeared in *Socialisme ou barbarie*—it was done by Mitch Abidor and published on the Marxists Internet Archive (https://www.marxists.org). Pannekoek wrote all the letters in English, but only the original handwritten drafts of the other two letters are available, so the first must be taken with a grain of salt. —Ed.

November 8, 1953

Dear Comrade Chaulieu,

I offer you many thanks for the series of eleven issues of *Socialisme ou barbarie* that you gave to comrade B . . . to give to me.[12] I read them (though I haven't yet finished) with great interest, because of the great agreement between us that they reveal. You probably remarked the same thing when reading my book *Les conseils ouvriers*.[13] For many years it seemed to me that the small number of Socialists who expounded these ideas hadn't grown; the book was ignored and was met with silence by almost the entire socialist press (except, recently, in the *Socialist Leader* of the ILP).[14] So I was happy to get to know a group that had arrived at the same ideas through an independent route. The complete domination by workers of their labor, which you express by saying: "The producers themselves organize the management of production," I described in the chapters on "the organization of workshops" and "social organization." The organisms the workers need for deliberations, formed of assemblies of delegates that you call "soviet organisms," are the same as those that we call "*conseils ouvriers*," "*arbeiterräte*," "workers' councils."

Certainly there are differences. I will deal with them, considering this as an essay in contribution to the discussion in your review. While you restrict the activity of these organisms to the organization of labor in factories after the taking of social power by the workers, we consider them as also being the organisms by means of which the workers will conquer this power. In the conquest of power we have no interest in a "revolutionary party" that will take the leadership of the proletarian revolution. This "revolutionary party" is a Trotskyist concept that (since 1930) has found adherents among many former partisans of the Communist Party who have been disappointed by the practice of the latter. Our opposition and criticism go back to the first years of the

---

12   [This comrade is most likely Cajo Brendel, a Dutch council communist, who had met members of *Socialisme ou barbarie* on a visit to Paris in 1953 and wrote to Pannekoek about them. —Ed.]

13   [*Workers' Councils*. —Ed.]

14   [Pannekoek is referring to the British Independent Labour Party. —Ed.].

Russian Revolution, and were directed at Lenin and were caused by his turn toward political opportunism. We have remained outside the Trotskyist road: we have never been under his influence. We consider Trotsky the most able spokesman for Bolshevism, and he should have been Lenin's successor. But after having recognized in Russia a nascent capitalism, our attention was principally on the western world of big capital where the workers will have to transform the most highly developed capitalism into real communism (in the literal sense of the word). By his revolutionary fervor Trotsky captivated all the dissidents that Stalinism had thrown out of the communist parties, and in inoculating them with the Bolshevik virus it rendered them almost incapable of understanding the great new tasks of the proletarian revolution.

Because the Russian Revolution and its ideas still have such a strong influence over people's spirits, it's necessary to more profoundly penetrate its fundamental character. In a few words, it was the last bourgeois revolution, though carried out by the working class. "Bourgeois revolution" signifies a revolution that destroys feudalism and opens the way to industrialization, with all the social consequences this implies. The Russian Revolution is thus in the direct line of the English Revolution of 1647, and the French Revolution of 1789, as well as those that followed in 1830, 1848, and 1871. During the course of these revolutions the artisans, the peasants, and the workers furnished the massive strength needed to destroy the *ancien régime*. Afterward, the committees and political parties of the men representing the rich strata that constituted the future dominant class came to the forefront and took control of governmental power. This was a natural result, since the working class was not yet mature enough to govern itself. In this new class society, where the workers were exploited, such a dominant class needs a government composed of a minority of functionaries and politicians. In a more recent era, the Russian Revolution seemed to be a proletarian revolution, the workers having been its authors through their strikes and mass actions. Nevertheless, the Bolshevik party, little by little, later succeeded in appropriating power (the laboring class being a small minority among the peasant population). Thus the bourgeois character (in the largest sense of the term) of the Russian Revolution became dominant and took the form of state capitalism. Since then, due to its ideological and spiritual influence in the world, the Russian Revolution has become the exact opposite of a proletarian revolution that liberates the workers and renders them masters of the productive apparatus.

For us the glorious tradition of the Russian Revolution consists in the fact that in its first explosions, in 1905 and 1917, it was the first to develop and show to the workers of the whole world the organizational form of their autonomous revolutionary action: the soviets. From that experience, confirmed later on, on a smaller scale in Germany, we drew our ideas on the forms of mass action that are proper to the working class, and that it should apply in order to obtain its own liberation.

Precisely opposed to this are the traditions, the ideas, and the methods that come from the Russian Revolution when the Communist Party takes power. These ideas, which only serve as obstacles to correct proletarian action, constituted the essence and the basis of Trotsky's propaganda.

Our conclusion is that the forms of organization of autonomous power, expressed by the terms "soviets" or "workers' councils" must serve as much in the conquest of power as in the direction of productive labor after this conquest. In the first place this is because the power of the workers over society cannot be obtained in any other way, for example by what is called a revolutionary party; in the second place, because these soviets, which will later be necessary for production, can only be formed through the class struggle for power.

It seems to me that in this concept the "knot of contradictions" of the problem of "revolutionary leadership" disappears. For the source of contradictions is the impossibility of harmonizing the power and the freedom of a class governing its own destiny, with the requirement that it obey a leadership formed by a small group or party. But can such a requirement be maintained? It clearly contradicts the most quoted idea of Marx's, i.e., that the liberation of the workers will be the task of the workers themselves. What is more, the proletarian revolution can't be compared to a simple rebellion or a military campaign led by a central command, nor even to a period of struggle similar, for example, to the great French revolution, which itself was nothing but an episode in the bourgeois ascension to power. The proletarian revolution is much more vast and profound; it is the accession of the mass of the people to the consciousness of their existence and their character. It will not be a simple convulsion; it will form the content of an entire period in the history of humanity, during which the working class will have to discover and realize its own faculties and potential, as well as its own goals and means of struggle. I attempted to elaborate on certain aspects of this revolution in my book *Les conseils ouvriers* in the chapter entitled "The Workers' Revolution." Of course, all of this only provides an abstract schema that can be used to bring to the forefront the diverse forces in action and their relations.

It's possible that you will now ask: Within the framework of this orientation what purpose does a party or a group serve, and what are its tasks? We can be sure that our group won't succeed in commanding the working masses in their revolutionary action: besides us there are a half dozen or more groups or parties who call themselves revolutionary, but who all differ in their programs and ideas, and compared to the great Socialist Party, these are nothing but Lilliputians. Within the framework of the discussion in issue number 10 of your review it was correctly asserted that our task is essentially theoretical: to find and indicate, through study and discussion, the best path of action for the working class. Nevertheless, the education based on this should not be intended solely for members of a group or party, but the masses of the working class. It will be up to them to decide the best way to act in their factory meetings and their councils. But in order for them to decide in the best way possible they must be enlightened by well-considered advice coming from the greatest number of people possible. Consequently, a group that proclaims that the autonomous action of the working class is the principal form of the socialist revolution will consider that its primary task is to go talk to the workers, for example by means of popular tracts that will clarify the ideas of the workers by explaining the important changes in society, and the need for the workers to lead themselves in all their actions, including in future productive labor.

Here you have some of the reflections raised by the reading of the very interesting discussions published in your review. In addition, I'd like to say how satisfied I was by the articles on "The American Worker," which clarifies a large part of the enigmatic problem of that working class without socialism, and the instructive article on the working class in East Germany. I hope that your group will have the chance to publish more issues of its review.

You will excuse me for having written this letter in English; it's difficult for me to express myself satisfactorily in French.

Sincerely yours,

Ant. Pannekoek

June 15, 1954[15]

Dear Comrade Chaulieu,

It was a great satisfaction for me to see that you printed a translation of my letter of Nov. 8 in no. 14 of your review *Socialisme ou barbarie*, and added your critical remarks, in this way involving your readers in a discussion of principles. There is one place in the translation where, probably by lack of clearness in my English, just the reverse has come out of what I meant to say: page 40 line 13 I intended to say: pour conquérir

---

15   [This is a transcription of a draft of Pannekoek's letter (the Dutch *"klad"* is written in the top left corner). It is uncertain if what he ultimately sent was drastically different from this or merely cleaned up, but there is certainly value in reproducing it here. Like other manuscripts of his, there are clear edits throughout, for example, words changed or added and whole sentences crossed out. To respect Pannekoek's choices of how he wanted to express his ideas, what is here is only what he apparently wanted. For those interested, they can read the scanned handwritten draft letter on Archives Autonomies (https://archivesautonomies.org) to see what he crossed out and what slight change of words he went with. —Ed.]

le pouvoir nous ne pouvons*pas* faire usage d'un "parti révolutionnaire."[16] Because you express the wish to continue the discussion I will present here some remarks on your response. Of course there remain differences of opinion, which by discussion may come to the fore with greater clarity. Such differences usually have their origin in a difference of the points of chief interest, proceeding either from different practical experiences or from living in a different milieu. For me it was the study of the political strikes and mass actions of the workers, in Belgium 1893, in Russia 1905 and 1917, in Germany 1918–19, from which I tried to get a clear understanding of the fundamental character of such actions. Your group is living and working among the tumultuous working-class movements of a big industrial town; so your attention is directed to the practical problem of how efficient modes of fight may develop out of the present often inefficient party strife and partial strikes.

Surely I do not suppose that the revolutionary actions of the working class will take place all in a sphere of peaceful discussion. But what I contend is that the final result of the often violent struggles is determined not by accidental facts but by what stands behind them in the minds of the workers, as a basis of firm convictions acquired by experience, study, and discussion of arguments. When the personnel in a shop has to decide on strike or not it is not by fists and violence but usually by argument that the decision is taken.

You put the dilemma in an entirely practical way: what shall the party do when it has 45% of the (council) members as its adherents and expects that another party (neo-Stalinist, aspiring at totalitarian state power) will try to seize power by violent action? Your answer is: forestall them by doing ourselves what we fear they will do. What will be the final result of such an action? Look at what happened in Russia. There was a party with excellent revolutionary principles, imbued with Marxism; it could moreover lean upon soviets already formed by the workers; yet it had to seize power for itself and the result was the totalitarian system

---

16   ["To conquer power, we cannot make use of a 'revolutionary party.'" —Ed.]

of Stalinism. (This "had to" means that the conditions were not yet ripe for a real proletarian revolution; in the highly capitalistic Western world they certainly are more ripe; how much more can only be shown by the course of the class struggle). So the question must be posed: the action of the party you suppose will it save the workers' revolution? It seems to me that it would rather be a step toward new despotism.

Certainly there are difficulties in either way. When the situation in France or in the world should call for mass actions of the working class, then immediately the Communist Party will try to bend the action into a pro-Russian party demonstration. And you will have to wage a strenuous fight with them. But it is not by copying its methods that we can defeat the Communist Party. This can be achieved only by applying our own method—the genuine mode of action of the fighting class—by the strength of argument based on the great principles of self-determination.[17] The workers can prevent mastery of the Communist Party only by developing and strengthening their own class power, i.e., their united will to seize and control themselves the production apparatus.

The main condition for the working class to win freedom is that the ideas of self-rule and self-management of the production apparatus have

---

17   [This sentence was followed by the following, though Pannekoek crossed it out:
      "The argument with the 45% example fits entirely in the parliamentarian world of
      fighting parties each with a certain percentage of followers. In the workers' revolution
      which we foresee it is the class that rises into action; there all the conditions, e.g.,
      of party-adherence, have changed. We do not say: it shall be our party with its most
      excellent program that has to seize power and it is our task to call upon the workers
      to sustain us against the others. We say it is our task to arouse and induce the work-
      ers to establish their own class-power in the shops and enterprises. The difference
      may be expressed in another more fundamental way. Your point of view seems to
      me to be: the worst that could happen to the liberation of the working class is the
      domination of party-communism; for then the workers will have lost the possibility
      to propagate and develop their ideas of freedom by means of council organisation.
      Or, expressed in another way: our first duty is to prevent the Communist Party and
      thereby establishing a totalitarian state power and to defend against them the western
      parliamentary democracy. It looks quite sensible and logical; it has the same sense
      and logics as had reformism when it said: revolution is far away; let us for the present
      by reform make capitalism tolerable for the workers. Marxist argument then replied:
      reforms the workers will get not by conciliatory tactics but by increasing their fighting
      power. So now we may reply:" —Ed.]

taken deep roots in the mind of the masses. There is a certain analogy with what Jaurès wrote in his *Histoire socialiste*, on the Constituante: "Cette Assemblée, touteneuve aux choses de la politique, sut, à peineréunie, déjouertoutes les manoeuvres de la Cour. Pourquoi? Parcequ'elleportait en ellequelquesidéesabstraiteset grandes, fortement et longuement méditées, qui luiétaientune lumière."[18] The cases are different, surely; instead of the grand political ideas of the revolutionary bourgeoisie we will have the grander social ideas of the workers, the ideas of control of production in organized collaboration; instead of the six hundred delegates elevated by the abstract ideas they had studied we will have the millions guided by their life experience of exploitation in productive work. Hence I see it to be the noblest and most useful task of a revolutionary party, by its propaganda in thousands of leaflets, pamphlets, and papers, to awaken these feelings to ever greater consciousness and clarity.

As to the character of the Russian Revolution: the translation of middle-class revolution into révolution bourgeoise (en Allemand on dit: bürgerliche Revolution) ne rend pas exactementits essence.[19] When in England the so-called middle class rose to power it consisted of a numerous class of mostly small capitalists or businessmen, owners of the (industrial) productive apparatus of society. Though the putting down of aristocratic power needed actions of the masses, these were not yet able to lay hands upon the production apparatus; this spiritual, moral, and organizational capability can be acquired by the workers only by means of their class struggle in a highly developed capitalism. In Russia there was no bourgeoisie of any importance; so a new "middle class," as directors of the productive work had to arise out of the avant-garde of the revolution and to take possession of the production apparatus, not as individual owners each of a small part but as collective owners of the

---

18   ["This [Constituent] Assembly, quite new to political affairs, was able, shortly after it began meeting, to foil all the court's maneuvers. Why? Because it bore within itself a few grand and abstract ideas it had vigorously meditated upon at length, which were to it a shining light." —Ed.]

19   ["Bourgeois revolution (in German we say: *bürgerliche* revolution) does not render exactly." —Ed.]

totality. Generally we can say: When the working masses (because they come out of precapitalist conditions) are not yet capable to take the production in their own hands, the result, inevitably, is a new ruling class, master of the production. This similarity is why I called the Russian Revolution (in its lasting character) a middle-class revolution. Surely the mass force of the proletarian class was needed to destroy the old system (and this was a school for workers all over the world). But a revolution of society can achieve no more than corresponds to the nature of the relevant social classes, and when the greatest radicalism was needed to overcome the resistances it has afterward to retrace its steps. This seems to be a common rule in the revolutions till now; thus up to 1793 the French Revolution became ever more radical, until the peasants at last were definitely free masters of the soil and the foreign armies were repelled; then the Jacobins were massacred and capitalism presented itself as the new master. Seen in this way the Russian Revolution falls in line with its predecessors, all vanquishing feudal power, in England, France, Germany. It was not an abortive proletarian revolution; the proletarian revolution is a thing of the future, before us.

I hope that these expositions, though they contain no new arguments, may serve to clarify some of the differences in our points of view.

September 3, 1954[20]

Dear Comrade Chaulieu. Thanks for your letter of August 22.

As to the other point, my letter of June 15: in writing it, it was not my intention that it should be printed, or rather: it was my idea that it would not be printed, so that I have the remembrance that it was not written with great care. If, however, you think that some of its parts may clarify the ideas, then I advise to select and print these parts only, in order that

20   [Those interested can read the scanned handwritten letter on the Association Archives Antonie Pannekoek (https://aaap.be) to see what he crossed out and what slight change of words he went with. Furthermore, I have omitted the first paragraph of this letter, for it merely touched on the potential publication of an article Pannekoek sent with his brief letter of August 10, 1954. —Ed.]

my remarks shall not occupy too much space. I have the impression that the exposure of my views in *Workers' Councils* may give a broader and more general basis. I will send you a reprint of one of its chapters which lately has been prepared and published by our English friends of the ILP[21] There is something abrupt in it, since the arguments are based on the former chapters that here are lacking; the ILP comrades apparently had the idea that just for the passive unrevolutionary English workers a little bit of discussion of the revolution may be a healthy stuff.

I have the impression that we stand at opposite extremes of opinion about proletarian class action, by each emphasizing one of its different sides. Always the fact appears that some persons stand out in activity, in courage or in clearness of vision, in speech or in rapidity of action; these persons together constitute an actual avant-garde which we see appear in every action. They become factual leaders; they may incite the activity of the masses, and by their broader view can give good advice in the actions. When they combine into fixed groups or parties with established programs these fluid relations become petrified. Then as leaders ex officio they feel themselves responsible and wish to be followed and obeyed. At the other side we see that in all mass or revolutionary actions there appears a deep common feeling, not clearly conscious—as shown by the fluctuations in taking part in the action—but based on very real conditions, securing the unity of action needed for positive results. Here the leading personalities become unimportant accidentals. The real and lasting gain of progress for society consists in what the total class, the working *masses* change in their inner character (acquiring independence, defiance, losing their servility); this takes place only by their own activity and initiative, not by following others. Between these two points of view the practice of the class struggle may take all grades of intermediate or combined forms.

There may still be made a remark on mass actions. Looking at the present life conditions in our Western countries it may seem (and is

---

21   [Anton Pannekoek, *The Way to Workers' Control* (London, 1953). This is a reprint of chapter 6, section II, of Pannekoek's book *Workers' Councils*. —Ed.]

widely accepted) that such mass actions ever more become impossible and unnecessary. Impossible because of the enormously increased power and violence of the governments backed by big capital. (If an industrial region should be in the hands of the workers one atom bomb may destroy it). Unnecessary because working and living conditions, as well as political rights for the working class become ever better and more secured (see USA). Yet we are certain that the threat of capitalism is heavier and more dangerous than ever before. Now world war is its most important form. The impending destruction and misery of mankind threatens the entire population, intellectuals and trades people as well as workers, though the latter form the most numerous part. So mass actions will be necessary more than in the past, and they lose their strict class character such as they had in the past (Belgium, Russia). They are the only way in which the masses of the peoples may exhibit their will in what constitutes their life interest. Yet you never find them mentioned, neither in political discussions and papers, nor in "socialist" reviews. Is it the fear to be identified with Russian communism? Or, more generally, the fear of all leading groups for the working masses taking action themselves?

ANTON PANNEKOEK BY PAUL MATTICK

The following article by Pannekoek's fellow council communist Paul Mattick was published in *New Politics* (1962), two years after Pannekoek's death. The transcription is from Marxists Internet Archive (https://www.marxists.org). —Ed.

Anton Pannekoek's life span coincided with what was almost the whole history of the modern labor movement; he experienced its rise as a movement of social protest, its transformation into a movement of social reform, and its eclipse as an independent class movement in the contemporary world. But Pannekoek also experienced its revolutionary potentialities in the spontaneous upheavals which, from time to time, interrupted the even flow of social evolution. He entered the labor movement a Marxist and he died a Marxist, still convinced that if there is a future, it will be a socialist future.

As have many prominent Dutch Socialists, Pannekoek came from the middle class and his interest in socialism, as he once remarked, was due to a scientific bent strong enough to embrace both society and nature. To him, Marxism was the extension of science to social problems, and the humanisation of society. His great interest in social science was entirely compatible with his interest in natural science; he became not only one of the leading theoreticians of the radical labor movement but also an astronomer and mathematician of world renown.

This unifying attitude regarding natural and social science and philosophy determined the character of most of Pannekoek's work. One of his earliest publications, *Marxism and Darwinism*, elucidates the relationship between the two theories; one of his last, *Anthropogenesis*, deals with the origin of man. "The scientific importance of Marxism as well as of Darwinism," he wrote, "consists in their following out the theory of evolution, the one upon the domain of the organic world, the other upon the domain of society." What was so important in Darwin's work was the recognition that "under certain circumstances some animal-kinds will necessarily develop into other animal-kinds." There was a "mechanism," a "natural law," which explained the evolutionary process. That Darwin identified this "natural law" with a struggle for existence analogous to capitalist competition did not affect his theory, nor did capitalist competition become therewith a "natural law."

It was Marx who formulated the propelling force for social development. "Historical materialism" referred to society; and though the world consists of both nature and society—as expressed in the need for man to eat in order to live—the laws of social development are not "laws of nature." And, of course, all "laws," whether of nature or society, are not absolute. But they are reliable enough, as verified by experience, to be considered "absolute" for purposes of human practice. At any rate, they deny sheer arbitrariness and free choice and relate to observed rules and regularities which allow for expectations that form the rationale for human activities.

With Marx Pannekoek held that it is "the production of the material necessities of life which forms the main structure of society and determines the political relations and social struggles." It is by way of class struggle that decisive social changes have been brought about and these changes have led from a less to a more productive level of social production. Socialism, too, implies the further development of the social forces of production, which are now hampered by the prevailing class relations. And this can only be done by a laboring population able to base its expectations on the emergence of a classless society. In known history, stages of human and social existence are recognizable through changing tools and forms of production that alter the productivity of social labor. The "origin" of this process is lost in prehistory, but it is reasonable to assume that it is to be found in man's struggle for existence in a natural setting which enabled and forced him to develop a capacity for work and social organisation. Since Friedrich Engels wrote *The Part Played by Labour in the Transformation of Ape into Man*, a whole literature has been built around the question of tools and human evolution.

In *Anthropogenesis*, Pannekoek returned to problems raised in his early *Marxism and Darwinism*. Just as there are "mechanisms" that account for social development and natural evolution, so there must be a "mechanism" that explains the rise of man in the animal world. Society, mutual aid, and even the use of "tools" are characteristic of other species besides man; what is specific to man is language, reason, and the making of tools. It is the last, the making of tools, which in all probability accounts for the simultaneous development of language and thought. Because the use of tools interposes itself between an organism and the outer world, between stimulus and action, it compels action, and hence thinking, to make a detour, from sense impressions by way of the tool, to the object.

Speech would be impossible without human thinking. The human mind has the capacity for abstract thought, of thinking in concepts. While mental life for both man and animal starts from sensations, which combine into images, the human mind differentiates between perceptions and actions by way of thought, just as the tool intervenes between man and that which he seeks to attain. The break between perceptions and actions, and the retention of past perceptions, allows for consciousness and thought, which establishes the interconnections of perceptions and formulates theories applicable to practical actions. Natural science is a living proof of the close connection that exists between tools and thinking. Because the tool is a separate and dead object which can be replaced when damaged, can be changed for a better one and differentiated into a multiplicity of forms for various uses, it assured man's extraordinary and rapid development; its use, in turn, assured the development of his brain. Labor, then, is the making and the "essence" of man, however much the worker may be despised and alienated. Work and the making of tools lifted man out of the animal world to the plane of social actions in order to cope with life's necessities.

The change from animal to man must have been a very long process. But the change from primitive to modern man is relatively short. What distinguishes primitive from modern man is not a different brain capacity but a difference in the uses of this capacity. Where social production stagnates, society stagnates; where the productivity of labor develops slowly, social change is also tardy. In modern society social production developed rapidly, creating new and destroying old class relationships. Not the natural struggle for existence but the social struggle for one or another concept of social organisation has determined social development.

From its very beginning, socialism has been both theory and practice. It is thus not restricted to those who are thought to benefit by the transformation from capitalism to socialism. Being concerned with the classless society and the ending of social strife, and by attracting intelligent men from all layers of society, socialism demonstrated its possible realisation in advance. Already as a young student of the natural sciences, specialising in astronomy, Pannekoek entered the Sociaal-Demokratische Arbeiterspartij (SDAP) and found himself, at once, in its left wing, on the side of Herman Gorter and Henriette Roland-Holst.

This party had been preceded by the Sociaal-Demokratische Bond (SDP) which under the influence of Domela Nieuwenhuis dissociated itself from the Second International. Antimilitarism was its foremost concern, and Nieuwenhuis advocated the use of the general strike for the prevention of war. He could not get a majority for his proposals and he detected, quite early, the trend toward class collaboration within the International. He opposed the exclusion of the anarchists from the International, and his experiences as a member of parliament led him to reject parliamentarism as a weapon of social emancipation. The "anarchist-syndicalist" tendencies, represented by Nieuwenhuis, split the organization, and the new Socialist Party, more akin to the "model" German social democracy, came into being. However, the radical ideology of the old party entered the traditions of the Dutch Socialist movement.

This traditional radicalism found expression in the new party's monthly, *De NieuweTijd*, particularly in the contributions of Gorter and Pannekoek who fought the growing opportunism of the party leaders. In 1909 the left wing group around Gorter was expelled and established a new organization, the Sozial-Demokratische Partij. Pannekoek had meanwhile gone to Germany. He lectured in the party schools of the German Sozial-Demokratische Partei, wrote for its theoretical publications and for various other papers, especially the *Bremer Burgerzeitung*. He associated himself with Gorter's new organization which, years later, under the leadership of van Revesteyn, Wijnkoop, and Ceton became the Moscow-oriented Communist Partij.

Though in the tradition of the "libertarian socialism" of Nieuwenhuis, Pannekoek's opposition to reformism and social-democratic "revisionism" was a Marxist opposition to the "official Marxism" in both its "orthodox" and "revisionist" forms. In its "orthodox" form, Marxism served as an ideology that covered up a non-Marxian theory and practice. But Pannekoek's defense of Marxism was not that of the doctrinaire; more than anyone else he recognized that Marxism is not a dogma but a method of thinking about social issues in the actual process of social transformation. Not only were certain aspects of Marxist theory superseded by the development of Marxism itself, but some of its theses, brought forth under definite conditions, would lose their validity when conditions changed.

The First World War brought Pannekoek back to Holland. Prior to the war, together with Radek, Paul Frölich, and Johann Knief, he had been active in Bremen. The Bremen group of left radicals, the International Communists, later amalgamated with the Spartakus Bund, thus laying the foundation for the Communist Party of Germany. Antiwar groups in

Germany found their leaders in Karl Liebknecht, Rosa Luxemburg, and Franz Mehring; antiwar sentiment in Holland centred around Herman Gorter, Anton Pannekoek, and Henriette Roland-Holst. In Zimmerwald and Kienthal[22] these groups joined Lenin and his followers in condemning the imperialist war and advocating proletarian actions for either peace or revolution. The Russian Revolution of 1917, hailed as a possible beginning of a world-revolutionary movement, was supported by both Dutch and German radicals despite previous basic differences between them and the Leninists.

While still in prison, Rosa Luxemburg expressed misgivings about the authoritarian tendencies of Bolshevism. She feared for the socialist content of the Russian Revolution unless it should find a rectifying support in a proletarian revolution in the West. Her position of critical support toward the Bolshevik regime was shared by Gorter and Pannekoek. They worked nevertheless in the new Communist Party and toward the establishment of a new International. In their views, however, this International was to be new not only in name but also in outlook, and with regard to both the socialist goal and the way to reach it. The social-democratic concept of socialism is state socialism, to be won by way of democratic parliamentary procedures. Universal suffrage and trade unionism were the instruments to accomplish a peaceful transition from capitalism to socialism. Lenin and the Bolsheviks did not believe in a peaceful transformation and advocated the revolutionary overthrow of capitalism. But their concept of socialism was still that of social democracy, and instrumentalities to this end still included parliamentarism and trade unionism.

However, czarism was not overthrown by democratic processes and trade union activities. The organization of the revolution was that of

22   [With the outbreak of the First World War, the reformist leaders of various Socialist parties within the Second International betrayed internationalism in favor of bourgeois nationalism. In response to this, a wide range of anti-militarists held conferences to discuss how to move forward against the imperialist war—first in Zimmerwald, Switzerland, on September 5–8, 1915, and then in Kienthal, Switzerland, on April 24–30, 1916. —Ed.]

spontaneously evolving soviets, of workers' and soldiers' councils, which soon gave way, however, to the Bolshevik dictatorship. Just as Lenin was ready to make use of the soviet movement, so was he ready to utilize any other form of activity, including parliamentarism and trade unionism, to gain his end—dictatorial power for his party camouflaged as the "dictatorship of the proletariat." Having reached his goal in Russia, he tried to consolidate his regime with the help of revolutionary movements in Western Europe and, should this fail, by trying to gain sufficient influence in the Western labor movement to secure at least its indirect support. Because of the immediate needs of the Bolshevik regime, as well as the political ideas of its leaders, the Communist International was not the beginning of a new labor movement but merely an attempt to gain control of the old movement and use it to secure the Bolshevik regime in Russia.

The social patriotism of the Western labor organizations and their policy of class collaboration during the war convinced the revolutionary workers of Western Europe that these organizations could not be used for revolutionary purposes. They had become institutions bound to the capitalist system and had to be destroyed together with capitalism. However unavoidable and necessary for the early development of socialism and the struggle for immediate needs, parliamentarism and trade unionism were no longer instruments of class struggle. When they did enter the basic social conflict, it was on the side of capital. For Pannekoek this was not a question of bad leadership, to be solved by a better one, but of changed social conditions wherein parliamentarism and trade unionism played no longer an emancipatory role. The capitalist crisis in the wake of the war posed the question of revolution and the old labor movement could not be turned into a revolutionary force since socialism has no room for trade unions or formal bourgeois democracy.

Wherever, during the war, workers fought for immediate demands they had to do so against the trade unions, as in the mass strikes in Holland, Germany, Austria, and Scotland. They organized their activities by way of shop committees, shop stewards, or workers' councils, independently of existing trade unions. In every truly revolutionary situation, in Russia in 1905 and again in 1917, as well as in the Germany and Austria of 1918, workers' and soldiers' councils (soviets) arose spontaneously and attempted to organize economic and political life by extending the council system on a national scale. The rule of workers' councils is the dictatorship of the proletariat, for the councils are elected at the point of production, thus leaving unrepresented all social layers not associated with production. In itself, this may not lead to socialism, and, in fact, the German workers' councils voted themselves out of existence by supporting the National Assembly. Yet, proletarian self-determination requires a social organization which leaves the decision-making power over production and distribution in the hands of the workers.

In this council movement, Pannekoek recognized the beginnings of a new revolutionary labor movement which, at the same time, was the beginning of a socialist reorganization of society. This movement could arise and maintain itself only in opposition to the old labor movement. Its principles attracted the most militant sector of the rebellious proletariat, much to the chagrin of Lenin who could not conceive of a movement not under the control of a party, or the state, and who was busy emasculating the soviets in Russia. But neither could he agree to an international communist movement not under the absolute control of his own party. At first by way of intrigue, and then openly, after 1920, the Bolsheviks tried to get the communist movement away from its antiparliamentary and anti–trade union course, under the pretext that it was necessary not to lose contact with the masses which still adhered to the old organizations. Lenin's *"Left-Wing" Communism: An Infantile Disorder* was directed first of all against Gorter and Pannekoek, the spokesmen of the communist council movement.

The Heidelberg Convention in 1919 split the German Communist Party into a Leninist minority and a majority adhering to the principles of antiparliamentarism and anti–trade unionism on which the party had originally been based. But there was now a new dividing question, namely, that of party or class dictatorship. The non-Leninist communists adopted the name, Communist Workers Party of Germany (KAPD), and a similar organization was later founded in Holland. Party communists opposed council communists, and Pannekoek sided with the latter. The council communists attended the Second Congress of the Third International in the capacity of sympathizers. The conditions of admission to the International—complete subordination of the various national organizations to the will of the Russian party—divorced the new council movement from the Communist International altogether.

The activities of the Communist International against the "ultraleft" were the first direct Russian interventions in the life of communist organizations in other countries. The pattern of control never changed and subordinated, eventually, the whole world communist movement to the specific needs of Russia and the Bolshevik state. Although the Russian-dominated movement, as Pannekoek and Gorter had predicted, never "captured" the Western trade unions or dominated the old socialist organizations by divorcing their followers from their leaders, they did destroy the independence and radical character of the emerging new communist labor movement. With the enormous prestige of a successful political revolution on their side, and with the failure of the German revolution, they could not fail to win a large majority in the communist movement to the principles of Leninism. The ideas and the movement of council communism declined steadily and practically disappeared altogether in the fascist reign of terror and the Second World War.

While Lenin's fight against the "ultraleft" was the first indication of the "counterrevolutionary" tendencies of Bolshevism, Pannekoek's and Gorter's struggle against the Leninist corruption of the new labor movement was the beginning of anti-Bolshevism from a proletarian point of view. And this, of course, is the only consistent anti-Bolshevism there is. Bourgeois "anti-Bolshevism" is the current ideology of imperialist capital competition, which waxes and wanes according to changing national power relations. The Weimar Republic, for instance, fought Bolshevism on the one hand and on the other made secret deals with the Red Army and open business deals with Bolshevism in order to bolster its own political and economic position within the world competitive process.

There was the Hitler-Stalin pact and the invasion of Russia. The Western allies of yesterday are the Cold War enemies of today, to mention only the most obvious of "inconsistencies" which, in fact, are the "politics" of capitalism, determined as they are, by nothing but the profit and power principles.

Anti-Bolshevism must presuppose anticapitalism since Bolshevik state capitalism is merely another type of capitalism. This was not as obvious, of course, in 1920 as it is now. It required experience with Russian Bolshevism to learn how socialism cannot be realized. The transfer of control of the means of production from private owners to the state and the centralistic and antagonistic determination of production and distribution still leaves intact capital labor relations as a relation between exploiters and exploited, rulers and ruled. In its development, it merely leads to a more modern form of capitalism where capital is directly—and not indirectly, as it was previously—the collective property of a politically maintained ruling class. It is in this direction that all capitalist systems move, thus reducing capitalist "anti-Bolshevism" to a mere imperialist struggle for world control

In retrospect it is easy to see that the differences between Pannekoek and Lenin could not be resolved by way of argument. In 1920, however, it was still possible to hope that the Western working class would take an independent course not toward a modified capitalism but toward its abolition. Answering Lenin's *"Left-wing" Communism: An Infantile Disorder,* Gorter still tried to convince the Bolsheviks of the "errors" of their ways, by pointing to the differences in socioeconomic conditions between Russia and the West, and to the fact that the "tactics" which brought Bolshevism to power in Russia could not possibly apply to a proletarian revolution in the West. The further development of Bolshevism revealed, that the "bourgeois" elements in Leninism were due not to a "faulty theory," but had their source in the character of the Russian Revolution itself, which had been conceived and was carried out as a state capitalist revolution sustained by a pseudo-Marxian ideology.

In numerous articles in anti-Bolshevik communist journals, and until the end of his life, Pannekoek elucidated upon the character of Bolshevism and the Russian Revolution. Just as he did in his earlier criticism of social democracy, so here, too, he did not accuse the Bolsheviks of a "betrayal" of working-class principles. He pointed out that the Russian Revolution, though an important episode in the development of the working-class movement, aspired only to a system of production which could be called state socialism, or state capitalism, which are one and the same thing. It did not betray its own goal any more than trade unions "betray" trade unionism. Just as there cannot be any other type of trade unionism than the existing one, so one cannot expect state capitalism to be something other than itself.

The Russian Revolution, however, had been fought under the banner of Marxism, and the Bolshevik state is almost generally considered a Marxist regime. Marxism, and soon Marxism-Leninism-Stalinism, remained the ideology of Russian state capitalism. To show what the "Marxism" of Leninism really implied, Pannekoek undertook a critical examination of its philosophical basis, published under the title *Lenin as Philosopher*, in 1938.

Lenin's philosophical ideas appeared in his work *Materialism and Empirio-criticism*, in Russian in 1908 and in German and English translations in 1927. Around 1904 certain Russian Socialists, Bogdanov in particular, had taken an interest in modern Western natural philosophy, especially in the ideas of Ernst Mach, and tried to combine these with Marxism. They gained some influence within the Russian Socialist Party, and Lenin set out to destroy this influence by attacking its apparent philosophical source.

Though not in a philosophical sense, Marx had called his system of thought materialism. It referred to the material base of all social existence and change and grew out of his rejection of both the philosophical materialism of Feuerbach and the philosophical idealism of Hegel. For bourgeois materialism, nature was objectively given reality and man was determined by natural laws. This direct confrontation of individual man and external nature, and the inability to see society and social labor as an indivisible aspect of the whole of reality, distinguished middle-class materialism from historical materialism.

Early bourgeois materialism, or natural philosophy, had held that through sense experience and the intellectual activity derived therefrom, it would be possible to gain absolute, valid knowledge of physical reality—thought to be made up of matter. In an attempt to carry the materialist representation of the objective world to the process of knowledge itself, Mach and the positivists denied the objective reality of matter, since physical concepts must be constructed from sense experience and thus retain their subjectivity. This disturbed Lenin greatly, because for him, knowledge was only what reflects objective truth, truth, that is, about matter. In Mach's influence in socialist circles, he saw a corruption of Marxian materialism. The subjective element in Mach's theory of knowledge became, in Lenin's mind, an idealist aberration and a deliberate attempt to revive religious obscurantism.

It was true, of course, that the critical progress of science found idealistic interpreters who would give comfort to the religionists. Some Marxists began to defend the materialism of the once revolutionary bourgeoisie against the new idealism—and the new science as well—of the established capitalist class. To Lenin this seemed particularly important as the Russian revolutionary movement, still on the verge of the bourgeois revolution, waged its ideological struggle to a large extent with the scientific and philosophical arguments of the early Western bourgeoisie.

By confronting Lenin's attack on "Empirio-criticism" with its real scientific content, Pannekoek not only revealed Lenin's biased and distorted exposition of the ideas of Mach and Avenarius, but also his inability to criticize their work from a Marxian point of view. Lenin attacked Mach not from the point of view of historical materialism, but from that of an earlier and scientifically less developed bourgeois materialism. In this use of middle-class materialism in defense of "Marxism" Pannekoek saw an additional indication of the half-bourgeois, half-proletarian character of Bolshevism and of the Russian Revolution itself. It went together with the state capitalist concept of "socialism," with the authoritarian attitudes toward spontaneity and organization, with the outdated and unrealizable principle of national self-determination, and with Lenin's conviction that only the middle-class intelligentsia is able to develop a revolutionary consciousness and is thus destined to lead the masses. The combination of bourgeois materialism and revolutionary Marxism which characterized Lenin's philosophy reappeared with the victorious Bolshevism as the combination of neocapitalist practice and socialist ideology.

However the Russian Revolution was a progressive event of enormous significance comparable to the French Revolution. It also revealed that a capitalist system of production is not restricted to the private property relations which dominated its laissez-faire period. With the subsiding feeble wave of revolutionary activities in the wake of the First World War, capitalism reestablished itself, despite the prevailing crisis conditions, by way of increasing state interventions in its economy. In the weaker capitalist nations this took the form of fascism and led to the intensification of imperialist policies which, finally, led to the Second World War. Even more than the First, the Second World War showed clearly that the existing labor movement was no longer a class movement but part and parcel of contemporary capitalism.

In Occupied Holland, during the Second World War, Pannekoek began his work on *Workers' Councils*, which he completed in 1947. It was a summing-up of his life experience with the theory and practice of the international labor movement and the development and transformation of capitalism in various nations and as a whole. This history of capitalism, and of the struggle against capitalism, ends with the triumph of a revived, though changed, capitalism after the Second World War, and with the utter subjugation of working-class interests to the competitive needs of the two rival capitalist systems preparing for a new world war. While in the West, the still existing labor organizations aspire, at best, to no more than the replacement of monopoly by state capitalism, the so-called communist world movement hopes for a world revolution after the model of the Russian Revolution. In either case, socialism is confounded with public ownership where the state is master of production and workers are still subjected to a ruling class.

The collapse of the capitalism of old was also the collapse of the old labor movement. What this movement considered to be socialism turns out to be a harsher form of capitalism. But unlike the ruling class, which adapts itself quickly to changed conditions, the working class, by still adhering to traditional ideas and activities, finds itself in a powerless and apparently hopeless situation. And as economic changes only gradually change ideas, it may still take considerable time before a new labor movement—fitted to the new conditions—will arise. For labor's task is still the same, that is, the abolition of the capitalist mode of production and the realization of socialism. And this can be brought about only when the workers organize themselves and society in such a way as to assure a planned social production and distribution determined by the producers themselves. When such a labor movement arises, it will recognize its origins in the ideas of council communism and in those of one of its most consistent proponents—Anton Pannekoek.

ARTICLE VERSIONS OF MANUSCRIPT CHAPTERS

The following were edited into stand-alone articles and published in various editions of *International Council Correspondence* during 1935–36. They are reproduced here in their order of publication as articles, which is different than the order of their corresponding chapters within the manuscript of *The Workers' Way to Freedom*. —Ed.

THE INTELLECTUALS

This edited version of chapter 8 of *The Workers' Way to Freedom* was published in *International Council Correspondence* vol. 1, no. 12 (October 1935). —Ed.

The intellectual middle class, the engineers, scientists, technical employees, etc., are a necessary part of industrial production, quite as indispensable as the workers themselves. Technical progress, in replacing workers by machines, tends to increase their number. Therefore their class interests and their class character must be of increasing importance in the social struggles.

Their growing numbers reflect the growing importance of science and theory in the production of life necessities. In a communist society all will partake of scientific knowledge. In capitalist society it is the privilege and the speciality of a separate class, the intellectual middle class.

The members of this class, contrary to the old independent middle class of small businessmen, live by selling their labor power to the capitalists. Their salaries indicate a higher cost of living and a more expensive education than that of the common workers. In the socialist press they are called proletarians (indeed, they are not owners of instruments of production) who need must join the workers. But it is only their lower ranks that merge gradually into skilled labor; the higher ranks, by origin and standard of living, by relationship, social standing and culture, feel themselves middle-class men, who can rise even to the position of a director, and thus be ranked with the big capitalists. Some of them sympathized with social democracy, but the bulk was filled with the capitalist spirit of striving for a better position for themselves only. In Italy and Germany they form the intellectual backbone of fascism.

What are the social ideals of this class?

They realize that capitalism is not eternal; they already perceive the signs of its decline: in economic crisis, in political revolts and revolutions, in social struggles, in world war. It is not the exploitation of labor that annoys them in capitalism; it is the disorder in capitalism, the anarchy in production that provokes their criticism. Where they rule in the factory, the efficiency of labor by means of strict order and conscious regulation is raised to the highest degree. But outside the factory, in society, where capitalists, stock gamblers, and politicians rule, they see the worst disorder and inefficiency, a scandalous waste of human labor, and the inevitable consequence: poverty and ruin for the whole of society.

What they want, therefore, is organization of production, conscious regulation of labor over the whole of society. They feel themselves the spiritual leaders, the class of intellect and knowledge, destined to take over the lead from the incapable hands of the present rulers. In America the ideas of "technocracy" are the first tokens of such a mode of thinking. By a scientific management of the whole of production under a central direction which does away with competition and which divests the individual capitalists from their arbitrary power, the amount of product can be raised to such a height that there will be abundance for everybody.

This social ideal of the intellectual middle class is a kind of socialism, but it is not necessarily directed against the capitalist class. It gees not mean to expropriate them or to take their profits away from them. On the contrary, in depriving them of their arbitrary power to damage one another, in abolishing the enormous waste, it will raise the productivity of labor to such a degree that the profits will increase considerably. And at the same time it renders possible an increase and securing of the workers' portion, so that all reason for revolt or revolution is taken away.

It is not a socialism of the workers, but a socialism for the workers; a socialism made by others, also for the benefit of the workers. The exploitation of the workers will not cease, it will be made more rational. With equal justice this social system may be called "organized capitalism."

There is, of course, no place for democracy in this system. Democracy means, at least formally, rule of the mass, of the whole people. But this socialism is founded upon the rule, the leadership of the few, of the intellectual minority. In present-day capitalism the technical middle class are leaders and directors of the labor process; they command the workers. They can imagine an ideal society only with this leading and commanding function preserved and extended. The intellectual class does not admit differences founded on noble birth or riches; but it admits differences in brains, in mental capacity and it considers itself as the class of men with the best brains, selected to lead the great masses of the ungifted common people, destined to be common workers.

Hence the political system belonging to this middle-class socialism can never be democracy; it must be the dictatorship of a leading bureaucracy. The socialism once proclaimed as their social goal by the vanguard of the working class was international. Because they saw production as a worldwide unit process and the class struggle of the workers as the common cause of the working class of the whole world. The intellectual class, however, owing to its middle-class origin to the close connection with the capitalist class, has a strong national feeling. Moreover, the instrument necessary for the regulation of production exists as a power organ of the state. Its socialist goal therefore means a national state socialism. Its rule is the rule of a state bureaucracy, its system of production is state capitalism. International world unity is a faraway dream to them, not a matter of practical ideals.

Some characteristics of the social ideals of the intellectual class are found in social democracy, especially in its state-socialist program, though its relation of leaders to masses has a more democratic stamp. In German national socialism some others of these characteristics are perceptible. The tendencies of a class are never reproduced purely in a political party or a political movement. They are the underlying basis, the underground stream, taking its course and growing after fixed laws, determined by class interests, by needs of social development, by the deepest subconscious feelings which the social conditions produce in a class. They are not adequately represented in the surface phenomena, in the political events, the party platforms, the government's changes, the measures taken, the revolutions, the programs—because in all these the traditions, the existing power factors, the relative force of contesting or cooperating classes, groups, parties, play a role. But then always anew, the realities hidden beneath the surface break through, upset the old and determine the new ideas and political events. So we have to look into these events for the class forces at work in them, just as for the forces of nature we look into the natural phenomena.

In fascism and national socialism the class spirit of the intellectual middle classes appears in its first germs. We see as yet only a common revolt against democracy, with only a faint and vague desire for an economically constructive policy. Nevertheless, the spiritual force of the national socialist slogans of the intellectual class was sufficient to carry away numbers of workers who saw in it an organizing power against capitalist disorder.

Is it possible that these parties will realize, or try to realize the class ideals of the intellectual class? This class is well-nigh powerless against the capitalist class. The social power of the intellectuals, measured by their number, their class consciousness, their social feeling, is still far below the power which the working class had long ago already attained. The capitalist class in Europe and America is so powerful that it does not need to tolerate any organization or regulation of production beyond its own interests. It is only when capitalism feels itself extremely weakened and endangered, by hard and long crisis, by workers' revolts, by world war, that conditions are different. Then the intellectuals, together with part of the workers, may be called upon to introduce constructive policy, tending toward state-capitalistic experiments.

When, however, the working class, rising against the unbearable oppression of monopolistic capitalism, by means of revolutionary movements, should succeed in beating down capitalist power, what will the intellectual class do? Then the position will be reversed; the working class, by its mighty fighting power, carries the other discontented classes along with it, in a common assault on capitalism. Then great parts of the intellectual class will join them, won over by the great socialist and communist ideals, and will consider them as their common cause. In every revolutionary movement in history we see great numbers joining it in a common enthusiasm for aims more radical than their own ideals, thereby making victory more easy. But afterward it appeared that each of the allies interpreted the slogans and aims in his own way, thus causing dissensions and new fights between the former comrades. The same will doubtlessly be the case in future revolutionary movements.

The slogans against capitalism, for socialism or communism, will be common to the revolutionary classes. But for each class they mean a different form of social organization. The working class has to build up production from below, by their direct hold over the factories, and to organize them by means of their workers' councils into a democratic commonwealth. The intellectual class will try to install a centrally organized state socialism, directed by a leading bureaucracy.

Is not the intellectual class right in this? Is it not necessary that in these most difficult times of fighting and social reconstruction the ignorant masses should be directed by those who have the best brains? Is it not true, that for that period this selected minority class, trained in science, in general and special knowledge, are the natural leaders, till up to the time when new generations have been born?

No, this is not true. The organization of society is not a matter of technics, of scientific knowledge. The technics of production are excellent already. Capitalism has developed the science of the forces of nature and its application to a high level. This is the domain of the superior knowledge of the intellectuals. As technical experts in the process of production they may apply their brains for the benefit of the community.

But social organization has to deal with other things: with social forces and with the knowledge of social forces. It is an organization of men. And here the intellectuals have no special capacities. What they bring along is only the haughty prejudices of the capitalist class. In social insight, in knowledge of the real class relations of society, the intellectuals stand below the working class. Because their mind clings to ideas belonging to a passing period. Because outside of their physical machines, in matters of human relationship, they are wont to deal not with the realities of social life itself, but with their spiritual images, conceptions, theories, abstractions.

Social organization does not depend on qualities of the intellect of a minority. It depends on qualities of character of the whole working people. It is the consolidation of the workers into one unity, through strong moral and economic forces, which cannot be commanded by leaders but must grow up in the masses in their fight for freedom.

Thus the social ideals and aims of the intellectuals and of the working class oppose one another. The intellectual class, when it should try to establish some social order, must call upon old instincts of obedience, upon the slave feelings of a bygone humanity. For its state-socialist aims it will find allies in social-democratic and party-communist platforms, in union leaders, in the capitalistic ideas of timid and backward workers, who think communist freedom too high for them, and in the beaten remnants of the capitalist force. Then the working class, finding itself opposed by this bloc trying under the banner of "socialism against anarchy" to preserve the domination of a ruling class over the working class, will need all its wisdom and all its unity to find and to fight its way to freedom.

TRADE UNIONISM

This edited version of chapter 3 of *The Workers' Way to Freedom* was published in *International Council Correspondence* vol. 2, no. 2 (January 1936). —Ed.

How must the working class fight capitalism in order to win? This is the all-important question facing the workers every day. What efficient means of action, what tactics can they use to conquer power and defeat the enemy? No science, no theory, could tell them exactly what to do. But spontaneously and instinctively, by feeling out, by sensing the possibilities, they found their ways of action. And as capitalism grew and conquered the earth and increased its power, the power of the workers also increased. New modes of action, wider and more efficient, came up beside the old ones. It is evident that the changing conditions, the forms of action, the tactics of the class struggle have to change also. Trade unionism is the primary form of labor movement in fixed capitalism. The isolated worker is powerless against the capitalistic employer. To overcome this handicap, the workers organized into unions. The union binds the workers together into common action, with the strike as their weapon. Then the balance of power is relatively equal, or is sometimes even heaviest on the side of the workers, so that the isolated small employer is weak against the mighty union. Hence in developed capitalism, trade unions and employer's unions (associations, trusts, corporations, etc.) stand as fighting powers against each other.

Trade unionism first came up in England, where industrial capitalism first developed. Afterward it spread to other countries, as a natural companion of capitalist industry. In the United States there were very special conditions. In the beginning, the abundance of free unoccupied land, open to settlers, made a shortage of workers in the towns and relatively high wages and good conditions. The American Federation of Labor became a power in the country, and generally was able to uphold a relatively high standard of living for the workers who were organized in unions.

It is clear that under such conditions the idea of overthrowing capitalism could not for a moment arise in the minds of the workers. Capitalism offered them a sufficient and fairly secure living. They did not feel themselves a separate class whose interests were hostile to the existing order; they were part of it; they were conscious of partaking in all the possibilities of an ascending capitalism in a new continent. There was room for millions of people, coming mostly from Europe. For these increasing millions of farmers, a rapidly increasing industry was necessary, where, with energy and good luck, workmen could rise to free artisans, to small businessmen, even to rich capitalists. It is natural that here a true capitalist spirit prevailed in the working class.

The same was the case in England. Here it was due to England's monopoly of world commerce and big industry, to the lack of competitors on the foreign markets, and to the possessions of rich colonies, which brought enormous wealth to England. The capitalist class had no need to fight for its profits and could allow the workers a reasonable living. Of course, at the first, fighting was necessary to urge this truth upon them; but then they could allow unions and grant wages in exchange for industrial peace. So here the working class was also imbued with the capitalist spirit.

Now this is entirely in harmony with the innermost character of trade unionism. Trade unionism is an action of the workers, which does not go beyond the limit of capitalism. Its aim is not to replace capitalism by another form of production, but to secure good living conditions within capitalism. Its character is not revolutionary, but conservative.

Certainly, trade union action is class struggle. There is a class antagonism in capitalism—capitalists and workers have opposing interests—not only on the question of conservation of capitalism, but also within capitalism itself, with regard to the division of the total product. The capitalists attempt to increase their profits, the surplus value, as much as possible, by cutting down wages and increasing the hours or the intensity of labor. On the other hand, the workers attempt to increase their wages and to shorten their hours of work. The price of labor power is not a fixed quantity, though it must exceed a certain hunger minimum; and it is not paid by the capitalist of his own free will. Thus this antagonism becomes the object of a contest, the real class struggle. It is the task, the function of the trade unions to carry on this fight.

Trade unionism was the first training school in proletarian virtue, in solidarity as the spirit of organized fighting. It embodied the first form of proletarian organized power. In the early English and American trade unions this virtue often petrified and degenerated into a narrow craft-corporation, a true capitalistic state of mind. It was different, however, where the workers had to fight for their very existence, where the utmost efforts of their unions could hardly uphold their standard of living, where the full force of an energetic, fighting, and expanding capitalism attacked them. There they had to learn the wisdom that only the revolution could definitely save them.

So there comes a disparity between the working class and trade unionism. The working class has to look beyond capitalism. Trade unionism lives entirely within capitalism and cannot look beyond it. Trade unionism can only represent a part, a necessary but narrow part, in the class struggle. And it develops aspects which bring it into conflict with the greater aims of the working class.

With the growth of capitalism and big industry, the unions too must grow. They become big corporations with thousands of members, extending over the whole country, having sections in every town and every factory. Officials must be appointed: presidents, secretaries, treasurers, to conduct the affairs, to manage the finances, locally and centrally.

They are the leaders, who negotiate with the capitalists and who by this practice have acquired a special skill. The president of a union is a big shot, as big as the capitalist employer himself, and he discusses with him, on equal terms, the interests of his members. The officials are specialists in trade union work, which the members, entirely occupied by their factory work, cannot judge or direct themselves.

So large a corporation as a union is not simply an assembly of single workers; it becomes an organized body, like a living organism, with its own policy, its own character, its own mentality, its own traditions, its own functions. It is a body with its own interests, which are separate from the interests of the working class. It has a will to live and to fight for its existence. If it should come to pass that unions were no longer necessary for the workers, then they would not simply disappear. Their funds, their members, and their officials, all these are realities that will not disappear at once, but continue their existence as elements of the organization.

The union officials, the labor leaders, are the bearers of the special union interests. Originally workmen from the shop, they acquire, by long practice at the head of the organization, a new social character. In each social group, once it is big enough to form a special group, the nature of its work, molds and determines its social character, its mode of thinking and acting. Their function is entirely different from that of the workers. They do not work in factories, they are not exploited by capitalists, their existence is not threatened continually by unemployment. They sit in offices, in fairly secure positions. They have to manage corporation affairs and to speak at workers meetings and discuss with employers. Of course, they have to stand for the workers, and to defend their interests and wishes against the capitalists. This is, however, not very different from the position of the lawyer who, appointed secretary of an organization, will stand for its members and defend their interests to the full of his capacity.

However, there is a difference. Because many of the labor leaders came from the ranks of workers, they have experienced for themselves what wage slavery and exploitation means. They feel as members of the working class and the proletarian spirit often acts as a strong tradition in them. But the new reality of their life continually tends to weaken this tradition. Economically they are not proletarians any more. They sit in conferences with the capitalists, bargaining over wages and hours, pitting interests against interests, just as the opposing interests of the capitalist corporations are weighed one against the other. They learn to understand the capitalists' position just as well as the workers' position; they have an eye for "the needs of industry"; they try to mediate. Personal exceptions occur, of course, but as a rule they cannot have that elementary class feeling of the workers that does not understand and weigh capitalist interests over against their own, but will fight for their proper interests. Thus they get into conflict with the workers.

The labor leaders in advanced capitalism are numerous enough to form a special group or class with a special class character and interests. As representatives and leaders of the unions they embody the character and the interests of the unions. The unions are necessary elements of capitalism, so the leaders feel as necessary items, as most useful citizens in capitalist society. The capitalist function of unions is to regulate class conflicts and to secure industrial peace. So labor leaders see it as their duty as citizens to work for industrial peace and mediate in conflicts. The test of the union lies entirely within capitalism; so labor leaders do not look beyond it. The instinct of self-preservation, the will of the unions to live and to fight for existence, is embodied in the will of the labor leaders to fight for the existence of the unions. Their own existence is indissolubly connected with the existence of the unions. This is not meant in a petty sense, that they only think of their personal jobs when fighting for the unions. It means that primary necessities of life and social functions determine opinions. Their whole life is concentrated in the unions, only here have they a task. So the most necessary organ of society, the only source of security and power is to them the union; hence it must be preserved and defended with all possible means. Even when the realities of capitalist society undermine this position. This capitalism does, when with its expansion class conflicts become sharper.

The concentration of capital in powerful concerns and their connection with big finance renders the position of the capitalist employers much stronger than the workers. Powerful industrial magnates are reigning as monarchs over large masses of workers, they keep them in absolute subjection and do not allow "their" men to go into unions. Now and then the heavily exploited wage slaves break out in revolt, in a big strike. They hope to enforce better terms, shorter hours, more human conditions, the right to organize. Union organizers come to aid them. But then the capitalist masters use their social and political power. The strikers are driven from their homes; they are shot by militia or hired thugs; their spokesmen are railroaded into jail; their relief actions are prohibited by court injunctions. The capitalist press denounces their cause as disorder, murder, and revolution; public opinion is aroused against them. Then, after months of standing firm and of heroic suffering, exhausted by misery and disappointment, unable to impress the capitalist steel structure, they have to submit and to postpone their claims to more opportune times.

In the trades where unions exist as mighty organizations, their position is weakened by this same concentration of capital. The large funds they had collected for strike support are insignificant in comparison to the money power of their adversaries. A couple of lockouts may completely drain them. No matter how hard the capitalist employer presses upon the worker by cutting wages and intensifying their hours of labor, the union cannot wage a fight. When tariffs have to be renewed, the union feels itself the weaker party. It has to accept the bad terms the capitalists offer; no skill in bargaining avails. But now the trouble with the rank and file members begins. The men want to fight; they will not submit before they have fought; and they have not much to lose by fighting. The leaders, however, have much to lose—the financial power of the union, perhaps its existence. They try to avoid the fight, which they consider hopeless. They have to convince the men that it is better to come to terms. So, in the final analysis, they must act as spokesmen of the employers to force the capitalists' terms upon the workers. It is even worse when the workers insist on fighting, in opposition to the decision of the unions. Then the union's power must be used as a weapon to subdue the workers.

So the labor leader has become the slave of his capitalistic task of securing the industrial peace—now at the cost of the workers, though he meant to serve them as best he could. He cannot look beyond capitalism, and within the horizon of capitalism with a capitalist outlook, he is right when he thinks that fighting is of no use. The criticism can only mean that trade unionism stands here at the limit of its power.

Is there another way out then? Could the workers win anything by fighting? Probably they will lose the immediate issue of the fight; but they will gain something else. By not submitting without having fought, they rouse the spirit of revolt against capitalism. They proclaim a new issue. But here the whole working class must join in. To the whole class, to all their fellow workers, they must show that in capitalism there is no future for them, and that only by fighting, not as a trade union, but as a class unity, they can win. This means the beginning of a revolutionary struggle. And when their fellow workers understand this lesson, when simultaneous strikes break out in other trades, when a wave of rebellion goes over the country, then in the arrogant hearts of the capitalists there may appear some doubt as to their omnipotence and some willingness to make concessions.

The trade union leader does not understand this point of view, because trade unionism cannot reach beyond capitalism. He opposes this kind of fight. Fighting capitalism in this way, means at the same time rebellion against the trade unions. The labor leader stands beside the capitalist in their common fear for the workers' rebellion.

When the trade unions fought against the capitalist class for better working conditions, the capitalist class hated them, but it had not the power to completely destroy them. If the trade unions would try to raise all the forces of the working class in their fight, the capitalist class would persecute them with all its means. They may see their actions repressed as rebellion, their offices destroyed by militia, their leaders thrown in jail and fined, their funds confiscated. On the other hand, if they keep their members from fighting, the capitalist class may consider them as valuable institutions to be preserved and protected, and their leaders as deserving citizens. So the trade unions find themselves between the devil and the deep sea; on the one side persecution, which is a tough thing to bear for people who meant to be peaceful citizens; on the other side, the rebellion of the members, which may undermine the unions. The capitalist class, if it is wise, will recognize that a bit of sham fighting must be allowed to uphold the influence of the labor leaders over the members.

The conflicts arising here are not anyone's fault; they are an inevitable consequence of capitalistic development. Capitalism exists, but it is at the same time on the way to perdition. It must be fought as a living thing, and at the same time, as a transitory thing. The workers must wage a steady fight for wages and working conditions, while at the same time communistic ideas, more or less clear and conscious, awaken in their minds. They cling to the unions, feeling that these are still necessary, trying now and then to transform them into better fighting institutions. But the spirit of trade unionism, which is in its pure form a capitalist spirit, is not in the workers. The divergence between these two tendencies in capitalism and in the class struggle appears now as a rift between the trade union spirit, mainly embodied in their leaders, and the growing revolutionary feeling of the members. This rift becomes apparent in the opposite positions they take in various important social and political questions.

Trade unionism is bound to capitalism; it has its best chances to obtain good wages when capitalism flourishes. So in times of depression it must hope that prosperity will be restored, and it must try to further it. To the workers as a class, the prosperity of capitalism is not at all important. When it is weakened by crisis or depressions, they have the best chance to attack it, to strengthen the forces of the revolution and to take the first steps toward freedom.

Capitalism extends its dominion over foreign continents, seizing their natural treasures in order to make big profits. It conquers colonies, subjugates the primitive population and exploits them, often with horrible cruelties. The working class denounces colonial exploitation and opposes it, but trade unionism often supports colonial politics as a way to capitalist prosperity.

With the enormous increases of capital in modern times, colonies and foreign countries are being used as places in which to invest large sums of capital. They become valuable possessions as markets for big industry and as producers of raw materials. A race for getting colonies, a fierce conflict of interests over the dividing of the world arises between the great capitalist states. In these politics of imperialism the middle classes are whirled along in a common exultation of national greatness. Then the trade unions side with the master class, because they consider the prosperity of their own national capitalism to be dependent on its success in the imperialist struggle. For the working class, imperialism means increasing power and brutality of their exploiters.

These conflicts of interests between the national capitalisms explode into wars. World war is the crowning of the policy of imperialism. For the workers, war is not only the destroying of all their feelings of international brotherhood, it also means the most violent exploitation of their class for capitalist profit. The working class, as the most numerous and the most oppressed class of society, has to bear all the horrors of war. The workers have to give not only their labor power, but also their health and their lives.

Trade unionism, however, in war must stand upon the side of the capitalist. Its interests are bound up with national capitalism, the victory of which it must wish with all its heart. Hence it assists in arousing strong national feelings and national hatred. It helps the capitalist class to drive the workers into war and to beat down all opposition.

Trade unionism abhors communism. Communism takes away the very basis of its existence. In communism, in the absence of capitalist employers, there is no room for the trade union and labor leaders. It is true that in countries with a strong socialist movement, where the bulk of the workers are socialists, the labor leaders must be socialists too, by origin as well as by environment. But then they are right-wing socialists; and their socialism is restricted to the idea of a commonwealth, where instead of greedy capitalists, honest labor leaders will manage industrial production.

Trade unionism hates revolution. Revolution upsets all the ordinary relations between capitalists and workers. In its violent clashes, all those careful tariff regulations are swept away; in the strife of its gigantic forces the modest skill of the bargaining labor leaders loses its value. With all its power, trade unionism opposes the ideas of revolution and communism.

This opposition is not without significance. Trade unionism is a power in itself. It has considerable funds at its disposal, as material element of power. It has its spiritual influence, upheld and propagated by its periodical papers as mental element of power. It is a power in the hands of leaders, who make use of it wherever the special interests of trade unions come into conflict with the revolutionary interests of the working class. Trade unionism, though built up by the workers and consisting of workers, has turned into a power over and above workers. Just as government is a power over and above the people.

The forms of trade unionism are different for different countries, owing to the different forms of development in capitalism. Nor do they always remain the same in every country. When they seem to be slowly dying away, the fighting spirit of the workers sometimes is able to transform them, or to build up new types of unionism. Thus in England, in the years 1880–90, the "new unionism" sprang up from the masses of poor dockers and the other badly paid, unskilled workers, bringing a new spirit into the old craft unions. It is a consequence of capitalist development that in founding new industries and in replacing skilled labor by machine power, it accumulates large bodies of unskilled workers, living in the worst of conditions. Forced at last into a wave of rebellion, into big strikes, they find the way to unity and class consciousness. They mold unionism into a new form, adapted to a more highly developed capitalism. Of course, when afterward capitalism grows to still mightier forms, the new unionism cannot escape the fate of all unionism, and then it produces the same inner contradictions.

The most notable form sprang up in America, in the Industrial Workers of the World. The IWW originated from two forms of capitalist expansion. In the enormous forests and plains of the West, capitalism reaped the natural riches by Wild West methods of fierce and brutal exploitation; and the worker-adventurers responded with as wild and jealous a defense. And in the eastern states new industries were founded upon the exploitation of millions of poor immigrants, coming from countries with a low standard of living and now subjected to sweatshop labor or other most miserable working conditions.

Against the narrow craft spirit of the old unionism, of the American Federation of Labor, which divided the workers of one industrial plant into a number of separate unions, the IWW put the principle: all workers of one factory as comrades against one master must form one union, to act as a strong unity against the employer. Against the multitude of often jealous and bickering trade unions, the IWW set up the slogan: one big union for all the workers. The fight of one group is the cause of all. Solidarity extends over the entire class. Contrary to the haughty disdain of the well-paid old American skilled labor toward the unorganized immigrants, it was these worst-paid proletarians that the IWW led into the fight. They were too poor to pay high fees and build up ordinary trade unions. But when they broke out and revolted in big strikes, it was the IWW who taught them how to fight; who raised relief funds all over the country; and who defended their cause in its papers and before the courts. By a glorious series of big battles it infused the spirit of organization and self-reliance into the hearts of these masses. Contrary to the trust in the big funds of the old unions, the Industrial Workers put their confidence in the living solidarity and the force of endurance, upheld by a burning enthusiasm. Instead of the heavy stonemasonry buildings of the old unions, they represented the flexible construction, with a fluctuating membership, contracting in time of peace, swelling and growing in the fight itself. Contrary to the conservative capitalist spirit of trade unionism, the Industrial Workers were anticapitalist and stood for revolution. Therefore they were persecuted with intense hatred by the whole capitalist world. They were thrown into jail and tortured on false accusations; a new crime was even invented on their behalf: that of "criminal syndicalism."

Industrial unionism alone as a method of fighting the capitalist class is not sufficient to overthrow capitalist society and to conquer the world for the working class. It fights the capitalists as employers on the economic field of production, but it has not the means to overthrow their political stronghold, the state power. Nevertheless, the IWW so far has been the most revolutionary organization in America. More than any other it has contributed to rouse class consciousness and insight, solidarity and unity in the working class, to turn its eyes toward communism, and to prepare its fighting power.

The lesson of all these fights is that against big capitalism, trade unionism cannot win. And if at times it wins, such victories give only temporary relief. And yet, these fights are necessary and must be fought. To the bitter end?—no, to the better end.

The reason is obvious. An isolated group of workers against an isolated capitalist employer, might be equal parties. But an isolated group of workers against an employer, backed by the whole capitalist class, is powerless. And such is the case here: the state power, the money power of capitalism, public opinion of the middle class, excited by the capitalist press, all attack the group of fighting workers.

But does the working class back the strikers? The millions of other workers do not consider this fight as their own cause. Certainly they sympathize, and often collect money for the strikers, and this may give some relief, provided its distribution is not forbidden by a judge's injunction. But this easygoing sympathy leaves the real fight to the striking group alone. The millions stand aloof, passive. So the fight cannot be won (except in some special cases, when the capitalists, for business reasons, prefer to grant concessions), because the working class does not fight as one undivided unit.

The matter will be different, of course, when the mass of the workers really consider such a contest as directly concerning them; when they find that their own future is at stake. If they go into the fight themselves and extend the strike to other factories, to ever more branches of industry. Then the state power, the capitalist power, has to be divided and cannot be used entirely against the separate group of workers. It has to face the collective power of the working class.

Extension of the strike, ever more widely, up to a general strike in the end, has often been advised as a means to avert defeat. But to be sure, this is not to be taken as a truly expedient pattern, accidentally hit upon, and ensuring victory. If such were the case, trade unions certainly would have made use of it repeatedly as regular tactics. It cannot be proclaimed at will by union leaders, as a simple tactical measure. It must come forth from the deepest feelings of the masses, as the expression of their spontaneous initiative; and this is aroused only when the issue of the fight is or grows larger than a simple wage contest of one group. Only then the workers will put all their force, their enthusiasm, their solidarity, their power of endurance into it.

And all these forces they will need. For capitalism also will bring into the field stronger forces than before. It may have been defeated and taken by surprise by the unexpected exhibition of proletarian force and thus have made concessions. But then afterward, it will gather new forces out of the deepest roots of its power and proceed to win back its position. So the victory of the workers is neither lasting nor certain. There is no clear and open road to victory; the road itself must be hewn and built through the capitalist jungle at the cost of immense efforts.

But even so, it will mean great progress. A wave of solidarity has gone through the masses, they have felt the immense power of class unity, their self-confidence is raised, they have shaken off the narrow group egotism. Through their own deeds they have acquired new wisdom: what capitalism means and how they stand as a class against the capitalist class. They have seen a glimpse of their way to freedom.

Thus the narrow field of trade union struggle widens into the broad field of class struggle. But now the workers themselves must change. They have to take a wider view of the world. From their trade, from their work within the factory walls, their mind must widen to encompass society at large. Their spirit must rise above the petty things around them. They have to face the state; they enter the realm of politics. The problems of revolution must be dealt with.

WORKERS' COUNCILS

This edited version of chapter 10 of *The Workers' Way to Freedom* was published in *International Council Correspondence* vol. 2, no. 5 (April 1936). —Ed.

I

In its revolutionary struggles, the working class needs organization. When great masses have to act as a unit, a mechanism is needed for understanding and discussion, for the making and issuing of decisions, and for the proclaiming of actions and aims.

This does not mean, of course, that all great actions and universal strikes are carried out with soldierlike discipline, after the decisions of a central board. Such cases will occur, it is true, but more often, through their eager fighting spirit, their solidarity and passion, masses will break out in strikes to help their comrades, or to protest against some capitalist atrocity, with no general plan. Then such a strike will spread like a prairie fire all over the country.

In the Russian Revolution of 1905, the strike waves went up and down. Often the most successful were those that had not been decided in advance, while the strikes that had been proclaimed by the central committees often failed.

The strikers, once they are fighting, want mutual contact and understanding in order to unite in an organized force. Here a difficulty presents itself. Without strong organization, without joining forces and binding their will in one solid body, without uniting their action in one common deed, they cannot win against the strong organization of capitalist power. But when thousands and millions of workers are united in one body, this can only be managed by functionaries acting as representatives of the members. And we have seen that then these officials become masters of the organization, with interests different from the revolutionary interests of the workers.

How can the working class, in revolutionary fights, unite its force into a big organization without falling into the pit of officialdom? The answer is given by putting another question: if all that the workers do is to pay their fees and to obey when their leaders order them out and order them in, are they themselves then really fighting their fight for freedom?

Fighting for freedom is not letting your leaders think for you and decide, and following obediently behind them, or from time to time scolding them. Fighting for freedom is partaking to the full of one's capacity, thinking and deciding for oneself, taking all the responsibilities as a self-relying individual amidst equal comrades. It is true that to think for oneself, to think out what is true and right, with a head dulled by fatigue, is the hardest, the most difficult task; it is much harder than to pay and to obey. But it is the only way to freedom. To be liberated by others, whose leadership is the essential part of the liberation, means the getting of new masters instead of the old ones.

Freedom, the goal of the workers, means that they shall be able, man for man, to manage the world, to use and deal with the treasures of the earth, so as to make it a happy home for all. How can they ensure this if they are not able to conquer and defend this themselves?

The proletarian revolution is not simply the vanquishing of capitalist power. It is the rise of the whole working people out of dependence and ignorance into independence and clear consciousness of how to make their life.

True organization, as the workers need it in the revolution, implies that everyone takes part in it, body and soul and brains; that everyone takes part in leadership as well as in action, and has to think out, to decide and to perform to the full of his capacities. Such an organization is a body of self-determining people. There is no place for professional leaders. Certainly there is obeying; everybody has to follow the decisions which he himself has taken part in making. But the full power always rests with the workers themselves.

Can such a form of organization be realized? What must be its structure? It is not necessary to construct it or think it out. History has already produced it. It sprang into life out of the practice of the class struggle. Its prototype, its first trace, is found in the strike committees. In a big strike, all the workers cannot assemble in one meeting. They choose delegates to act as a committee. Such a committee is only the executive organ of the strikers; it is continually in touch with them and has to carry out the decisions of the strikers. Each delegate at every moment can be replaced by others; such a committee never becomes an independent power. In such a way, common action as one body can be secured, and yet the workers have all decisions in their own hands. Usually in strikes, the uppermost lead is taken out of the hands of these committees by the trade unions and their leaders.

In the Russian Revolution when strikes broke out irregularly in the factories, the strikers chose delegates which, for the whole town or for an industry or railway over the whole state or province, assembled to bring unity into the fight. They had at once to discuss political matters and to assume political functions because the strikes were directed against czarism. They were called soviets, councils. In these soviets all the details of the situation, all the workers' interests, all political events were discussed. The delegates went to and fro continually between the assembly and their factories. In the factories and shops the workers, in general meetings, discussed the same matters, took their decisions and often sent new delegates. Able Socialists were appointed as secretaries, to give advice based on their wider knowledge. Often these soviets had to act as political powers, as a kind of primitive government when the czarist power was paralyzed, when officials and officers did not know what to do and left the field to them. Thus these soviets became the permanent center of the revolution; they were constituted by delegates of all the factories, striking or working. They could not think of becoming an independent power. The members were often changed and sometimes the whole soviet was arrested and had to be replaced by new delegates. Moreover they knew that all their force was rooted in the workers' will to strike or not to strike; often their calls were not followed when they did not concur with the workers' instinctive feelings of power or weakness, of passion or prudence. So the soviet system proved to be the appropriate form of organization for a revolutionary working class. In 1917 it was at once adopted in Russia, and everywhere workers' and soldiers' soviets came into being and were the driving force of the revolution.

The complementary proof was given in Germany. In 1918, after the breakdown of the military power, workers' and soldiers' councils in imitation of Russia were founded. But the German workers, educated in party and union discipline, full of social-democratic ideas of republic and reform as the next political aims, chose their party and union officials as delegates into these councils. When fighting and acting themselves, they acted and fought in the right way, but from lack of self-confidence they chose leaders filled with capitalist ideas, and these always spoilted matters. It is natural that a "council congress" then resolved to abdicate for a new parliament, to be chosen as soon as possible.

Here it became evident that the council system is the appropriate form of organization only for a revolutionary working class. If the workers do not intend to go on with the revolution, they have no use for soviets. If the workers are not far enough advanced yet to see the way of revolution, if they are satisfied with the leaders doing all the work of speechifying and mediating and bargaining for reforms within capitalism, then parliaments and party and union congresses—called workers' parliaments because they work after the same principle—are all they need. If, however, they fight with all their energy for revolution, if with intense eagerness and passion they take part in every event, if they think over and decide for themselves all details of fighting because they have to do the fighting, then workers' councils are the organization they need.

This implies that workers' councils cannot be formed by revolutionary groups. Such groups can only propagate the idea by explaining to their fellow workers the necessity of council organization when the working class as a self-determining power fights for freedom. Councils are the form of organization only for fighting masses, for the working class as a whole, not for revolutionary groups.

They originate and grow up along with the first action of a revolutionary character. With the development of revolution, their importance and their functions increase. At first they may appear as simple strike committees, in opposition to the labor leaders when the strikes go beyond the intentions of the leaders, and rebel against the unions and their leaders.

In a universal strike the functions of these committees are enlarged. Now delegates of all the factories and plants have to discuss and to decide about all the conditions of the fight; they will try to regulate into consciously devised actions all the fighting power of the workers; they must see how they will react upon the governments' measures, the doings of soldiers or capitalist gangs. By means of this very strike action, the actual decisions are made by the workers themselves. In the councils, the opinions, the will, the readiness, the hesitation, or the eagerness, the energy and the obstacles of all these masses concentrate and combine into a common line of action. They are the symbols, the exponents of the workers' power; but at the same time they are only the spokesmen who can be replaced at any moment. At one time they are outlaws to the capitalist world, and at the next, they have to deal as equal parties with the high functionaries of government.

When the revolution develops to such power that the state power is seriously affected, then the workers' councils have to assume political functions. In a political revolution, this is their first and chief function. They are the central bodies of the workers' power; they have to take all measures to weaken and defeat the adversary. Like a power at war, they have to stand guard over the whole country, controlling the efforts of the capitalist class to collect and restore their forces and to subdue the workers. They have to look after a number of public affairs which otherwise were state affairs: public health, public security, and the uninterrupted course of social life. They have to take care of the production itself, the most important and difficult task and concern of the working class in revolution.

A social revolution in history never began as a simple change of political rulers who then, after having acquired political power, carried out the necessary social changes by means of new laws. Already, before and during the fight, the rising class built up its new social organs as new sprouting branches within the dead husk of the former organism. In the French Revolution, the new capitalist class, the citizens, the businessmen, the artisans, built up in each town and village their communal boards, their new courts of justice, illegal at the time, usurping simply the functions of the powerless functionaries of royalty. While their delegates in Paris discussed and made the new constitution, the actual constitution was made all over the country by the citizens holding their political meetings, building up their political organs afterward legalized by law.

In the same way during the proletarian revolution, the new rising class creates its new forms of organization which step by step in the process of revolution supersede the old state organization. The workers' councils, as the new form of political organization, take the place of parliamentarism, the political form of capitalist rule.

2

Parliamentary democracy is considered by capitalist theorists as well as by Social Democrats as the perfect democracy, conforming to justice and equality. In reality, it is only a disguise for capitalist domination, and contrary to justice and equality. It is the council system that is the true workers' democracy.

Parliamentary democracy is foul democracy. The people are allowed to vote once in four or five years and to choose their delegates; woe to them if they do not choose the right man. Only at the polls the voters can exert their power; thereafter they are powerless. The chosen delegates

are now the rulers of the people; they make laws and constitute governments, and the people have to obey. Usually, by the election mechanism,
only the big capitalist parties with their powerful apparatus, with their
papers, their noisy advertising, have a chance to win. Real trustees of
discontented groups seldom have a chance to win some few seats.

In the soviet system, each delegate can be repealed at any moment.
Not only do the workers continually remain in touch with the delegate,
discussing and deciding for themselves, but the delegate is only a temporary messenger to the council assemblies. Capitalist politicians denounce
this "characterless" role of the delegate, in that he may have to speak
against his personal opinion. They forget that just because there are no
fixed delegates, only those will be sent whose opinions conform to those
of the workers.

The principle of parliamentary representation is that the delegate
in parliament shall act and vote according to his own conscience and
conviction. If on some question he should ask the opinion of his voters,
it is only due to his own prudence. Not the people, but he on his own
responsibility has to decide. The principle of the soviet system is just the
reverse; the delegates only express the opinions of the workers.

In the elections for parliament, the citizens are grouped according
to voting districts and counties; that is to say according to their dwelling
place. Persons of different trades or classes, having nothing in common,
accidentally living near one another, are combined into an artificial group
which has to be represented by one delegate.

In the councils, the workers are represented in their natural groups,
according to factories, shops, and plants. The workers of one factory or
one big plant form a unit of production; they belong together by their
collective work. In revolutionary epochs, they are in immediate contact
to interchange opinions; they live under the same conditions and have
the same interests. They must act together; the factory is the unit which
as a unit has to strike or to work, and its workers must decide what they
collectively have to do. So the organization and delegation of workers in
factories and workshops is the necessary form.

It is at the same time the principle of representation of the communist order growing up in the revolution. Production is the basis of society, or, more rightly, it is the contents, the essence of society; hence the order of production is at the same time the order of society. Factories are the working units, the cells of which the organism of society consists. The main task of the political organs, which mean nothing else but the organs managing the totality of society, concerns the productive work of society. Hence it goes without saying that the working people, in their councils, discuss these matters and choose their delegates, collected in their production units.

We should not believe, though, that parliamentarism, as the political form of capitalism, was not founded on production. Always the political organization is adapted to the character of production as the basis of society. Representation, according to dwelling place, belongs to the system of petty capitalist production, where each man is supposed to be the possessor of his own small business. Then there is a mutual connection between all these businessmen at one place, dealing with one another, living as neighbors, knowing one another and therefore sending one common delegate to parliament. This was the basis of parliamentarism. We have seen that later on this parliamentary delegation system proved to be the right system for representing the growing and changing class interests within capitalism.

At the same time it is clear now why the delegates in parliament had to take political power in their hands. Their political task was only a small part of the task of society. The most important part, the productive work, was the personal task of all the separate producers, the citizens as businessmen; it required nearly all their energy and care. When every individual took care of his own small lot, then society as their totality went right. The general regulations by law, necessary conditions, doubtlessly, but of minor extent, could be left to the care of a special group or trade, the politicians. With communist production the reverse is true. Here the all-important thing, the collective productive work, is the task of society as a whole; it concerns all the workers collectively. Their personal work does not claim their whole energy and care; their mind is turned to the collective task of society. The general regulation of this collective work cannot be left to a special group of persons; it is the vital interest of the whole working people.

There is another difference between parliamentarism and the soviet system. In parliamentary democracy, one vote is given to every adult man and sometimes woman on the strength of their supreme, inborn right of belonging to mankind, as is so beautifully expressed in celebration speeches. In the soviets, on the other hand, only the workers are represented. Can the council system then be said to be truly democratic if it excludes the other classes of society?

The council system embodies the dictatorship of the proletariat. Marx and Engels, more than half a century ago, explained that the social revolution was to lead to the dictatorship of the working class as the next political form and that this was essential in order to bring about the necessary changes in society. Socialists, thinking in terms of parliamentary representation only, tried to excuse or to criticize the violation of democracy and the injustice of arbitrarily excluding persons from the polls because they belong to certain classes. Now we see how the development of the proletarian class struggle in a natural way produces the organs of this dictatorship, the soviets.

It is certainly no violation of justice that the councils, as the fighting centers of a revolutionary working class, do not include representatives of the opposing class. And thereafter the matter is not different. In a rising communist society there is no place for capitalists; they have to disappear and they will disappear. Whoever takes part in the collective work is a member of the collectivity and takes part in the decisions. Persons, however, who stand outside the process of collective production, are, by the structure of the council system, automatically excluded from influence upon it. Whatever remains of the former exploiters and robbers has no vote in the regulation of a production in which they take no part.

There are other classes in society that do not directly belong to the two chief opposite classes: small farmers, independent artisans, intellectuals. In the revolutionary fight they may waver to and fro, but on the whole they are not very important, because they have less fighting power. Mostly their forms of organization and their aims are different. To make friends with them or to neutralize them, if this is possible without impeding the proper aims or to fight them resolutely if necessary, to decide upon the way of dealing with them with equity and firmness, will be the concern, often a matter of difficult tactics, of the fighting working class. In the production system, insofar as their work is useful and necessary, they will find their place and they will exert their influence after the principle that whoever does the work has a chief vote in regulating the work.

More than half a century ago, Engels said that through the proletarian revolution the state would disappear; instead of the ruling over men would come the managing of affairs. This was said at a time when there could not be any clear idea about how the working class would come into power. Now we see the truth of this statement confirmed. In the process of revolution, the old state power will be destroyed, and the organs that take its place, the workers' councils, for the time being, will certainly have important political functions still to repress the remnants of capitalist power. Their political function of governing, however, will be gradually turned into nothing but the economic function of managing the collective process of production of goods for the needs of society.

THE POWER OF THE CLASSES

This edited version of chapter 2 of *The Workers' Way to Freedom* was published in *International Council Correspondence* vol. 2, no. 6 (May 1936). —Ed.

I

The power of the capitalist class is enormous. Never in history was there a ruling class with such power. Their power is first, money power. All the treasures of the world are theirs, and modern capital, produced by the ceaseless toil of millions of workers, exceeds all the treasures of the old world. The surplus value is partly accumulated into ever more and new capital; partly it must be spent by the capitalists. They buy servants for their personal attendants; they also buy people to defend them, to safeguard their power and their dominating position. In capitalism everything can be bought for money; muscles and brain as well as love and honor have become market goods. Said old John D. Rockefeller: "Everyone can be bought if you only know his price." The statement is not exactly true, but it shows the capitalist's view of the world.

The capitalists buy young proletarians to form a fighting force. In the same way as they buy Pinkertons against strikers, they will, in times of greater danger, organize huge armies of volunteers provided with the best modern arms, well-fed and well-paid, to defend their sacred capitalist order.

But capitalism cannot be defended by brutal force alone. Being itself the outcome of a high development of intellectual forces, it must consequently be defended by these same intellectual forces. Behind the physical struggle in the class war, stands the spiritual contest of ideas. Capitalists know that, often better than the workers. Hence they buy all the good brains they can. Often in a coarse, open way; most often however, indirectly. This is done, for instance, by donating money for cultural purposes. Numerous students of science the world over have profited in their researches from the Rockefeller Foundation. Thus the name "Rockefeller" has a reputation in the field of natural sciences where "Ludlow" is never heard of. This kind of philanthropy serves capitalism well. Capitalists have founded universities all over the United States where among other sciences sociology is taught, to demonstrate the impossibility and wickedness of communism. The young people leave the universities imbued with these ideas and they know high salaries and public honor await them if they do not deviate from the straight path of capitalism.

The capitalists buy the press; they buy the editors; they buy all the means of publicity, and in this way they mold public opinion. It is an invisible spiritual despotism by which the entire nation is made to think as the capitalist class wish it to think. Money reigns over the world, thus it can buy the brain power available.

Capitalist power in the second place is political. The state is the organization of the capitalist class. Its task is to render possible private production, and to enable the individual capitalists to carry on their businesses by protecting and regulating their intercourse.

The government makes laws for the protection of "honest" businessmen against "thieves" and "murderers." Against strikers and revolutionists, who are far more dangerous to the existing social order, laws even more drastic are made. For the enforcing of these laws, the police and jail are used. In every strike, in every political demonstration, the workers find the police arrayed against them, clubbing and throwing them into jail for the benefit of the capitalist class and to protect the capitalists profits. Gangs of hired thugs are sworn in as deputy sheriffs and given police authority; and when the workers cannot be subdued in this way, militia and citizen guards are mobilized against them.

In each capitalist country the army is the strongest force in the service of the capitalist class because, for its wars with other countries, it needs the fighting power of the whole country, all classes included.

The army is an organized body bound together by the strictest military discipline, provided with the most cruel, refined, and effective means of killing and destroying. If it is used in political wars, where in the worst case the capitalist class suffers only heavy losses, is it not to be used then in case of revolution where the capitalist class is menaced with complete loss of all it possesses?

Thus the nation is the stronghold of capitalism. As a strongly organized power, nationwide, directed by the uniform will of the central government, provided with a powerful army, it protects the capitalist class. Physical force, however, is not sufficient to subdue a people or a class. How many strong governments in history, though well-armed, have been overthrown by rebellions. Spiritual forces in most cases are decisive above mere physical power. In capitalism the rule holds good that in the long run it is more effectual to fool people than to beat them.

So capitalist power consists thirdly in its intellectual power. The ideas of a ruling class pervade the majority of the members of society. Certainly the capitalist class could not buy guards and intellectuals if these fellows did not share its ideology and sentiments. Capitalist government could not govern, even with its strong physical force, if the mass of the people were not filled with the same spirit as the government itself. How is it possible that in the mass of the people, even in the working class, this capitalist spirit prevails?

The main force is tradition and inheritance. The ideology of the capitalist class is nothing but the ideology of the former middle classes, the petty producers. The idea of private property as a natural right, the belief that everyone should build his own fortune and that free competition guarantees the best results, the maxim that everyone has only to care for himself and God will take care of the rest, the conviction that thrift and industry are the virtues which secure prosperity, and that America is the best country and should be defended against other nations, all these beliefs are inherited from the time and the class of small business. And this is the very creed big business wants the masses to believe in as eternal truths today.

The fathers or grandfathers of the proletarians of today were such small businessmen themselves; small farmers, settlers, craftsmen, even small capitalists, ridden down by competition. They, too, have inherited these ideas, and in their youth found them to be true. Then society changed rapidly and big industry developed, and they became forever proletarians. Their ideas, however, could not change so rapidly and their mind clings to the old ideology.

Still, the school of life is powerful and impresses the mind with new ideas in line with the changing world. But now the capitalist school comes into action. With all available means, the capitalist ideas are propagated and artificially forced upon the minds of the people. At first in the schools when the children's minds are flexible and impressionable; afterward for the adults from the pulpit, in the daily press, by the radio, the movies, etc. Their task is not only to keep the capitalistic way of thinking alive in the working-class minds, but still more, to prevent them thinking at all. By filling their time and their minds with exciting futilities, they kill every wish for serious reading and thinking.

May this be called fooling the workers? The capitalistic class is sincere in this propaganda; it believes what it tries to urge upon the workers. But capitalistic ideology is foolishness for the workers. The workers have to foster the new ideas that are growing out of the changing world; they have to acquire the knowledge of the evolution of labor and of the class struggle as the way to communism.

Thus the power of the capitalist class is more than their money and political power alone. The small businessmen, the small farmers, who believe they will succeed by personal effort—as sometimes they do— are a part of the capitalist power. Every workman who only cares for himself and not for the future of his class, every workman who only reads capitalist newspapers and finds his chief interest in boxing matches, etc., by so doing contributes to the power of the capitalist class.

In the rapid development of technical and economic forms of production, the mind of man is left behind. This mental backwardness of the working masses is the chief power of the capitalist class.

II

What power can the working class set forth against it? First, the working class is the most numerous class in society. By the growth of industry it continually increases, whereas the number of independent businessmen has relatively decreased. The available statistics show that in the United States the working class is the largest class. Only the farmers and the salaried employees follow at some distance as important classes. The capitalist class proper is insignificant in numbers; and the small and middle-class men and petty dealers are much less numerous than the wage workers. But number is not the only thing that counts. A number of millions, dispersed in widely separated homes all over the land, cannot exert the same power as the same number of millions pressed together in the towns. The big towns are the centers of economic, cultural, and political life. The millions of workers, forming the majorities in the population in these centers, assembled into big class agglomerations, must under these conditions exert a strong social power.

In ancient Rome the proletarians were numerous also, and strongly concentrated. Their social power, however, was nothing because they did not work. They were parasites; they lived from public moneys. With the modern proletarians, the matter is the reverse.

The second element of power for the working class is its importance in human society. It is on their work that society is founded. The capitalists might be dismissed, the petty producers and dealers might be dispensed with, without impairing the production of life necessities which mostly takes place in the big factories. But the working class cannot be dispensed with. With its essential, fundamental role only the work of the farmers can be compared.

The workers have their hand on the production apparatus. They manage it; they work it; they command it; they have direct power over it. Not legally, for legally they have to obey the capitalists, and police and soldiers may come to enforce this legal right. But actually it is theirs, for without them the living producing machinery is a dead carcass. If they refuse to work, society cannot exist. It has happened already, that a general strike has paralyzed the entire economic and social life, and thereby wrung important concessions from the unwilling ruling class. Then for a moment, like a flash of lightning, that mighty power of the proletarian class, its intimate connection with the production apparatus, was disclosed.

To be sure, if this possible power is to become a living, actual power, a weighty condition must be fulfilled. Such united action of the whole class is not possible, if it is not sustained by a strong moral force. So, as the third element of proletarian power, we find solidarity, the spirit of unity, organization. Solidarity is the bond that unites the will of all the separate individuals into one common will, thus achieving one mighty organized action.

Is it right to speak of a specifically proletarian virtue? Does not capitalism itself practice organization and united action in its factories, in its trusts, in its armies? Here the unity is based upon command, upon fines, upon penalties. Certainly, for common interests combined action must take place in each class, but here again the true economic position manifests itself, that capitalists are competitors, and workers are comrades.

Capitalism is based upon private business, private interests. The more eagerly the capitalist pursues his personal interests, the better for his business. Hence a hard egotism is developed that submerges natural human sympathies. The workers, on the other hand, cannot win anything by egotism. So long as they face capital individually, they are powerless and miserable; only by collective action can they win better conditions. The more they pursue personal interests, the more they are beaten down. The more they develop a feeling of fellowship, of mutual aid, of self-sacrifice for their class, the better it is for their interests.

When at the dawn of civilization, private property came into being, men separated, each to work on his own lot, in order to develop productivity of labor in mutual competition. In this century-long development, from small crafts to modern industry, civilized man rose to a sturdy self-determinism, to independence, to confidence in his own powers and to a strong feeling of individualism. All his energies and faculties were awakened to the service or his fighting powers. But this was at the cost of moral losses; egotism and cruelty grew in mankind, and distrust and enmity sprang up amid fellow men.

Now the modern proletariat is coming up, for the first time a class without property, hence without real interests one against the other. Still endowed with the personal energies and faculties inherited from their ancestors, they are trained by the machine into the discipline of common action. And though their attempts for a better living standard are helplessly beaten down by the overwhelming power of capitalism, much good comes from these attempts. Their common interests against the capitalist class awakens in them the feelings of brotherhood.

As the working class finds strength in its moral superiority over the capitalist class, it also finds strength in its intellectual superiority. To the feeling is added the knowledge. First comes the deed, the action of solidarity, that springs spontaneously from the depth of emotion and passion. After that comes the insight that there is an unavoidable conflict of opposing interests. It is the first form of class consciousness. With the deepening of knowledge, the ways of action, the fighting conditions are seen more clearly; and as is the case of all science, this insight will lead future actions along the most efficient ways of getting results.

After their number, their social importance, their moral force of solidarity, this knowledge is the fourth element in proletarian power. It is the science developed chiefly by Marx and Engels which explains, first, the course of history from the growth of society in its primitive beginnings, through feudalism and capitalism, thence to communism, basing this analysis upon the development of labor and its productivity. And second, it explains the structure of capitalist production and shows how capitalism must break down by means of its own forces, by developing and exploiting the proletarian class, by driving it into revolt through its own collapses, and by increasing thereby the proletarians fighting powers.

This science, Marxism, is a proletarian science. The capitalist class rejects it; its scientists deny its truth. Indeed, it is impossible for the capitalist class to accept it. No class can accept a theory that proclaims its own collapse and death; for by accepting it, it could not fight with full confidence and with full force. To fight against annihilation is a primary instinct, in a class as well as in an organism.

The capitalist class cannot see beyond the horizon of capitalism. So it sees the growing concentration of capital, the growing power of big finance, the heavy crises and the impending world wars, the rising tide of the proletarian fight with its threat of revolution, it sees all these phenomena without drawing one rational conclusion from them. It sees no sense in history, though its ablest scientists investigate every detail; it sees no light in the future, uncertainty and mysticism fill its mind. But it has one determination, to fight for its supremacy.

For the workers this science enlightens their arduous course to the future. It makes clear to them their life, their work, their poverty, their relation to their employers, and to the other classes. It explains to them the reality of the world as they experience it, different indeed from the capitalist teachings. Whereas the school of life impresses their minds with new ideas in line with the new world, it is this science of society that molds these ideas into a firm consistent knowledge. And so the workers will eventually acquire the wisdom they need in their fight for freedom.

ON THE COMMUNIST PARTY

This edited version of chapter 6 of *The Workers' Way to Freedom* was published in *International Council Correspondence* vol. 2, no. 7 (June 1936). —Ed.

I

During the world war small groups in all countries arose, convinced that out of this ordeal of capitalism, a proletarian revolution must ensue, and they were ready to prepare for it. They once more took the name of Communists, forgotten since the old times of Marx in 1848, to identify themselves from the old Socialist Parties. The Bolshevik party, then having its center in Switzerland, was one of them. After the war had ceased, they united into communist parties standing for the proletarian revolution, in opposition to the socialist parties who supported the war politics of the capitalist government, and represented the submissive, fearful tendencies in the working class. The communist parties gathered all the young fighting spirit in its ranks.

Contrary to the theory that not in a ruined but only in a prosperous capitalistic country the workers could build up a true commonwealth, the Communists put forth the truth that it was the very ruin of capitalist production which made a revolution necessary and would incite the working class to fight for revolution with all its energy.

Opposing the social-democratic view, that a parliament chosen by general suffrage was a fair representation of society and the basis of socialism, the Communists put forth the new truth, stated by Marx and Engels, that the working class, to attain its aims, had to take power entirely in its own hands, and had to set up its own dictatorship, excluding the capitalist class from any share in the government.

In opposition to parliamentarism, they put forth, following the Russian example, the soviets or workers' councils.

In the defeated Germany, November 1918, a vigorous communist movement sprang up and united the Spartacus group and other groups which had secretly grown up during the war. It was crushed the following January by the counterrevolutionary forces of the socialist government. This prevented the rise of an independent, strong communist power in Germany, animated by the spirit of a highly developed modern proletariat, therefore the Communist Party of Russia entirely dominated the young rising communist groups of the world. They united in the Third International, which was directed from Moscow. Now Russia remained the only center of world revolution; the interests of the Russian state directed the communist workers all over the world. The ideas of Russian Bolshevism dominated the communist parties in the capitalist countries.

Russia was attacked by the capitalist governments of Europe and America. In defense, Russia attacked these governments by inciting the working class to rebellion, by calling them to world revolution—a communist revolution, not in the future, but as soon as possible. And if they could not be won for communism, then at least for opposition to the policy of their governments. Hence the communist groups were forced to go into parliament and to go into trade unions, to drive them as an opposing force against their capitalist governments.

World revolution was the great battle cry. Everywhere in the world, in Europe, Asia, America, among the oppressed classes and the oppressed peoples, the call was heard and workers arose. They were animated by the Russian example, feeling that now through the war, capitalism was shaken from its foundations, that it was weakened still more by the economic disorders and crisis. They were just small minorities, but the masses of the workers stood waiting, looking with sympathy toward Russia, hesitating still because their leaders said that the Russians were a backward people and because the capitalist papers spoke of atrocities and predicted an inevitable and rapid breakdown. These very infamies of the capitalist press, however, showed how much the example was hated and feared.

Was a communist revolution possible? Could the working class conquer power and defeat capitalism in England, France, and America? Certainly not. It had not the strength that was needed. Perhaps in Germany only.

What ought to have been done then? The communist revolution, the victory of the working class, is not a matter of a few years; it is a whole period of rising and fighting. This crisis of capitalism could only be the starting point for this period. The task of the Communist Party was to build up the power of the working class in this period step by step. This perhaps is a long way, but there is no other.

The Russian Bolshevik leaders did not understand world revolution in this way. They meant it to come immediately, in the near future. That which had happened in Russia, why could it not happen in other countries? The workers there had only to follow the example of their Russian comrades. In Russia, a firmly organized party of some ten thousand of revolutionists, by means of a working class of hardly a million, within the population of a hundred million, had conquered power, and afterward by the right platform it stood for and by defending their interests, it won the masses to its side.

In the same way the rest of the world's communist parties comprising the most eager class conscious, able, and energetic minorities of the working class, led by capable leaders, could conquer political power if only the mass of the workers would follow them. Were not the capitalist governments ruling minorities also?

The whole of the working class which now suffers from this minority rule has only to back the Communist Party to vote for it, to its call, and the party will do the real work. It is the vanguard, it attacks, it defeats the capitalist government and replaces it, and when in power it will carry through communism, just as in Russia.

And the dictatorship of the working class? It is embodied in the dictatorship of the Communist Party, just as in Russia.

Do as we did! This was the advice, the call, the directive given by the Bolshevik party to the communist parties of the world. It was based upon the idea of equality of Russian conditions with the conditions in capitalist countries. The conditions, however, were so widely different that hardly any resemblance could be seen. Russia stood on the threshold of capitalism, at the beginning of industrialism. The great capitalist countries stood at the close of industrial capitalism. Hence the goals were entirely different. Russia had to be raised from primitive barbarism to the high level of productivity reached in America and Europe. This could only be done by a party, governing the people, organizing state capitalism. America and Europe with their high level of capitalist productivity have to transform themselves to communist production. This can only be done by the common effort of the working class in its entirety.

The working class in Russia was a small minority and nearly the whole population consisted of primitive peasants. In England, Germany, France, and America nearly half or even more than half of the population consisted of proletarians, wage workers. In Russia there was a very small, insignificant capitalist class without much power or influence. In England, Germany, France, America a capitalist class more powerful than the world had ever seen, dominated society, dominated the whole world.

The Communist Party leaders, by proclaiming that they (the party) should be able to beat the capitalist class, showed by this very assertion that they did not see the real power of this class. By setting Russia as the example to be followed, not only in heroism and fighting spirit, but also in methods and aims, they betrayed their inability to see the difference between the Russian czarist rule and the capitalist rule in Europe and America.

The capitalist class with its complete domination of the economic forces, with its money power, its intellectual power, does not allow a minority group to vanquish and destroy it. No party, though led by the ablest leaders, can defeat it. There is only one power strong enough to vanquish this mighty class. This power is the working class.

The essential basis of capitalist power is its economic power. No political laws issued from above can seriously affect it. It can only be attained by another economic power, by the opposing class, striking at its very roots. It is the entirety of the workers who have to come into the field, if capitalism is to be overthrown.

At first sight this appeal to the whole of the working class may appear illusionary. The masses, the majority, are not clearly class conscious; they are ignorant as to social development; they are indifferent to the revolution. They are more egotistic for personal interests than for solidarity for class interests, submissive and fearful, seeking futile pleasures. Is there much difference between such an indifferent mass and a population as in Russia? Can anything be expected from such a people rather than from that class conscious, eager, energetic, self-sacrificing, clear-minded communist minority?

This, however, is only relevant if it should be a question of a revolution of tomorrow, as conceived by the Communist Party.

For the real proletarian revolution, not the superficial chance character of today, is essential, which is determined by the present surrounding capitalist world. The real communist revolution depends on the deeper essential class nature of the proletariat.

The working class of Europe and America have qualities in itself that enable it to rise with a great force. They are descendants of a middle class of artisans and farmers who for many centuries have worked their own soil or their own shop as free people. They therefore acquired skill and independence, capability, and a strong individuality to act for themselves, persistent industry, and the habit of personal energy in work. These qualities the modern workers have inherited from their ancestors. Dominated thereafter during one or more generations by capitalism, they were trained by the machine to regular intensity and discipline in collective work. And after the first depression there grew in them, during continual fighting, the new rising virtue of solidarity and class unity.

On these foundations the future greatness of the revolutionary class will be built up. In Europe and in America there are hundreds of millions of people who possess these qualities. The fact that as yet they still stand before their task, that they have not yet finished it, that they hardly made a beginning, does not mean that they are not able to perform it. None other than their own power can tell them how to act; they have to find their way themselves by hard suffering and bitter experience. They have brains and they have hearts to find out and to do it and build up that class unity out of which the new mankind will arise.

They are not a neutral indifferent mass that does not count when a revolutionary minority tries to overthrow the ruling capitalist minority. As long as they do not actively take part, the revolution cannot be won; but when they do take part, they are not the people to be led in obedience by a party.

Certainly a party in its ascendance consists of the class's best elements, exceeding the mass as a whole. Its leaders usually are the prominent forces in the party, embodying the great aims in their names, admired, hated, honored. They stand at the front and when a great fight is lost, its great leaders are destroyed, the party is crushed. Knowing this, the secondary leaders, or the party officials, will often shrink from the supreme fight, from the boldest aims. The working class itself can be defeated, but it can never be crushed. Its forces are indomitable; its roots are in the firm earth; as growing green turf, the blooming tops which are mown always come up anew. The workers can temporarily desist from fighting when weakened, but their forces increase continually. A party that follows them in their retreat cannot recover, it must lose its character and repudiate its principles; it is lost forever. A party, a group, leaders, have limited force which is entirely spent, is sacrificed in honor, or in dishonor in the events of the class struggle; the class itself draws upon an unlimited store.

Prominent leaders can show the way, parties in their principles and platforms can express the ideas, the aims of the class only temporary.

At first the class follows them, but then it has to pass them up, putting up bolder aims, higher ideas, conforming to the widening and deepening of the class struggle. The party tries to keep the class at its former lower level, at its more moderate aims, and has to be discarded. The doctrine that a party stands above the class, that it should remain the leader always, being theoretically false, in practice means strangling the class and leading it to its defeat.

We will show how in the Communist Party this doctrine after its first glorious ascendance led to rapid decay.

II

These are the principles leading the Communist Party and determining its practice: the party has to win dictatorship, to conquer power, to make revolution, and by this to liberate the workers; the workers have to follow, to back the party and to bring it to power.

Hence its direct aim is: to win the masses of the workers as adherents, to bring them to its side; not to make them good independent fighters, able to find and to force their own way.

Parliamentary action is one of the means. Though the Communist Party declared that parliamentarism was useless for the revolution, still it went into parliament; this was called "revolutionary parliamentarism," to demonstrate in parliament the uselessness of parliamentarianism. In reality it was a means to get votes and voters, followers of the party. It served to detract the workers' votes from the Socialist Party. Numerous workers who were disillusioned by the capitalist policy of social democracy, who wished to stand for revolution, were won over by the big talk and the furious criticisms of the Communist Party against capitalism. Now this policy opened a new way for them, to stick to their old belief that by voting only and following leaders, this time better leaders, they would be liberated. These famous revolutionists, who in Russia had founded the state of the workers, told them this easy way was the right way.

Another means was trade unionism. Though the Communist Party declared the unions useless for the revolution, yet the Communists had to become members of them in order to win the unions for communism. This did not mean the making of the union members into clearly class-conscious revolutionists; it meant the replacing of the "corrupt" old leaders by Communist Party men. It meant the party controlling the ruling-class machine of the unions, that it might command the big armies of union members. Of course the old leaders were not willing to give way; they simply excluded the red opposition groups. Then new "red" unions were formed.

Strikes are the schools for communism. When the workers are on strike, fighting the capitalist class face to face, then they learn the real power of capitalism; they see all its forces directed against them. But then they realize more fully the necessary force of solidarity, the necessity for unity. They are more keen to understand, and their spirit is eager to learn. What they learn is the most important lesson, and that is that communism is the only salvation.

The Communist Party varied this truth according to its principles in each strike that it was present to take part, or rightly to take the lead. The direction must be taken out of the hands of the trade union leaders, who do not have the right fighting spirit. The workers should lead themselves. The reason for this statement was because the working class, as you know, is represented by the Communist Party, therefore the party should lead them. Each success was used to advertise the party. Instead of the communist education, which is a natural outcome of each big fight in capitalism, came the artificial aim: to increase the influence of the party on the masses.

Instead of the natural lesson, that communism is the salvation, came the artificial lesson that the Communist Party is the savior. By its revolutionary talk, they caught and absorbed all the eager fighting spirit of the strikers, but diverted it to its own aims. Quarrels which were injurious to the workers' cause were often the result.

A continual fight was made against the Social Democratic Party to detract its followers from it by criticism of its politics. Their leaders were denounced and were called by the most spicy names as accomplices of capital and traitors of the working class. Doubtlessly, a serious, critical exposition showing that social democracy had left the way of class struggle will open the eyes of many workers. But now, all at once, the scene changed and an alliance was offered to these "traitors" for a common fight against capitalism. This was called solemnly "the unity of the working class restored." In reality it would have been nothing but the temporary collaboration of two competing groups of leaders, both trying to keep or win obedient followers.

To win followers and votes, it is not necessary to call upon the working class alone. All the poor classes living miserably under capitalism will hail the new and better masters who promise them freedom. So they did as the Socialist Party did; the Communist Party addressed its propaganda to all who suffer.

Russia gave the example, The Bolshevik party, though a workers' party, had won power only by their alliance with the peasants. When, once in power, they were threatened by the capitalist tendencies in the wealthy peasants, they called upon the poor peasants as the allies of the workers. Then the communist parties in America and Europe always imitating Russian slogans directed their appeals to the workers and the poor peasants also. It forgot that in highly developed countries of capitalism there lives in the poor peasants the strong spirit of private ownership the same as in the big farmers, if they could be won over by promises they would be but unreliable allies ready to desert at the first contrariety.

The working class in its revolution can only rely upon its own force. Other poor classes of society will often join them, but they cannot give additional weight of importance because the strong innate force which proletarian solidarity and mastership over production gives to the working class is lacking in them. Therefore, even in rebellion, they are uncertain and fickle. What can be aimed at is that they will not be tools in the capitalists' hands. This cannot be obtained by promises. Promises and platforms count with parties, but classes are directed by deeper feelings and passions founded on interests. They can be reached only when their respect and their confidence is aroused because they see that the workers bravely and energetically attack the capitalist class.

The matter is different for a Communist Party wishing to win power for itself. All the poor who suffer under capitalism are equally as good as followers of the party. Their despair, seeing no sure way out by their own force, makes them the right adherents to a party that says it liberates them. They are apt to break out in explosions but not to climb in continuous fight. In the heavy world crisis of these last few years the increasing masses of the regularly unemployed, in which the need and the idea of a rapid immediate world revolution became dominant, also turned to the Communist Party. Especially by means of this army, the Communist Party hoped to conquer political supremacy for itself.

The Communist Party did not try to increase the power of the working class. It did not educate its adherents to clearness, to wisdom, to unity of all workers. It educated them into enthusiastic but blind, hence fanatical, believers and followers; into obedient subjects of the party in power. Its aim was not to make the working class strong, but to make the party powerful. Because its fundamental ideas originated from primitive Russian, not from highly developed capitalistic European and American conditions.

When a party wishes to win followers with all means and cannot attract them by arousing their interest in revolution, then it will try to win them by appealing to their reactionary prejudices. The strongest feeling which capitalism awakes and raises with all its might against revolution is nationalism. When in 1923 French troops occupied the Rhineland and everywhere in Germany the waves of nationalism went high, the Communist Party also played the nationalistic game trying to compete with the capitalistic parties. In the Reichstag it proposed a companionship of the communist armed forces, the "red guards," with the German capitalist army (Reichswehr). Here international politics played a part. Russia, at that time hostile to the Western victorious governments, tried to make an alliance with Germany, hence the German Communist Party had to make friends with its own capitalist government.

This was the chief character of all the communist parties affiliated to the Third International; they were directed by Moscow by the Russian

Communist leaders, so they were the tools of Russian foreign policies. Russia was "all the workers' fatherland," the center of communist world revolution. The interest of Russia should be the prominent interest of the communist workers all over the world. It was clearly stated by the Russian leaders that when a capitalist government should be the ally of Russia against other powers, the workers in that country had to stand by their government. They had to fight their government, in other countries. The class struggle between the capitalist and the workers' class had to be made subordinate to the temporary needs and fortunes of Russian foreign politics.

Its dependence on Russia, materially and spiritually, is at the root of all the weakness of the Communist Party. All the ambiguities in the Russian development are reflected in the position of the Communist Party. The Russian leaders have to tell their subjects that their state-capitalistic building up of industrialism is the building up of communism. Hence each new factory or electric power plant is hailed in the communist papers as a triumph of communism. In order to encourage the minds of the Russians in perseverance, they were told by their papers that [the] capitalist [world] was nearly succumbing to a world revolution and envious of Russia, meditated to make war with Russia. This was repeated in the communist papers all over the world, while at the same time Russia was concluding commercial treaties with these capitalist governments. When Russia made alliances with some capitalist states and took part in their diplomatic quarrels, the communist papers glorified this as a capitulation of the capitalist world before communism. The papers continually advertised Russian "communism" before the workers of the world.

Russia is the great example; hence the Russian example has to be imitated in the Communist Party. Just as in Russia, the party has to dominate the class. In the Russian party the leaders dominate because they have all the power factors in their hands. In the same way the Communist Party leaders dominate. The members have to show "discipline." Moscow, the "Comintern" (Central Committee of the Third International) are the highest leaders; at their command the leaders in every country are dismissed and replaced by others.

It is natural that in the other countries there are doubts that arise among the workers and members as to the rightness of these Russian methods. But such opposition was always beaten down and excluded from the party. No independent judgment was allowed; obedience was demanded.

After the revolution the Russians had built up a "red army" to defend their freedom against the attacks of the "white armies." In the same way the German Communist Party. formed a "red guard," bodies of armed young Communists, to fight against the armed nationalists.

It was not simply a workers' army against capitalism, but also a weapon against all the adversaries of the Communist Party. Wherever oppositions arose at meetings and other workers criticized the party politics, the red guards at the command of their leaders were to deal with them, with maltreatment. Not opening their brains, but breaking their skulls was the method employed against criticizing fellow workers. Thus young and eager fighters were educated into rowdies instead of educating them to become real Communists. When the national revolution came, when national violence proved too far stronger and more irresistible than communist violence, numerous young workers who had learned nothing but to beat their leaders' adversaries, at once changed their colors and became just as zealous nationalists as they were before zealous Communists.

Through the glory that radiated from the Russian Revolution, through its own gallant talk, the Communist Party assembled year by year all the ardent enthusiastic young workers under its colors. These young workers were used either in idle sham fights or spilt into useless party politics; all these valuable qualities were lost to the revolution. The best of them, disillusioned, turned their back on the party and tried to find new ground in founding separate groups.

Looking backward, we see the world war, as a culmination of capitalist oppression, arouse the revolutionary spirit of the workers everywhere.

Barbarous Russia, as the weakest of the governments, fell at the first stroke, and as a bright meteor the Russian Revolution rose and shone over the earth. It was another revolution than the workers needed. Its dazzling light, first filling them with hope and force, blinded them, so that they did not see their own way. Now they have to recover and to turn their eyes toward the dawn of their own revolution.

The Communist Party cannot recover. Russia is making its peace with the capitalist nations and taking its place among them with its own economic system. The Communist Party inseparably linked to Russia is doomed to live on sham fighting. Opposition groups split off ascribing the decay to false tactics of some particular leaders, to diversify from the right principles. In vain; the basis of the downfall lies in the principles themselves.

THE ROLE OF FASCISM

This edited version of chapter 7 of *The Workers' Way to Freedom* was published in *International Council Correspondence* vol. 2, no. 8 (July 1936). —Ed.

The chief characteristic of fascism is that of organizing the petty capitalist and middle class with their narrow-minded spirit of private business into a mass organization, strong enough to check and beat the proletarian organizations. This class, squeezed in between the capitalist and the working class, unable to fight capitalism, is always ready to turn against the workers' class struggle. Though it hates big capital and puts forth anticapitalistic slogans, it is a tool in the hands of capitalism, which pays and directs its political action toward the subduing of the workers.

Its ideas and theories are directed chiefly against the class struggle, against the workers feeling and acting as a separate class. Against this, it brings forward a strong nationalistic feeling, the idea of the unity of the nation against foreign nations. In this nation workers have their place, not as a separate class, but combined with the employers as industrial and agrarian groups of production. Representatives of these groups form advisory boards for the government. This is called the corporative state, founded on direct representation of the economic grouping of society, on capitalist labor. It is opposed to the parliamentary system for which fascism has hardly any use and which it denounces as a power of disruption, a mischievous preaching of internal dissension.

Parliamentarianism is the expression of supremacy of the people, the citizens, and of the dependence of the government. Fascism puts the state above the citizens. The state, as organization of the nation, is the superior objective to which the citizens are subordinate. Not democracy, not the people's right, but authority, the people's duties stand first. It places the party chief at the head of the state, as a dictator, to rule with his party companions without interference from parliamentary delegates.

It is clear that this form of government corresponds to the needs of modern capitalism. In a highly developed capitalism economic power is not rooted, as it was in the beginning, in a numerous class of independent producers, but in a small group of big capitalists. Their interests can be served better by influencing a small body of absolute rulers, and their operations seem more safely secured if all opposition of the workers and all public criticism is kept down with an iron fist. Hence a tendency is visible in all countries to increase the power of the central government and of the chieftains of the state. Though this is also sometimes called fascism, it makes some difference whether parliamentary control is maintained, or an open dictatorial rule is established, founded upon the terrorism of a mighty party organization.

In Germany an analogous development of the National Socialist movement took place somewhat later. The revolution of 1918 had brought socialism into power but this power was made use of to protect capitalism. The Socialists in the government let the capitalists operate as they liked. The petty capitalist classes seeing their antagonists on both sides now united and Socialist officials involved in foul capitalist affairs considered socialist state concern and capitalist speculation as one common principle of corruption of an international gang of grafters. It opposed to them the honest small business of petty capitalists and the conservative old-time farmers. Young intellectuals of the universities who found their former monopoly of public offices infringed upon by detested Socialist leaders, and former officers jobless through the diminution of the army, organized the first groups of National Socialists.

They were eager nationalists because they belonged to the capitalist middle classes and were opposed to the internationalism of the ruling social democracy. They called themselves Socialist, because their petty-capitalistic feeling was hostile to big business and big finance. They were strongly antisemitic, too. Firstly, because Jewish capital played an important role in Germany especially in the large stores, which stores caused the ruin of the small shopkeepers. Secondly, because numerous Jewish intellectuals flooded the universities and the learned professions, and by their keener wits often—e.g., as lawyers and physicians—left their German competitors behind them.

Financially these National Socialists were backed by many big capitalist concerns, especially by the armament industry which felt its interests endangered by the increasing disarmament conferences. They formed the illegal fighting groups of capitalism against rising Bolshevism. Then came the world crisis, aggravating the conditions in Germany exhausted as it was by the peace treaty indemnities. The revolt of the desperate middle classes raised the National Socialist Party to the position of the mightiest party and enabled it to seize the political power and to make its leader the dictator of Germany.

Seemingly this dictatorship of middle-class ideas is directed against big capitalism as well as against the working-class movement. It is clear, however, that a petty capitalist program of a return to former times of small business cannot be carried out. It soon became evident in Germany that big capitalism and the land-owning aristocracy are still the real masters behind the ruling National Socialist Party. In reality this party acts as an instrument of capitalism to fight and destroy the workers' organization.

So strong was the power of the new slogans that they drew even a large number of workers with them, who joined the National Socialist Party. The workers had learned to follow their leaders, but these leaders having disappointed them, were beaten by the stronger leaders. The splendor and the spiritual power of the socialist and communist ideals had waned. National socialism promised the workers a better socialism, by class peace instead of by class war. If offered them their appropriate place in the nation as members of the united people not as a separate class.

Due to the victory of fascism, or its equivalent, in certain countries, the working classes in these countries have been thrown back in their systematic upward strife for liberation. Their organizations have been wiped out, or in the case of the trade unions, put directly under the command of capitalist state officials. The workers' papers have been suppressed, free speech prohibited, socialist and communist propaganda forbidden and punished with imprisonment, concentration camps, or long incarceration. In the enforced uniformity of opinion there is no room for revolutionary teachings. The way of regular progress toward proletarian power in the development of insight and organization by means of propaganda and discussions, the way to revolution and freedom, is blocked by the concrete wall of reaction.

So it appears on the surface. But, looking deeper into the problem, it only means that for the workers the smooth and peaceful way of growing to power is blocked. We said before that the right of free speech, the right of organizing, the right of propaganda and of forming political parties, were necessary for capitalism. It means that they are necessary to ensure a regular working of capitalist production and capitalist development. It means that, once they are gone, the class antagonisms must at last explode in heavy uprisings and violent revolutionary movements. The capitalist class has to decide whether it prefers this way.

It has its reasons for taking this way. It strongly feels that the heavy world crisis of today is shaking the capitalist system in the heart. It knows that the diminished production is unable to feed the whole working class and at the same time to leave sufficient profits. It is resolved not to bear the losses itself. So it realizes that the workers, starved by unemployment, must rise and will rise in revolts. And it tries to forestall them by fortifying its own position, by forging the whole capitalist class into one strong unity, by putting the state power in strong armor, by tying the workers to this state by means of strong fetters, by robbing them of their old means of defense, their Socialist spokesmen and their organizations. This is the reason why in these last years fascism became powerful.

Capitalism at one time seemed to be on to the best way of fooling the workers by means of sham democracy and sham reforms. Now it is turning the other way, to heavy oppression. This must drive the workers to resistance and to determined class fighting. Why does capitalism do so? Not of its own free will, but compelled by material, economic forces inherent in its innermost nature: by the heavy crisis which endangers its profits and arouses its fears for revolution.

Triumphant fascism boasts that it has blocked the way to communism forever. Its claim for this is because it has crushed the workers' movement. What it really crushed were only the ineffective, primitive forms. It destroyed the illusions, the old socialist beliefs, the socialist and communist parties—all obsolete things hampering progress. It destroyed at the same time the old party divisions which incited workers against workers. It thereby has restored their natural class unity.

Parties are groups of common opinion; organizations are dependent on membership—both of these are secondary accidentals. Class is the primary reality founded in the nature of capitalism itself. By tradition the workers considered political opinion and organization membership as the real distinctions between workers and capitalists. They were thinking and feeling in terms of parties and unions—and by tradition may continue to do so for some time. Now they are constrained to think and feel in terms of class. Without any walls of partition, they stand one beside the other and they see that they are all comrades, subject to the same capitalist exploitation. No party discipline can call them to action; they will have to think out and make their own action when the burden of fascist capitalism makes itself too heavily felt. The mist of opposing party opinions, of political slogans, of union narrowness, which dimmed the natural class consciousness, has been destroyed. Sharp and relentless the reality of capitalism confronts them, and to fight it they have only themselves, their class unity to rely upon.

The political parties of the working class—we speak of Germany and Italy—have disappeared; only the leaders in exile continue to speak as if they were the parties. This does not mean that they have disappeared forever. If there should come an uprising of the working class, they will come back and present themselves again as leaders. They must he vanquished for the second time, now by the workers, by conscious recognition that they are obsolete.

This does not mean that there will be no more parties in the future, that their role is finished. New parties will arise undoubtedly in revolutionary periods to express in new situations the unavoidable differences of tactical opinions within the working class. Parties in this sense are necessary elements in social development. The working class cannot be given ready-made opinions and platforms from some dictator party, which claims to do the thinking work for it, and forbids independent opinion. The working class has to think out and to find out the way for itself. Then opinions as to what is and what must be done will differ because their lives—though in the main rather alike—were different in particulars. Groups of common opinion will be formed to discuss and to propagate their ideas, to fight the scientists of the capitalist class, to wage the spiritual contest with other groups. This is the way of self-education for the working class.

Parties in this sense may be called the scouting groups in the capitalist jungle. They have to investigate the ways, to study science and circumstances, to discuss these in mutual debate, to lay their ideas, their explanations, their advice before their fellow workers. In this way they are the necessary instruments to build up the intellectual power of the working class.

Their task is not to act instead of the workers, to do the real fighting work for the workers and to drag the class behind them. They will not have the power to put themselves in the place of the class. Class unity, class action will be paramount, party opinion subordinate.

II

There are points of similarity between fascist Italy and Germany, and Bolshevist Russia. They are ruled by dictators, the chiefs of dictator parties—the Communist Party in Russia, the Fascist Party in Italy, the National Socialist Party in Germany. These parties are large, strongly organized groups which by their zeal and enthusiasm, their devotion to the cause, by their discipline and energy are able to dominate state and country, and to enforce upon it the stamp of one hard, big unity.

This is a similarity in form; the contents are different. In Russia state capitalism builds up the productive forces; private capital is not tolerated. In Italy and Germany, the state and the ruling party are intimately connected with private large-scale capitalism. But here also a better economic organization is included in the fascist aims.

Big business always means a certain organization of production, transport and banking in the hands of a small number of directing individuals. And these comparatively few persons have control and power over the mass of lesser capitalists. Political rulers were already connected with these big capitalists before. Now the fascist program proclaims it to be the task of state power to direct and regulate the economic force. The increase of nationalism in all countries, and the preparing for world war, as expressed in the slogan of autarchy, i.e., the complete reliance of each state upon its own resources, imposes upon the political leaders a close cooperation with the leaders of industry. If in the old capitalism the state was a necessary instrument of industry, now industry becomes a necessary instrument of the state, too. Ruling the state and ruling industry is being merged into one. Imposing regulation upon private business now means that by the fascist power the bulk of the lesser capitalists are subjected still more completely to big business.

To be sure, in fascist capitalism the ruling class clings to the principle of private enterprise, if not for others, then at least for themselves. The silent contest of big capitalists, monopolists, bankers, for supremacy and profit goes on behind the scenes. If, however, the economic crisis lasts, then the increasing misery, the rebellions of workers or middle classes will compel the rulers to more efficient regulations of economic life. Already now, capitalist economists look to Russia and study its economics as a possible model, and as a way out. "Planned Economics" is the talk of politicians in many countries. A development of European and American capitalism in the direction of and into some form of state capitalism may offer itself as a means to prevent or to thwart or to turn back a proletarian revolution. This will be called socialism then. If we compare it to the last program, the "Plan" of the Belgian Social Democratic Party for regulating capitalism, the difference is not fundamental. The Belgian plan, indeed, may be called an attempt to compete with fascism in a salvation action for capitalism.

If now we compare these three parties, the Social Democratic Party, the Communist Party, the Fascist Party, we find that they have their chief aim in common. They want to dominate and rule the working class. Of course in order to save the worker, to make them happy, to make them free. They all say so.

Their means, their platforms are different; they are competitors, and each abuses the others calling them counterrevolutionaries or criminals.

Social democracy makes an appeal to democracy; the workers shall choose their masters by vote. The Communist Party resorts to revolution; the workers shall rise at the call of the Communist Party, overthrow capitalist rule and put the Communist Party into office. The fascists make an appeal to national feelings and petty-capitalist instincts. They all aspire to some form of state capitalism or state socialism where the working class is commanded and exploited by the state, by the community of leaders, directors, officials, the managers of production.

Their common basis is the opinion that the working masses are unable to conduct their own affairs. The incapable and stupid many, as they believe, must be led and educated by the capable few.

When the working class fights for its real freedom, in order to take the direction of the production, the rule of society into its own hands, it will find all these parties opposed to it.

INDEX

"Passim" (literally "scattered") indicates intermittent discussion of a topic over a cluster of pages.

ABOUT THE AUTHOR AND EDITOR

Anton Pannekoek (1873–1960) was a Dutch astronomer, Marxist revolutionary, and key theoretician of council communism—a Marxist alternative to both Leninism and social democracy that instead emphasized working-class self-emancipation through workers' councils. He developed his theories through witnessing the rise and fall of social democracy as well as the rise and fall of the Russian and German revolutions. He is most well-known by revolutionaries for his magnum opus *Workers' Councils* (AK Press, 2002) and his critical *Lenin as Philosopher* (Merlin Press, 1975), and by astronomers for his research of the Milky Way and astrophysics—for which he received an honorary degree from Harvard University in 1936; the Gold Medal of the Royal Astronomical Society in 1951; and had a crater on the moon, an asteroid, and the Anton Pannekoek Institute for Astronomy at the University of Amsterdam named after him.

Robyn K. Winters is a libertarian communist, amateur historian, and contributor of Working Class History. They currently work within the Canadian labour movement and reside on the unceded territories of the Musqueam, Squamish, and Tsleil-Waututh in Vancouver, British Columbia, Canada.

ABOUT PM PRESS

PM Press is an independent, radical publisher of books and media to educate, entertain, and inspire. Founded in 2007 by a small group of people with decades of publishing, media, and organizing experience, PM Press amplifies the voices of radical authors, artists, and activists. Our aim is to deliver bold political ideas and vital stories to all walks of life and arm the dreamers to demand the impossible. We have sold millions of copies of our books, most often one at a time, face to face. We're old enough to know what we're doing and young enough to know what's at stake. Join us to create a better world.

PM Press
PO Box 23912
Oakland, CA 94623
www.pmpress.org

PM Press in Europe
europe@pmpress.org
www.pmpress.org.uk

FRIENDS OF PM PRESS

These are indisputably momentous times—the financial system is melting down globally and the Empire is stumbling. Now more than ever there is a vital need for radical ideas.

In the many years since its founding—and on a mere shoestring—PM Press has risen to the formidable challenge of publishing and distributing knowledge and entertainment for the struggles ahead. With hundreds of releases to date, we have published an impressive and stimulating array of literature, art, music, politics, and culture. Using every available medium, we've succeeded in connecting those hungry for ideas and information to those putting them into practice.

Friends of PM allows you to directly help impact, amplify, and revitalize the discourse and actions of radical writers, filmmakers, and artists. It provides us with a stable foundation from which we can build upon our early successes and provides a much-needed subsidy for the materials that can't necessarily pay their own way. You can help make that happen—and receive every new title automatically delivered to your door once a month—by joining as a Friend of PM Press. And, we'll throw in a free T-shirt when you sign up.

Here are your options:

- **$30 a month** Get all books and pamphlets plus 50% discount on all webstore purchases

- **$40 a month** Get all PM Press releases (including CDs and DVDs) plus 50% discount on all webstore purchases

- **$100 a month** Superstar—Everything plus PM merchandise, free downloads, and 50% discount on all webstore purchases

For those who can't afford $30 or more a month, we have **Sustainer Rates** at $15, $10, and $5. Sustainers get a free PM Press T-shirt and a 50% discount on all purchases from our website.

Your Visa or Mastercard will be billed once a month, until you tell us to stop. Or until our efforts succeed in bringing the revolution around. Or the financial meltdown of Capital makes plastic redundant. Whichever comes first.

ABOUT US

Working Class History is an international collective of worker-activists focused on the research and promotion of people's history through our podcast, books, and social media channels.

We want to uncover stories of our collective history of fighting for a better world and tell them in a straightforward and engaging way to help educate and inspire new generations of activists.

Through our social media outlets with over one million followers, we reach an audience of over 20 million per month. So if you're on social media, you can connect with us in the following ways:

- ■ Instagram: @workingclasshistory
- ■ Facebook: facebook.com/workingclasshistory
- ■ Twitter: @wrkclasshistory
- ■ YouTube: youtube.com/workingclasshistory
- ■ Mastodon: mastodon.social/@workingclasshistory
- ■ Tumblr: workingclasshistory.tumblr.com

We receive no funding from any political party, academic institution, corporation or government. All of our work is funded entirely by our readers and listeners on patreon. So if you appreciate what we do, consider joining us, supporting our work, and getting access to exclusive content and benefits at patreon.com/workingclasshistory.

Working Class History: Everyday Acts of Resistance & Rebellion

Edited by Working Class History
Foreword by Noam Chomsky

ISBN: 978-1-62963-8-232 / 978-1-62963-8-874
Paperback / Hardcover
$20.00 / $59.95
6 x 9 • 352 pages

History is not made by kings, politicians, or a few rich individuals—it is made by all of us. From the temples of ancient Egypt to spacecraft orbiting Earth, workers and ordinary people everywhere have walked out, sat down, risen up, and fought back against exploitation, discrimination, colonization, and oppression.

Working Class History presents a distinct selection of people's history through hundreds of "on this day in history" anniversaries that are as diverse and international as the working class itself. Women, young people, people of color, workers, migrants, Indigenous people, LGBT+ people, disabled people, older people, the unemployed, home workers, and every other part of the working class have organized and taken action that has shaped our world, and improvements in living and working conditions have been won only by years of violent conflict and sacrifice. These everyday acts of resistance and rebellion highlight just some of those who have struggled for a better world and provide lessons and inspiration for those of us fighting in the present. Going day by day, this book paints a picture of how and why the world came to be as it is, how some have tried to change it, and the lengths to which the rich and powerful have gone to maintain and increase their wealth and influence.

This handbook of grassroots movements, curated by the popular Working Class History project, features many hidden histories and untold stories, reinforced with inspiring images, further reading, and a foreword from legendary author and dissident Noam Chomsky.

"This ingenious archive of working class history, organized as an extended calendar, is filled with little and better known events. Reading through the text, the power, fury, and persistence of the working-class struggles shine. 'Working class' is broader than unions and job struggles, and rather includes all emancipatory acts of working-class people, be they Indigenous peoples fighting for land rights, African Americans massively protesting police killings, anticolonial liberation movements, women rising up angry, or mass mobilizations worldwide against imperialist wars. It is international in scope as is the working class. This is a book the reader will open every day to recall and be inspired by what occurred on that date. I love the book and will look forward to the daily readings."
—Roxanne Dunbar-Ortiz, author of *An Indigenous Peoples' History of the United States*